INVADER ZIM

BEST OF SKOOL

™

Created by
JHONEN VASQUEZ

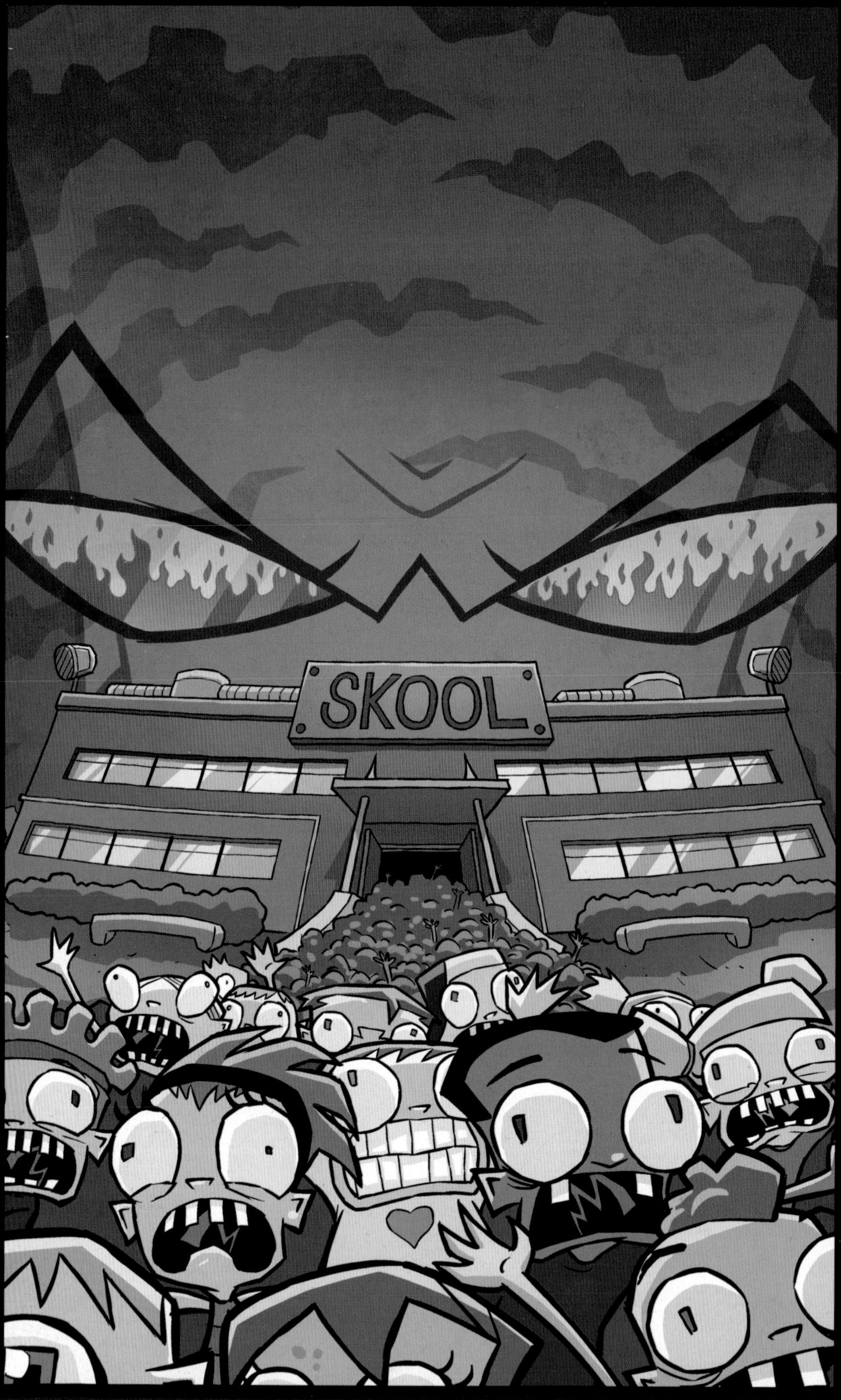
SKOOL

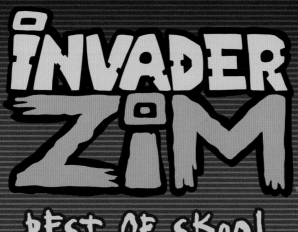

BEST OF SKOOL

Control Brain
JHONEN VASQUEZ

TALES OF BITTERS
Written and conceived by ERIC TRUEHEART
Illustrated by WARREN WUCINICH • Colored
by FRED C. STRESING

THE EVIL MS. BITTERS
Written by DANIELLE KOENIG • Illustrated by
WARREN WUCINICH • Colored by
FRED C. STRESING

BITTERS AND THE WITCH
Written, illustrated, colored, and lettered by
KC GREEN (with additional heads by
WARREN WUCINICH)

MS. BITTERS' BUGS
Written and pencilled by IAN MCGINTY
Inked by FRED C. STRESING and MEG CASEY
Colored by FRED C. STRESING

SWEETHEART BITTERS
Written by JAMIE SMART • Illustrated by
WARREN WUCINICH • Colored by
FRED C. STRESING

PHYSICAL PHITNESS
Written by ERIC TRUEHEART • Illustrated by
KATE SHERRON and MEG CASEY • Colored by
FRED C. STRESING • Lettered by
WARREN WUCINICH

OH BROTHER WHY ART THOU
Written by SAM LOGAN • Illustrated by KATE
SHERRON • Colored by FRED C. STRESING
Lettered by WARREN WUCINICH

LI'L MEAT MAN
Written by ERIC TRUEHEART • Illustrated and
lettered by WARREN WUCINICH
Colored by FRED C. STRESING

Retail cover illustrated by WARREN WUCINICH

Book design by KEITH WOOD with ANGIE KNOWLES
Edited by ROBIN HERRERA • Collection edited by JASMINE AMIRI

Special thanks to JOAN HILTY and LINDA LEE

Published by Oni-Lion Forge Publishing Group, LLC

James Lucas Jones, president & publisher • Charlie Chu, e.v.p. of creative & business development • Steve Ellis, s.v.p. of games & operations • Alex Segura, s.v.p of marketing & sales Michelle Nguyen, associate publisher • Brad Rooks, director of operations • Amber O'Neill, special projects manager • Margot Wood, director of marketing & sales • Katie Sainz, marketing manager • Tara Lehmann, publicist • Holly Aitchison, consumer marketing manager • Troy Look, director of design & production • Angie Knowles, production manager • Kate Z. Stone, senior graphic designer • Carey Hall, graphic designer • Sarah Rockwell, graphic designer Hilary Thompson, graphic designer • Vincent Kukua, digital prepress technician • Chris Cerasi, managing editor • Jasmine Amiri, senior editor • Shawna Gore, senior editor • Amanda Meadows, senior editor • Robert Meyers, senior editor, licensing • Desiree Rodriguez, editor Grace Scheipeter, editor • Zack Soto, editor • Ben Eisner, game developer • Jung Lee, logistics coordinator • Kuian Kellum, warehouse assistant

Joe Nozemack, publisher emeritus

This volume collects issues #15, #32, #37, and #45 of the Oni Press series *Invader Zim*.

Oni-Lion Forge Publishing Group, LLC
1319 SE Martin Luther King Jr. Blvd.
Suite 240
Portland, OR 97214

onipress.com	lionforge.com
facebook.com/onipress	facebook.com/lionforge
twitter.com/onipress	twitter.com/lionforge
instagram.com/onipress	instagram.com/lionforge

First edition: November 2021

ISBN: 978-1-62010-916-8 • eISBN: 978-1-62010-917-5

nickelodeon

Library of Congress Control Number: 2020939380

1 3 5 7 9 10 8 6 4 2

Printed in China.

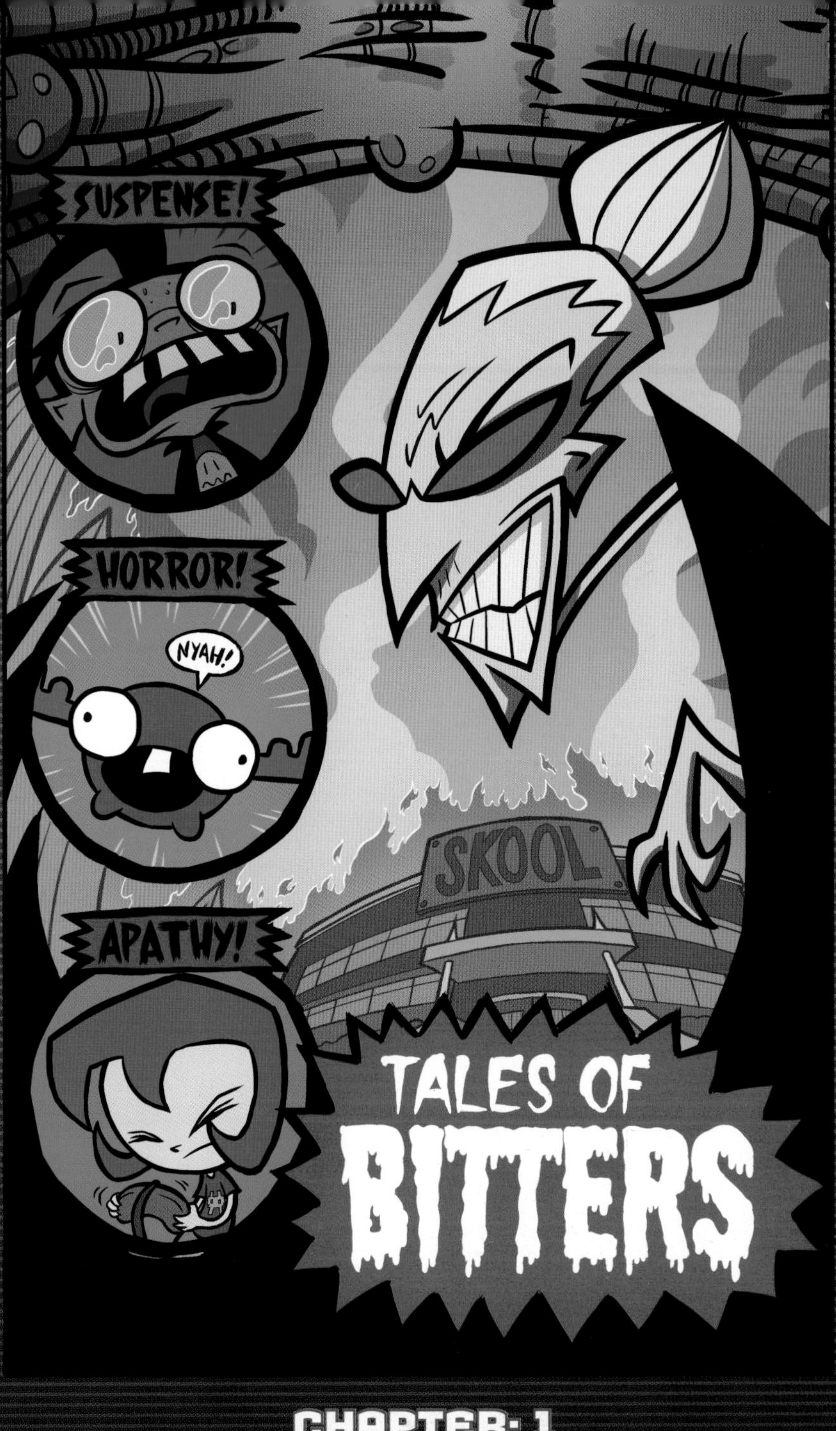
SUSPENSE!
HORROR!
NYAH!
APATHY!
SKOOL
TALES OF
BITTERS

CHAPTER: 1

illustration by Warren Wucinich

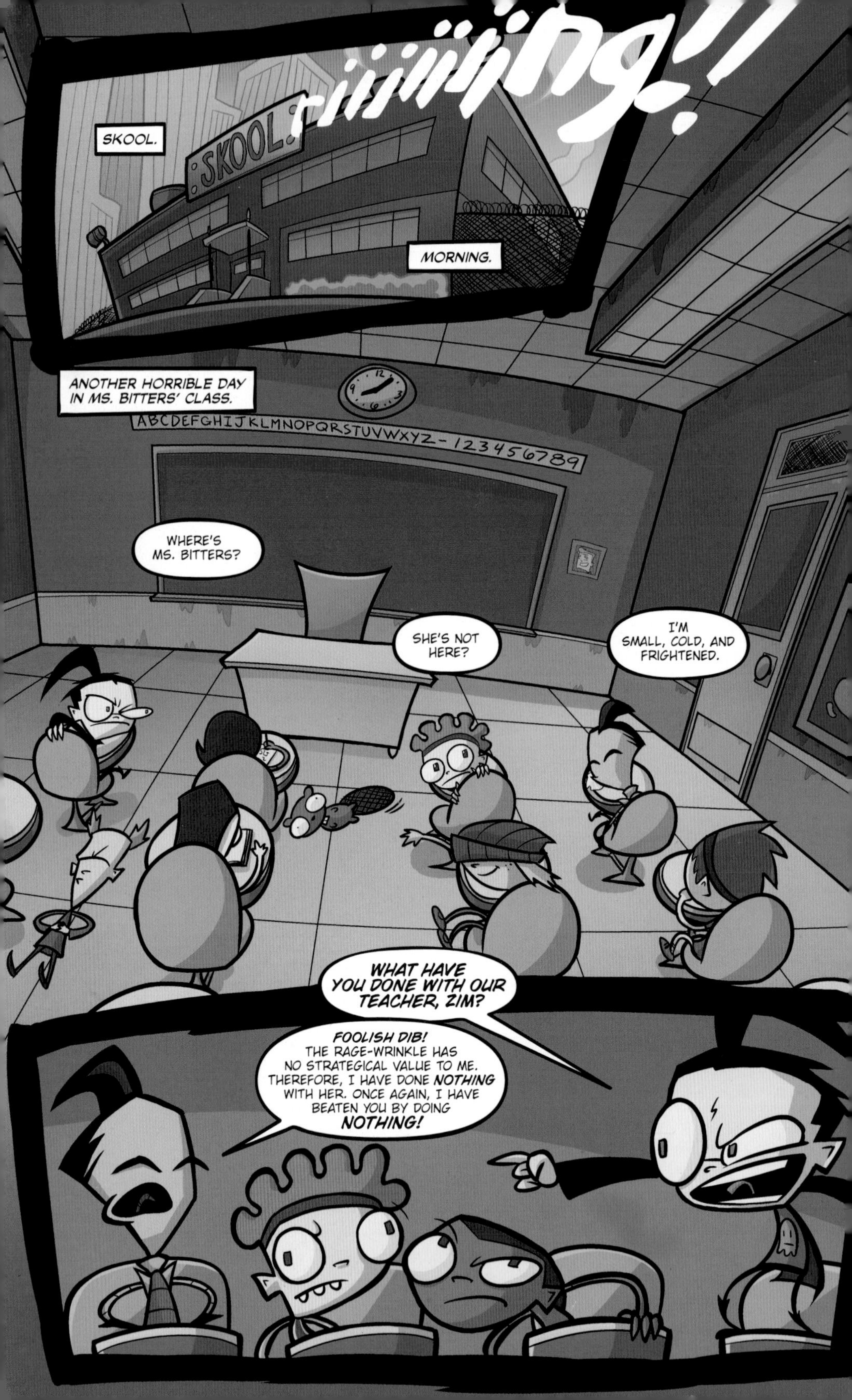

rIIIIIIING!!
SKOOL.
SKOOL
MORNING.
ANOTHER HORRIBLE DAY IN MS. BITTERS' CLASS.
ABCDEFGHIJKLMNOPQRSTUVWXYZ-123456789
WHERE'S MS. BITTERS?
SHE'S NOT HERE?
I'M SMALL, COLD, AND FRIGHTENED.
WHAT HAVE YOU DONE WITH OUR TEACHER, ZIM?
FOOLISH DIB! THE RAGE-WRINKLE HAS NO STRATEGICAL VALUE TO ME. THEREFORE, I HAVE DONE NOTHING WITH HER. ONCE AGAIN, I HAVE BEATEN YOU BY DOING NOTHING!

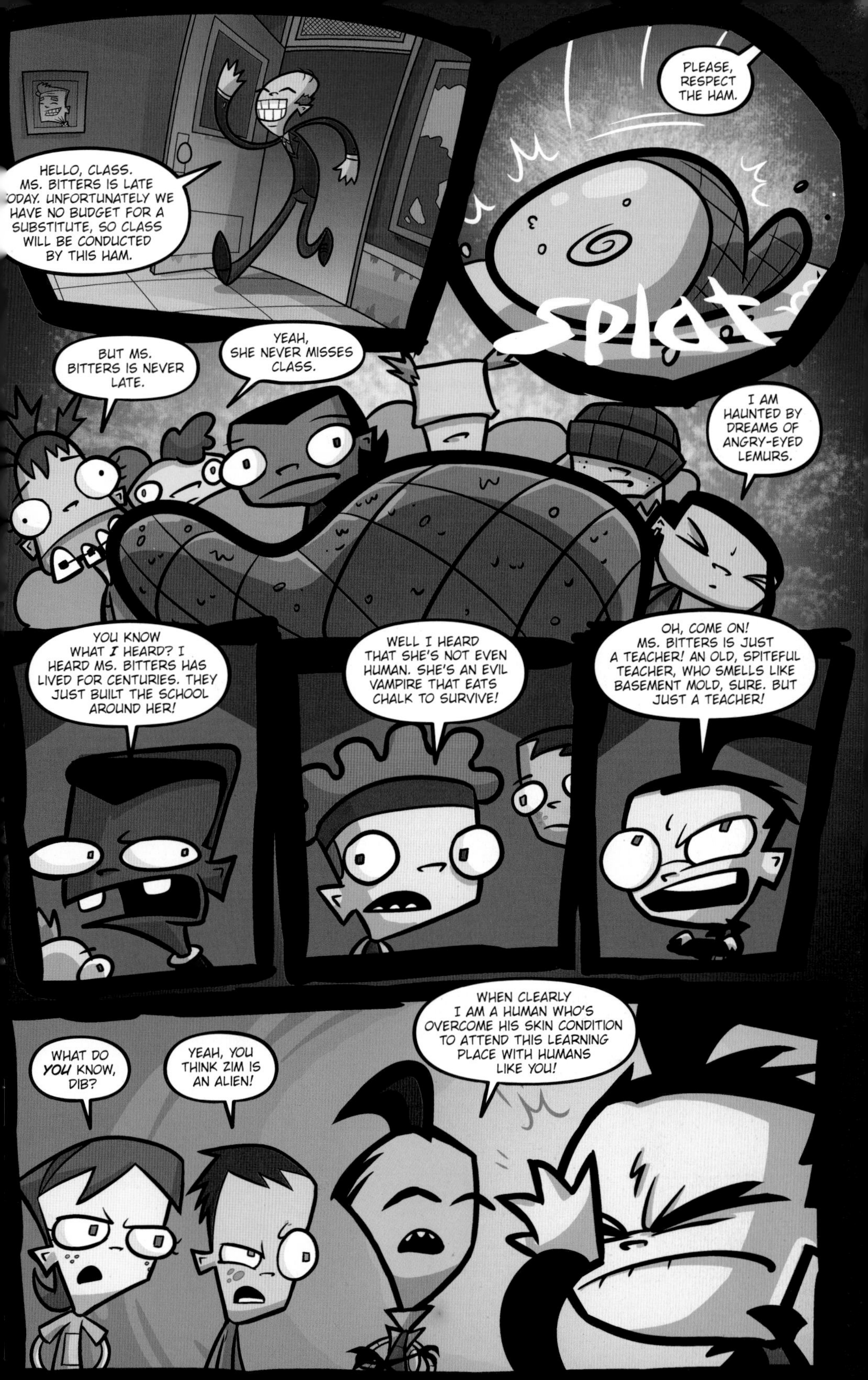
HELLO, CLASS. MS. BITTERS IS LATE TODAY. UNFORTUNATELY WE HAVE NO BUDGET FOR A SUBSTITUTE, SO CLASS WILL BE CONDUCTED BY THIS HAM.
PLEASE, RESPECT THE HAM.
SPLAT
BUT MS. BITTERS IS NEVER LATE.
YEAH, SHE NEVER MISSES CLASS.
I AM HAUNTED BY DREAMS OF ANGRY-EYED LEMURS.
YOU KNOW WHAT *I* HEARD? I HEARD MS. BITTERS HAS LIVED FOR CENTURIES. THEY JUST BUILT THE SCHOOL AROUND HER!
WELL I HEARD THAT SHE'S NOT EVEN HUMAN. SHE'S AN EVIL VAMPIRE THAT EATS CHALK TO SURVIVE!
OH, COME ON! MS. BITTERS IS JUST A TEACHER! AN OLD, SPITEFUL TEACHER, WHO SMELLS LIKE BASEMENT MOLD, SURE. BUT JUST A TEACHER!
WHAT DO ***YOU*** KNOW, DIB?
YEAH, YOU THINK ZIM IS AN ALIEN!
WHEN CLEARLY I AM A HUMAN WHO'S OVERCOME HIS SKIN CONDITION TO ATTEND THIS LEARNING PLACE WITH HUMANS LIKE YOU!

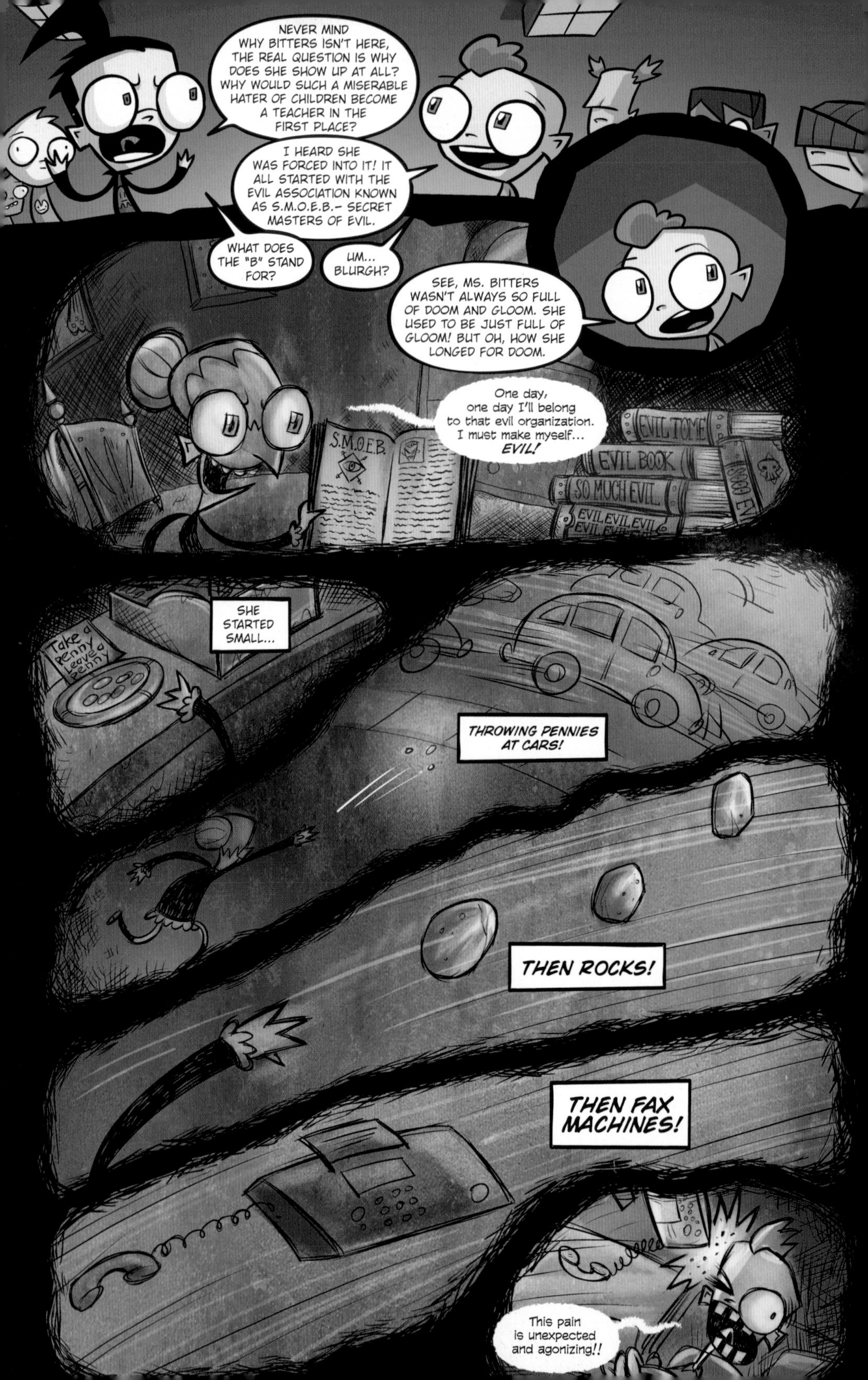
NEVER MIND WHY BITTERS ISN'T HERE, THE REAL QUESTION IS WHY DOES SHE SHOW UP AT ALL? WHY WOULD SUCH A MISERABLE HATER OF CHILDREN BECOME A TEACHER IN THE FIRST PLACE?
I HEARD SHE WAS FORCED INTO IT! IT ALL STARTED WITH THE EVIL ASSOCIATION KNOWN AS S.M.O.E.B.- SECRET MASTERS OF EVIL.
WHAT DOES THE "B" STAND FOR?
UM... BLURGH?
SEE, MS. BITTERS WASN'T ALWAYS SO FULL OF DOOM AND GLOOM. SHE USED TO BE JUST FULL OF GLOOM! BUT OH, HOW SHE LONGED FOR DOOM.
S.M.O.E.B.
One day, one day I'll belong to that evil organization. I must make myself... EVIL!
EVIL TOME
EVIL BOOK
SO MUCH EVIL
EVIL EVIL EVIL
SHE STARTED SMALL...
Take a penny Leave a penny
THROWING PENNIES AT CARS!
THEN ROCKS!
THEN FAX MACHINES!
This pain is unexpected and agonizing!!

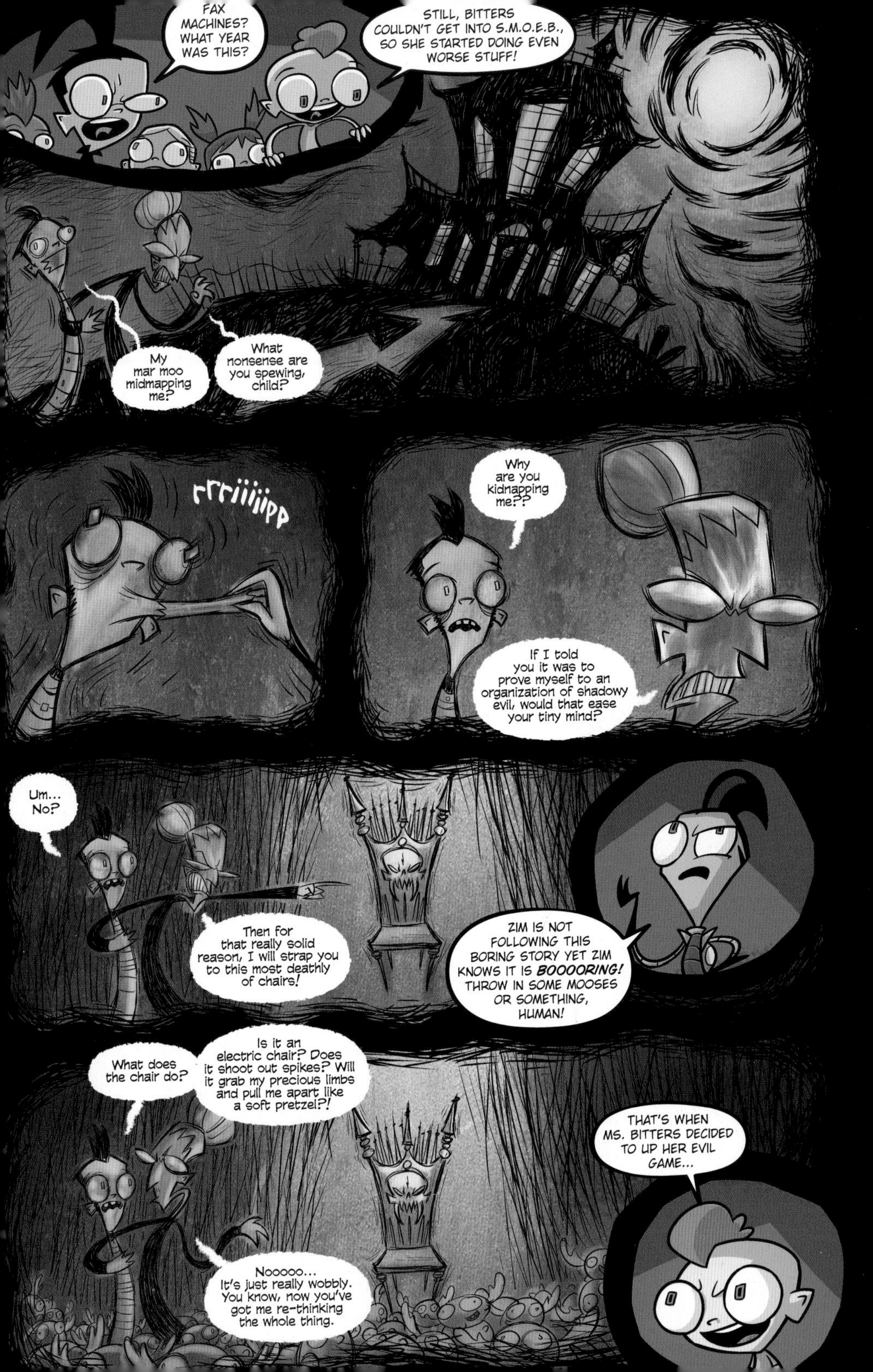

FAX MACHINES? WHAT YEAR WAS THIS?
STILL, BITTERS COULDN'T GET INTO S.M.O.E.B., SO SHE STARTED DOING EVEN WORSE STUFF!
My mar moo midmapping me?
What nonsense are you spewing, child?
rrriiiiipp
Why are you kidnapping me??
If I told you it was to prove myself to an organization of shadowy evil, would that ease your tiny mind?
Um... No?
Then for that really solid reason, I will strap you to this most deathly of chairs!
ZIM IS NOT FOLLOWING THIS BORING STORY YET ZIM KNOWS IT IS BOOOORING! THROW IN SOME MOOSES OR SOMETHING, HUMAN!
What does the chair do?
Is it an electric chair? Does it shoot out spikes? Will it grab my precious limbs and pull me apart like a soft pretzel?!
Nooooo... It's just really wobbly. You know, now you've got me re-thinking the whole thing.
THAT'S WHEN MS. BITTERS DECIDED TO UP HER EVIL GAME...

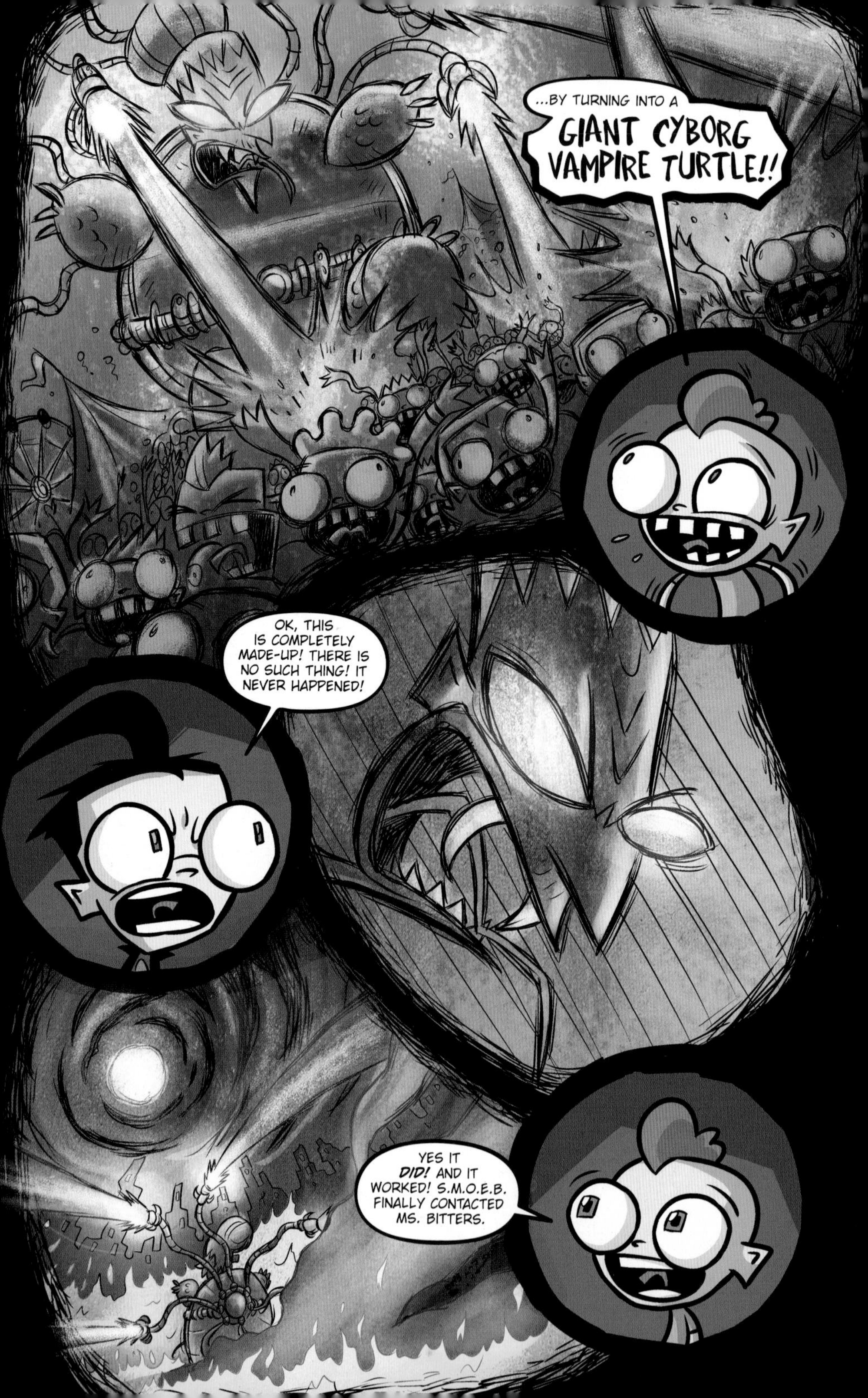
...BY TURNING INTO A GIANT CYBORG VAMPIRE TURTLE!!
OK, THIS IS COMPLETELY MADE-UP! THERE IS NO SUCH THING! IT NEVER HAPPENED!
YES IT DID! AND IT WORKED! S.M.O.E.B. FINALLY CONTACTED MS. BITTERS.

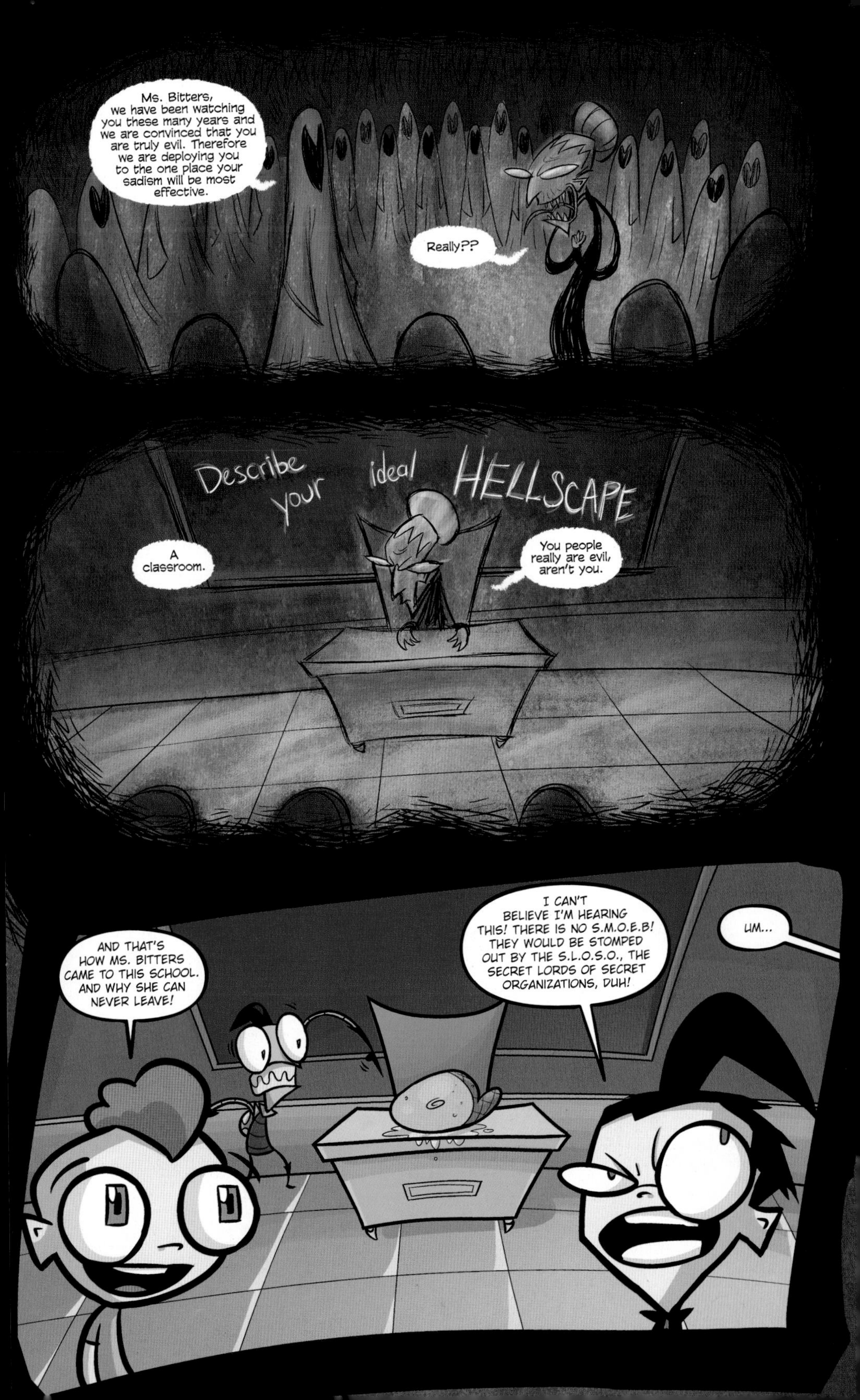
Ms. Bitters, we have been watching you these many years and we are convinced that you are truly evil. Therefore we are deploying you to the one place your sadism will be most effective.
Really??
Describe your ideal HELLSCAPE
A classroom.
You people really are evil, aren't you.
AND THAT'S HOW MS. BITTERS CAME TO THIS SCHOOL. AND WHY SHE CAN NEVER LEAVE!
I CAN'T BELIEVE I'M HEARING THIS! THERE IS NO S.M.O.E.B! THEY WOULD BE STOMPED OUT BY THE S.L.O.S.O., THE SECRET LORDS OF SECRET ORGANIZATIONS, DUH!
UM...

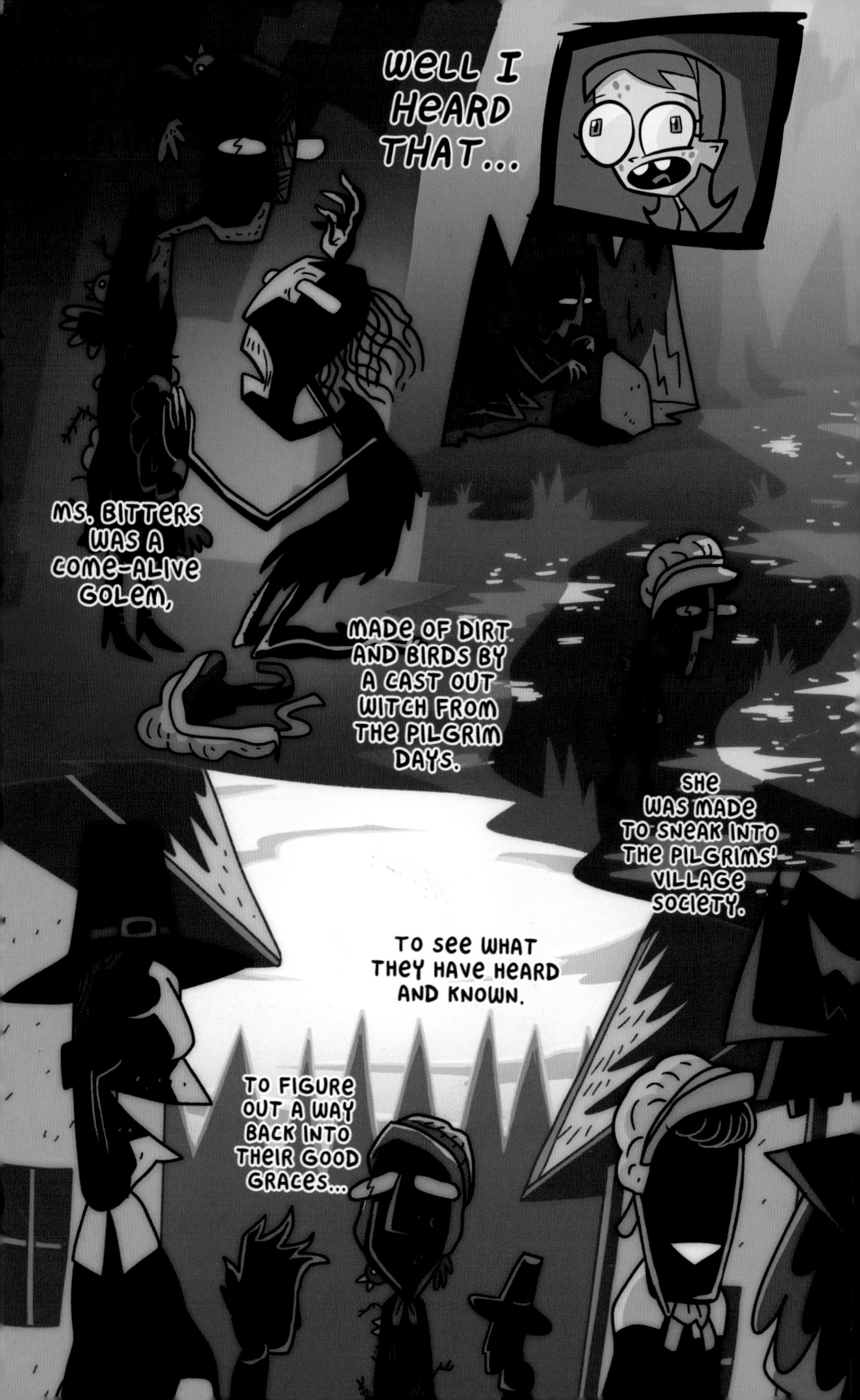
WELL I HEARD THAT...
MS. BITTERS WAS A COME-ALIVE GOLEM,
MADE OF DIRT AND BIRDS BY A CAST OUT WITCH FROM THE PILGRIM DAYS.
SHE WAS MADE TO SNEAK INTO THE PILGRIMS' VILLAGE SOCIETY.
TO SEE WHAT THEY HAVE HEARD AND KNOWN.
TO FIGURE OUT A WAY BACK INTO THEIR GOOD GRACES...

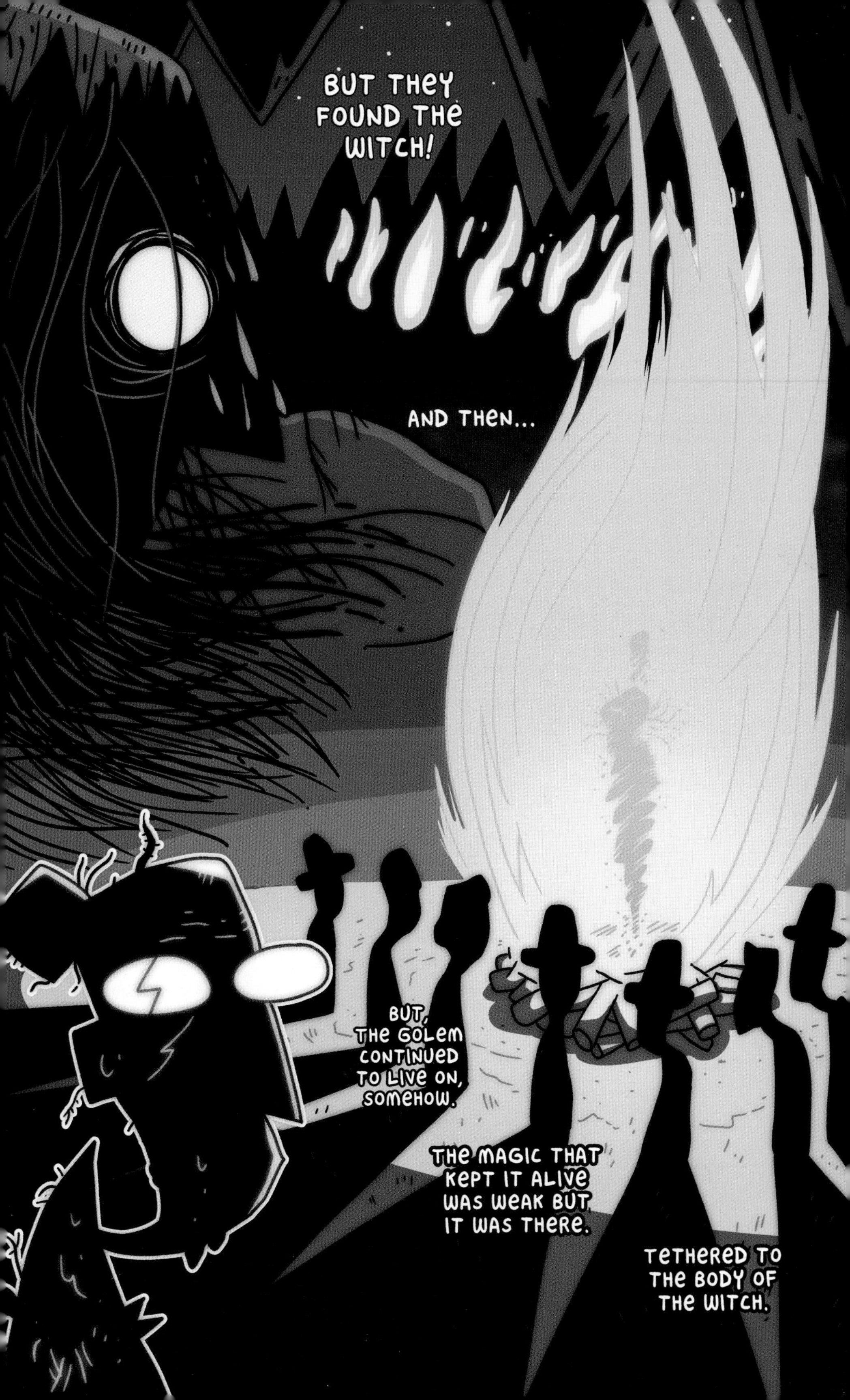
BUT THEY FOUND THE WITCH!
AND THEN...
BUT, THE GOLEM CONTINUED TO LIVE ON, SOMEHOW.
THE MAGIC THAT KEPT IT ALIVE WAS WEAK BUT IT WAS THERE.
TETHERED TO THE BODY OF THE WITCH.

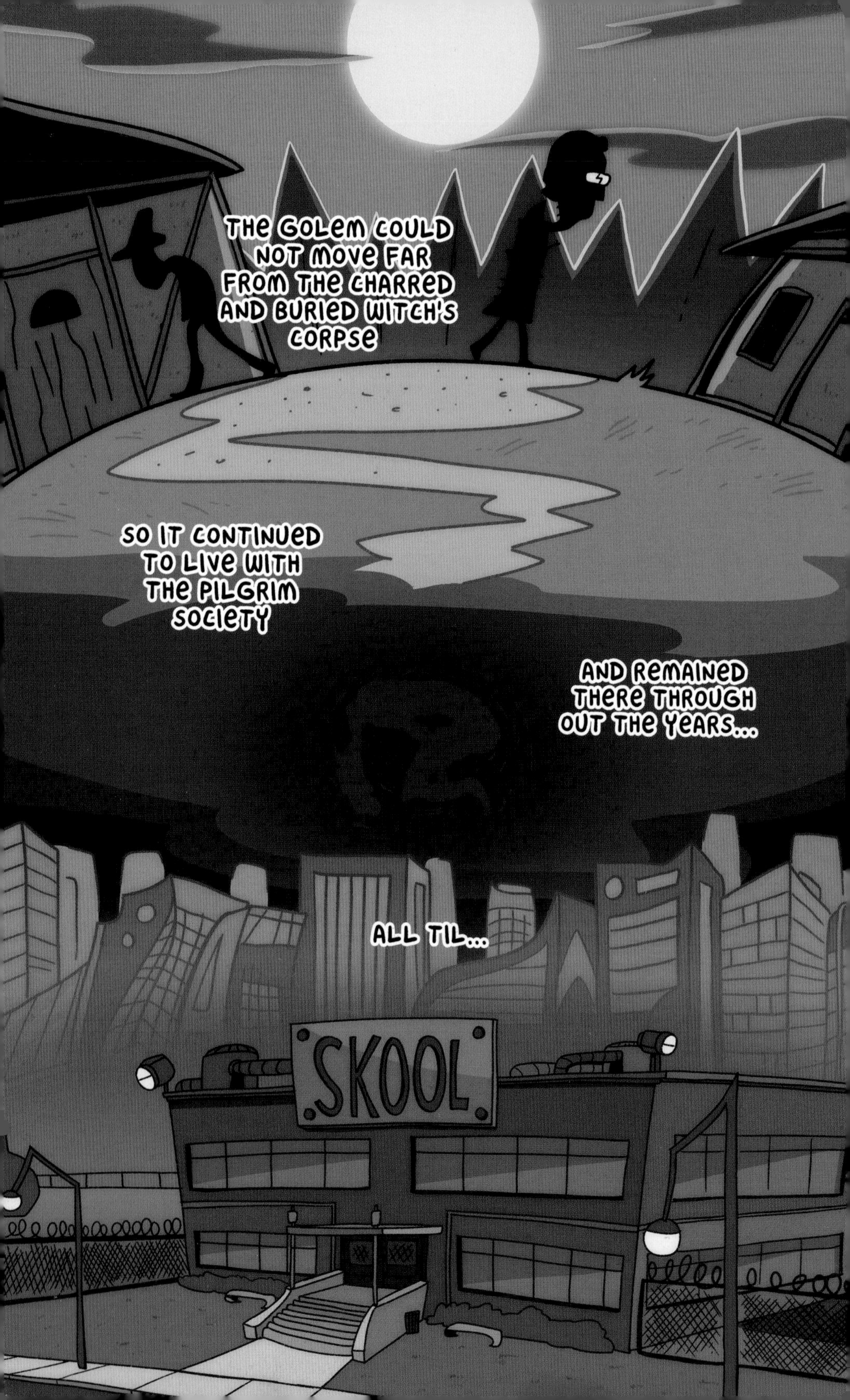
THE GOLEM COULD NOT MOVE FAR FROM THE CHARRED AND BURIED WITCH'S CORPSE
SO IT CONTINUED TO LIVE WITH THE PILGRIM SOCIETY
AND REMAINED THERE THROUGH OUT THE YEARS...
ALL TIL...
SKOOL

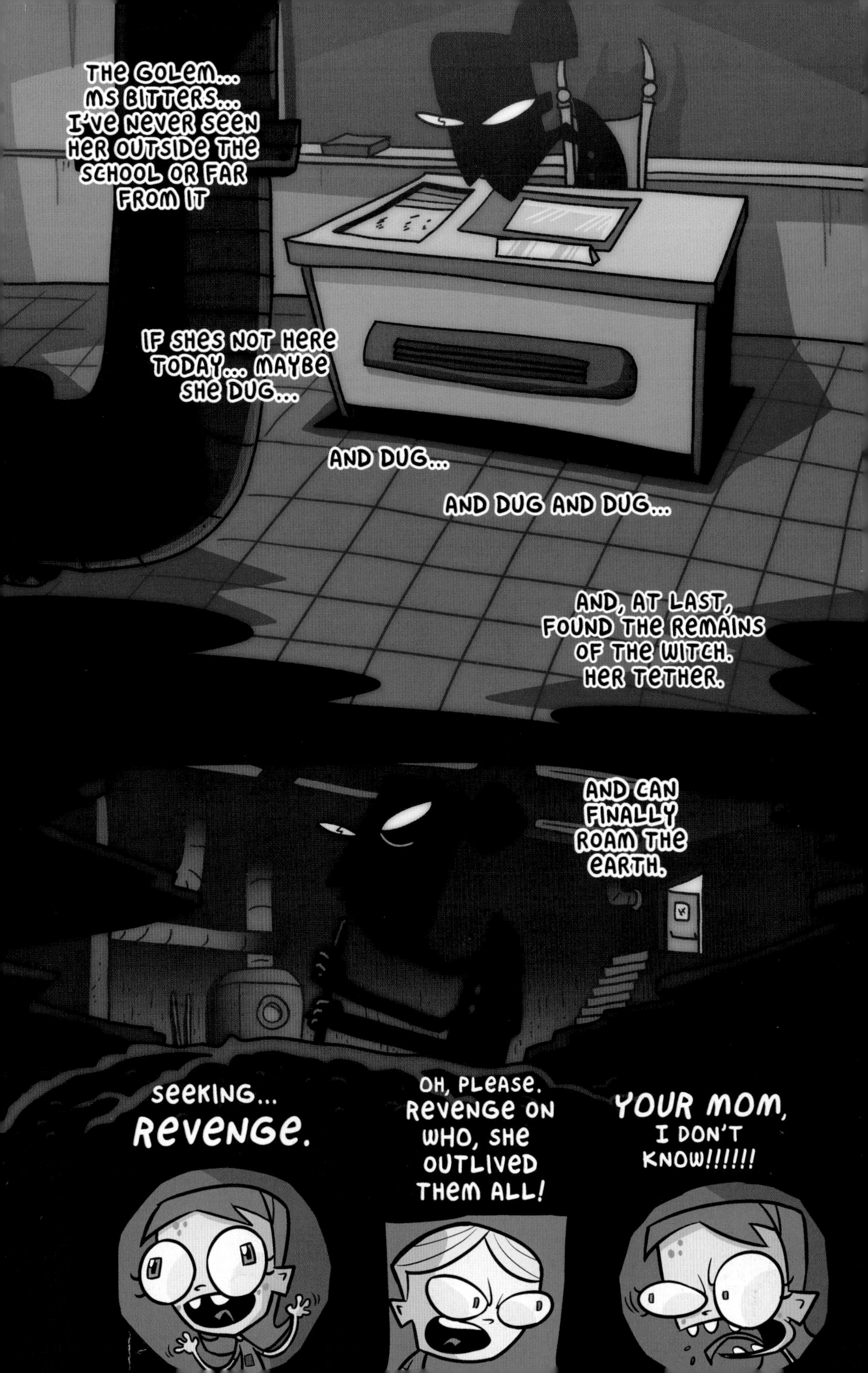
THE GOLEM... MS BITTERS... I'VE NEVER SEEN HER OUTSIDE THE SCHOOL OR FAR FROM IT
IF SHES NOT HERE TODAY... MAYBE SHE DUG...
AND DUG...
AND DUG AND DUG...
AND, AT LAST, FOUND THE REMAINS OF THE WITCH. HER TETHER.
AND CAN FINALLY ROAM THE EARTH.
SEEKING... REVENGE.
OH, PLEASE. REVENGE ON WHO, SHE OUTLIVED THEM ALL!
YOUR MOM, I DON'T KNOW!!!!!!

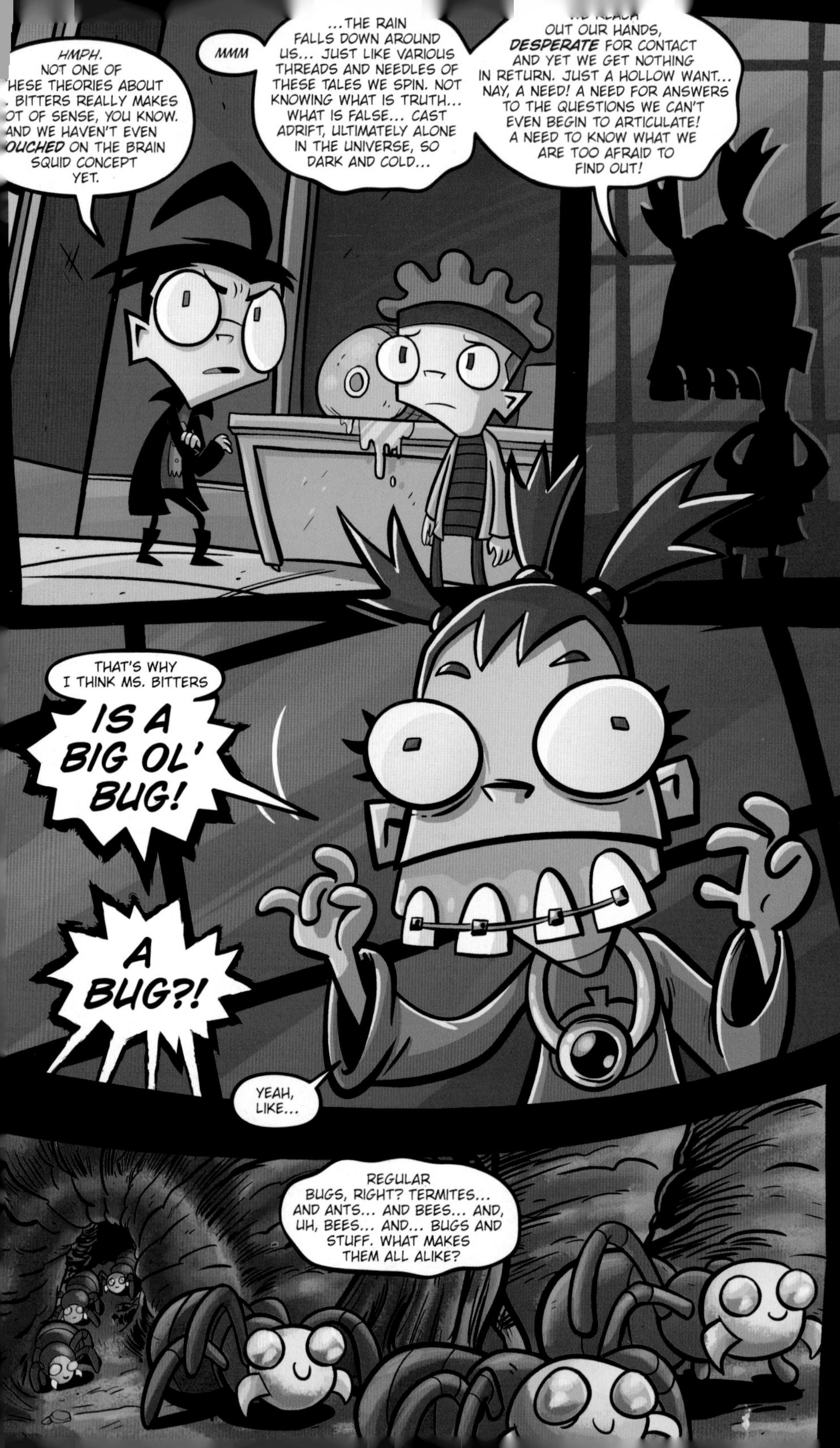
HMPH. NOT ONE OF
HESE THEORIES ABOUT
. BITTERS REALLY MAKES
OT OF SENSE, YOU KNOW.
AND WE HAVEN'T EVEN
OUCHED ON THE BRAIN
SQUID CONCEPT
YET.
MMM
...THE RAIN FALLS DOWN AROUND US... JUST LIKE VARIOUS THREADS AND NEEDLES OF THESE TALES WE SPIN. NOT KNOWING WHAT IS TRUTH... WHAT IS FALSE... CAST ADRIFT, ULTIMATELY ALONE IN THE UNIVERSE, SO DARK AND COLD...
OUT OUR HANDS, DESPERATE FOR CONTACT AND YET WE GET NOTHING IN RETURN. JUST A HOLLOW WANT... NAY, A NEED! A NEED FOR ANSWERS TO THE QUESTIONS WE CAN'T EVEN BEGIN TO ARTICULATE! A NEED TO KNOW WHAT WE ARE TOO AFRAID TO FIND OUT!
THAT'S WHY I THINK MS. BITTERS
IS A BIG OL' BUG!
A BUG?!
YEAH, LIKE...
REGULAR BUGS, RIGHT? TERMITES... AND ANTS... AND BEES... AND, UH, BEES... AND... BUGS AND STUFF. WHAT MAKES THEM ALL ALIKE?

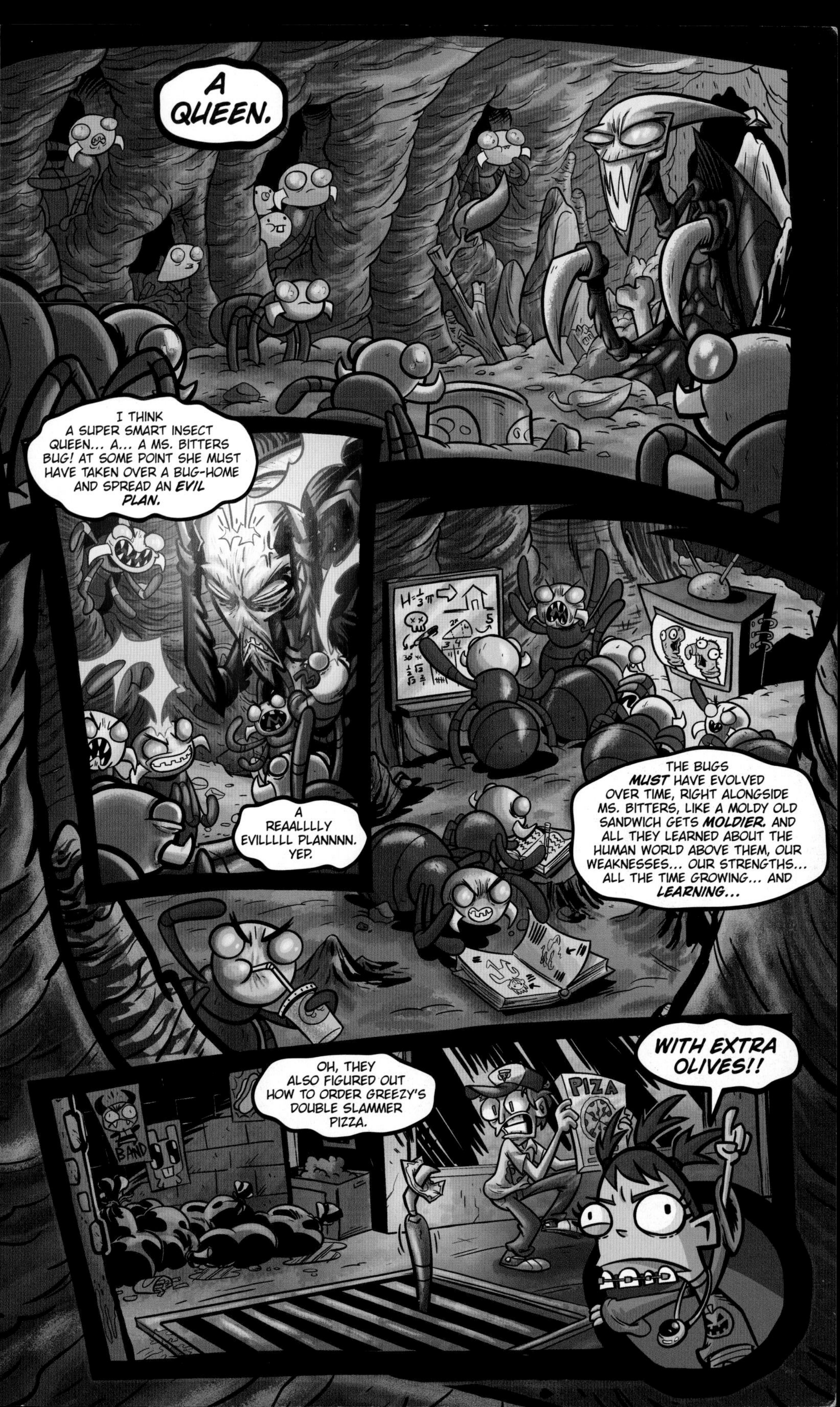
A QUEEN.
I THINK A SUPER SMART INSECT QUEEN... A... A MS. BITTERS BUG! AT SOME POINT SHE MUST HAVE TAKEN OVER A BUG-HOME AND SPREAD AN EVIL PLAN.
A REAALLLLY EVILLLLL PLANNNN. YEP.
THE BUGS MUST HAVE EVOLVED OVER TIME, RIGHT ALONGSIDE MS. BITTERS, LIKE A MOLDY OLD SANDWICH GETS MOLDIER. AND ALL THEY LEARNED ABOUT THE HUMAN WORLD ABOVE THEM, OUR WEAKNESSES... OUR STRENGTHS... ALL THE TIME GROWING... AND LEARNING...
OH, THEY ALSO FIGURED OUT HOW TO ORDER GREEZY'S DOUBLE SLAMMER PIZZA.
WITH EXTRA OLIVES!!
PIZA
BAND

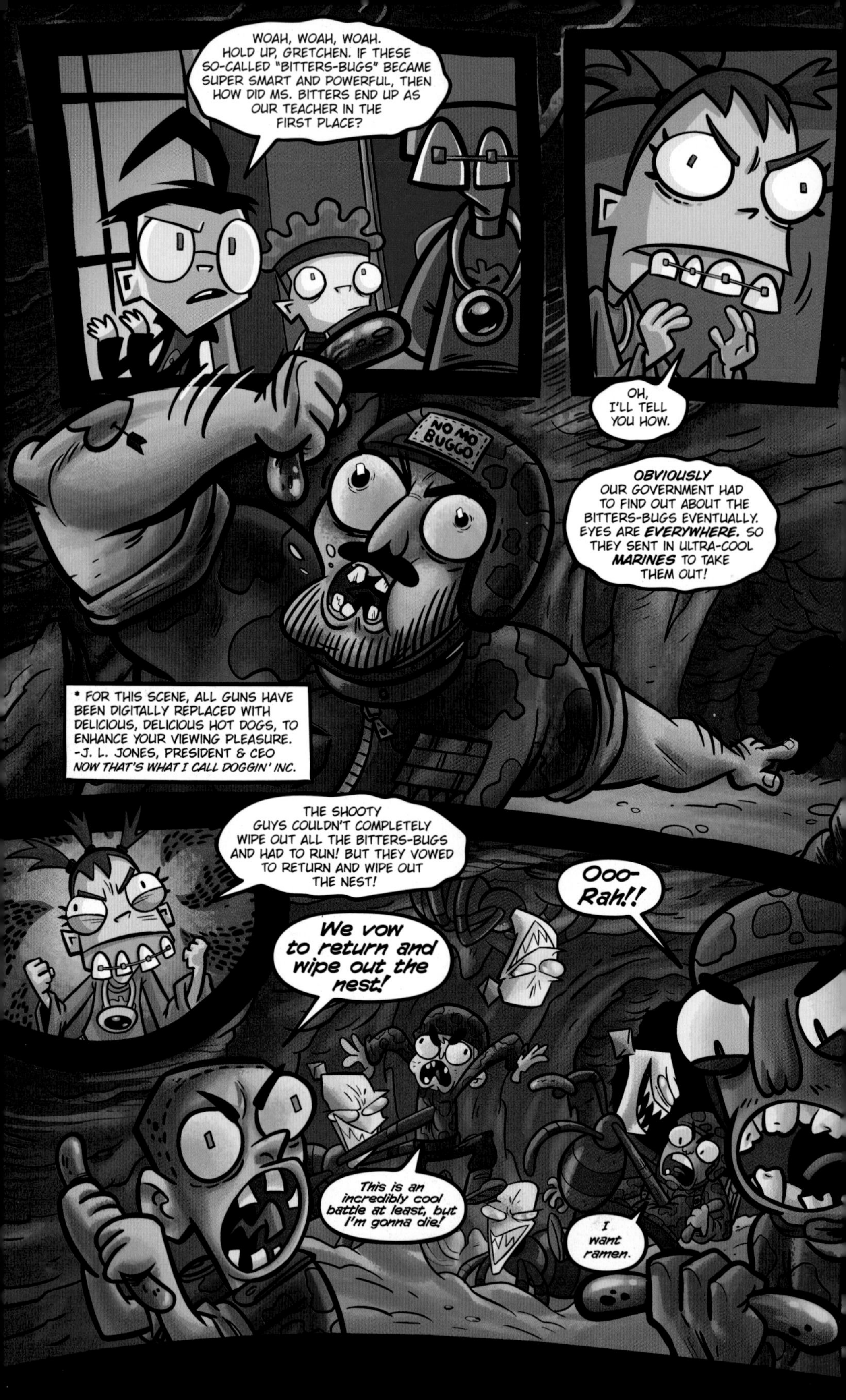
WOAH, WOAH, WOAH. HOLD UP, GRETCHEN. IF THESE SO-CALLED "BITTERS-BUGS" BECAME SUPER SMART AND POWERFUL, THEN HOW DID MS. BITTERS END UP AS OUR TEACHER IN THE FIRST PLACE?
OH, I'LL TELL YOU HOW.
NO MO BUGGO
OBVIOUSLY OUR GOVERNMENT HAD TO FIND OUT ABOUT THE BITTERS-BUGS EVENTUALLY. EYES ARE *EVERYWHERE.* SO THEY SENT IN ULTRA-COOL *MARINES* TO TAKE THEM OUT!
* FOR THIS SCENE, ALL GUNS HAVE BEEN DIGITALLY REPLACED WITH DELICIOUS, DELICIOUS HOT DOGS, TO ENHANCE YOUR VIEWING PLEASURE. -J. L. JONES, PRESIDENT & CEO *NOW THAT'S WHAT I CALL DOGGIN' INC.*
THE SHOOTY GUYS COULDN'T COMPLETELY WIPE OUT ALL THE BITTERS-BUGS AND HAD TO RUN! BUT THEY VOWED TO RETURN AND WIPE OUT THE NEST!
Ooo-Rah!!
We vow to return and wipe out the nest!
This is an incredibly cool battle at least, but I'm gonna die!
I want ramen.

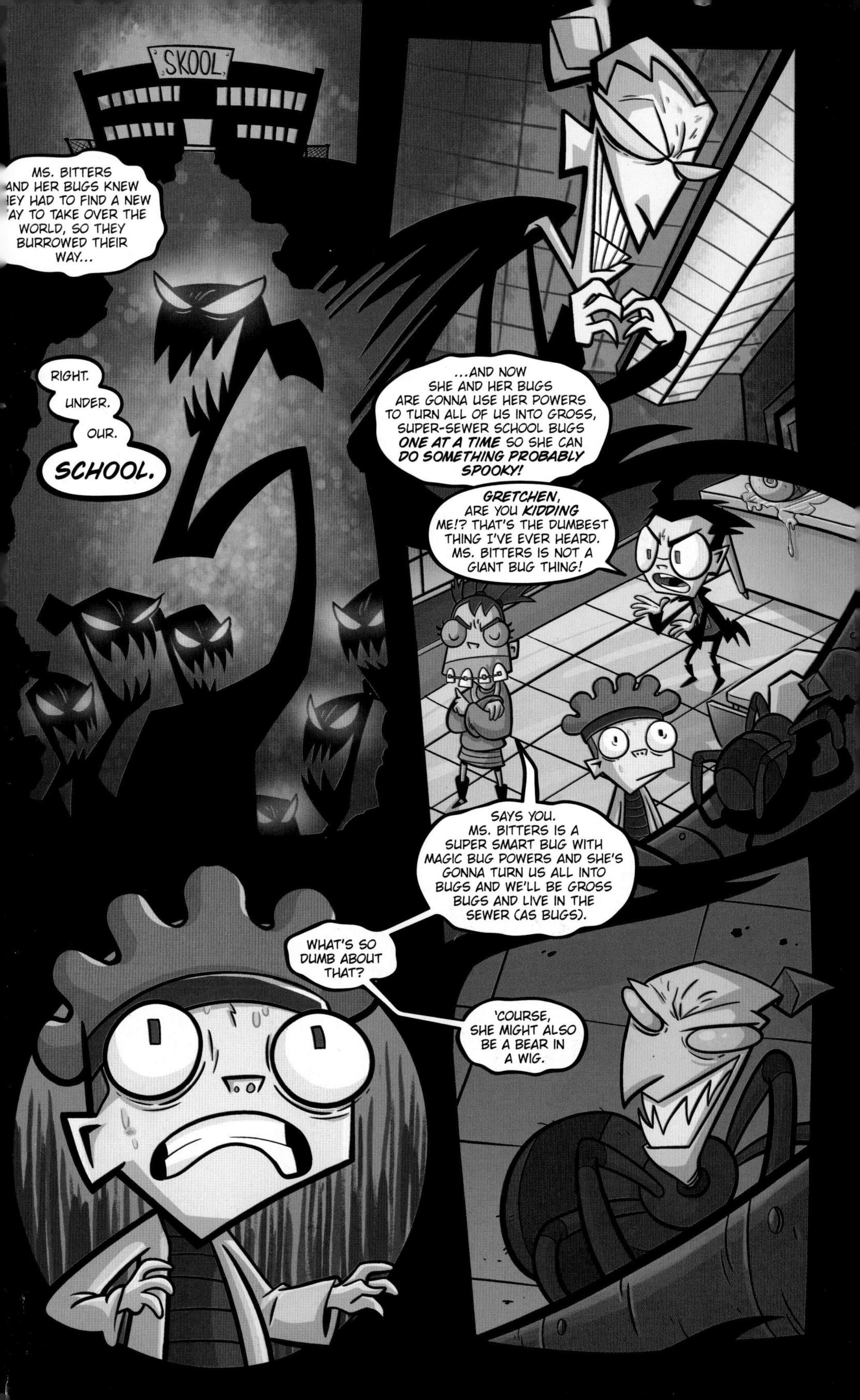
SKOOL
MS. BITTERS AND HER BUGS KNEW HEY HAD TO FIND A NEW AY TO TAKE OVER THE WORLD, SO THEY BURROWED THEIR WAY...
RIGHT.
UNDER.
OUR.
SCHOOL.
...AND NOW SHE AND HER BUGS ARE GONNA USE HER POWERS TO TURN ALL OF US INTO GROSS, SUPER-SEWER SCHOOL BUGS ONE AT A TIME SO SHE CAN DO SOMETHING PROBABLY SPOOKY!
GRETCHEN, ARE YOU KIDDING ME!? THAT'S THE DUMBEST THING I'VE EVER HEARD. MS. BITTERS IS NOT A GIANT BUG THING!
SAYS YOU. MS. BITTERS IS A SUPER SMART BUG WITH MAGIC BUG POWERS AND SHE'S GONNA TURN US ALL INTO BUGS AND WE'LL BE GROSS BUGS AND LIVE IN THE SEWER (AS BUGS).
WHAT'S SO DUMB ABOUT THAT?
'COURSE, SHE MIGHT ALSO BE A BEAR IN A WIG.

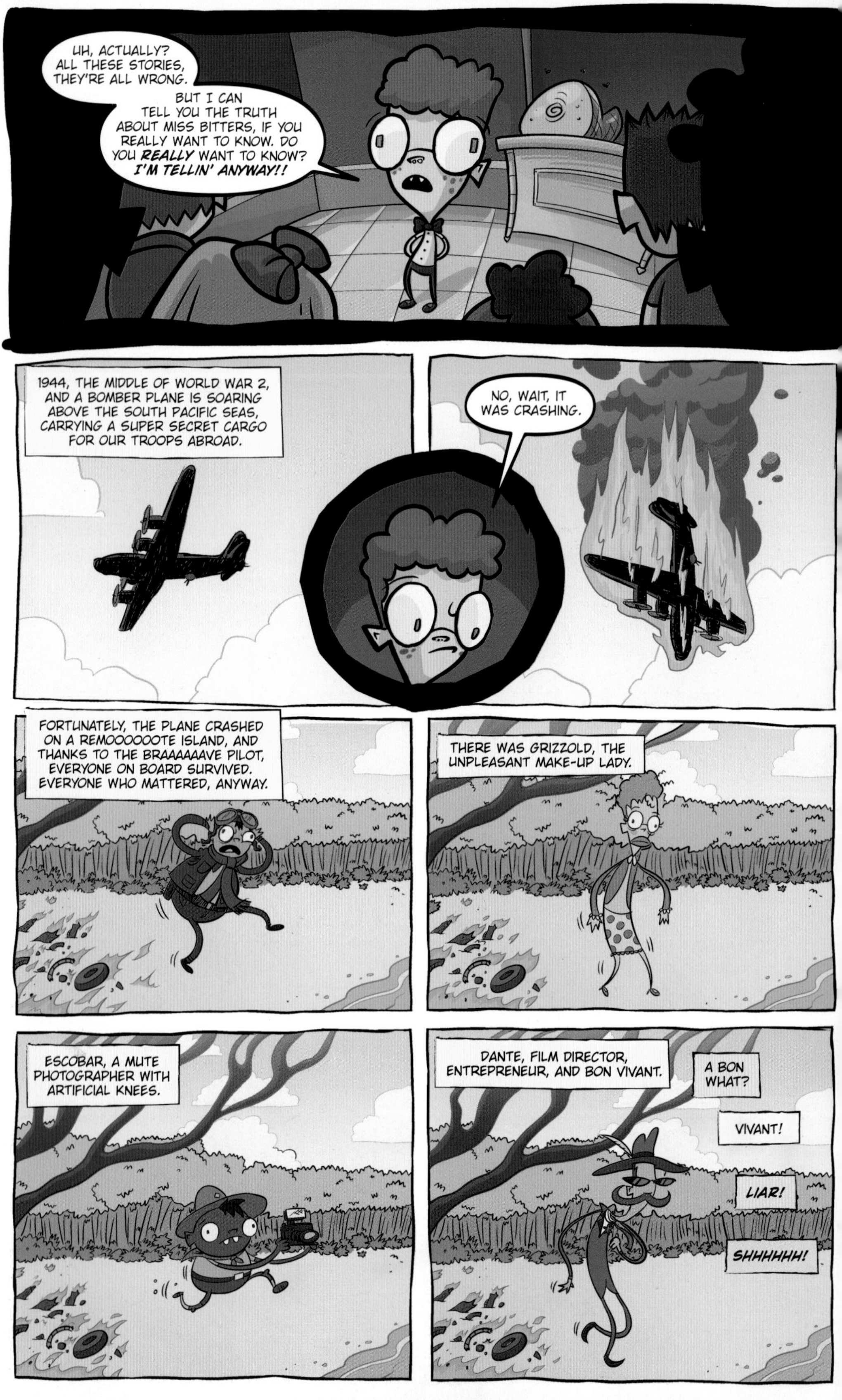
UH, ACTUALLY? ALL THESE STORIES, THEY'RE ALL WRONG.
BUT I CAN TELL YOU THE TRUTH ABOUT MISS BITTERS, IF YOU REALLY WANT TO KNOW. DO YOU **REALLY** WANT TO KNOW? ***I'M TELLIN' ANYWAY!!***
1944, THE MIDDLE OF WORLD WAR 2, AND A BOMBER PLANE IS SOARING ABOVE THE SOUTH PACIFIC SEAS, CARRYING A SUPER SECRET CARGO FOR OUR TROOPS ABROAD.
NO, WAIT, IT WAS CRASHING.
FORTUNATELY, THE PLANE CRASHED ON A REMOOOOOOTE ISLAND, AND THANKS TO THE BRAAAAAAVE PILOT, EVERYONE ON BOARD SURVIVED. EVERYONE WHO MATTERED, ANYWAY.
THERE WAS GRIZZOLD, THE UNPLEASANT MAKE-UP LADY.
ESCOBAR, A MUTE PHOTOGRAPHER WITH ARTIFICIAL KNEES.
DANTE, FILM DIRECTOR, ENTREPRENEUR, AND BON VIVANT.
A BON WHAT?
VIVANT!
LIAR!
SHHHHHH!

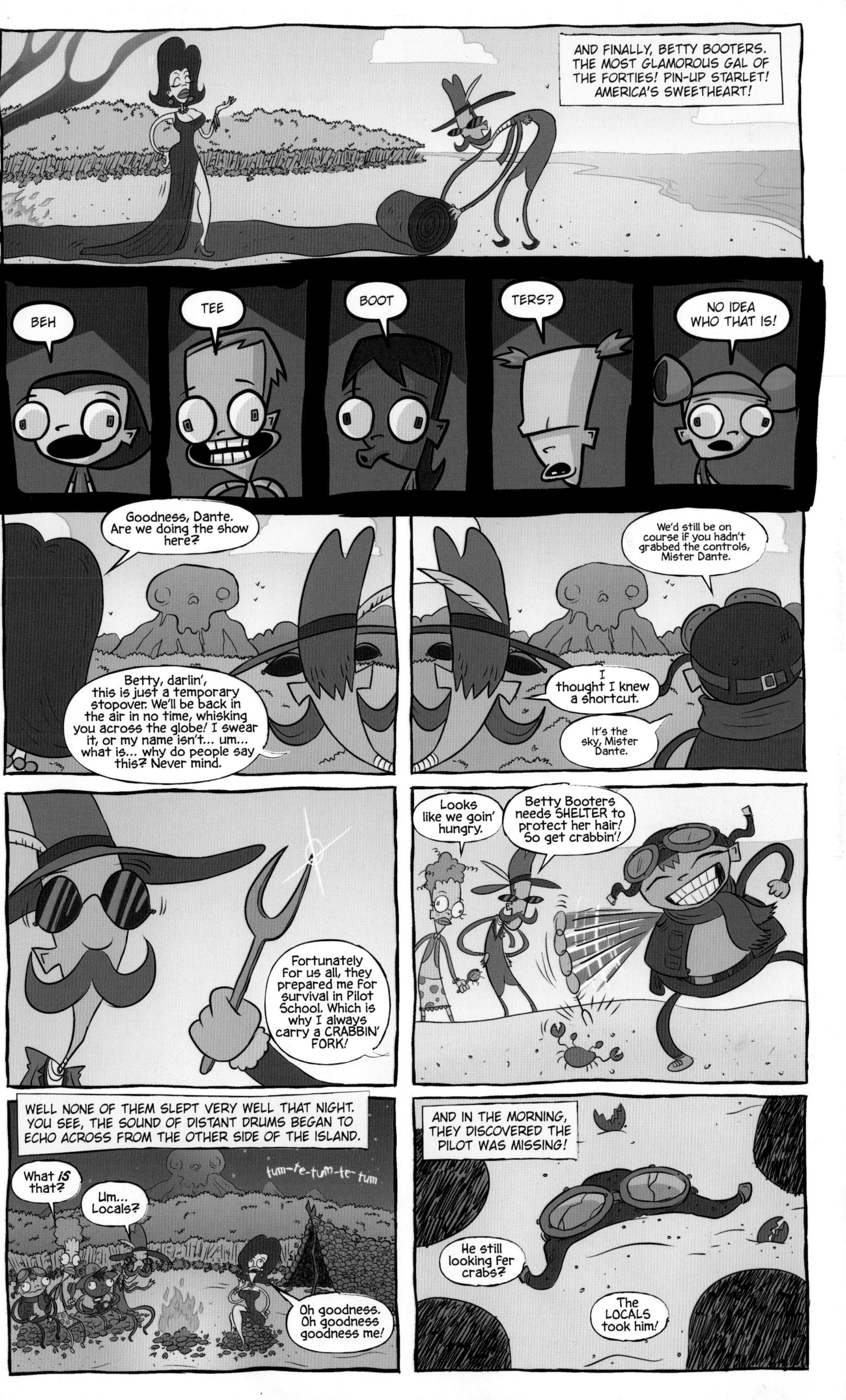

AND FINALLY, BETTY BOOTERS. THE MOST GLAMOROUS GAL OF THE FORTIES! PIN-UP STARLET! AMERICA'S SWEETHEART!
BEH
TEE
BOOT
TERS?
NO IDEA WHO THAT IS!
Goodness, Dante. Are we doing the show here?
Betty, darlin', this is just a temporary stopover. We'll be back in the air in no time, whisking you across the globe! I swear it, or my name isn't... um... what is... why do people say this? Never mind.
We'd still be on course if you hadn't grabbed the controls, Mister Dante.
I thought I knew a shortcut.
It's the sky, Mister Dante.
Fortunately for us all, they prepared me for survival in Pilot School. Which is why I always carry a CRABBIN' FORK!
Looks like we goin' hungry.
Betty Booters needs SHELTER to protect her hair! So get crabbin'!
WELL NONE OF THEM SLEPT VERY WELL THAT NIGHT. YOU SEE, THE SOUND OF DISTANT DRUMS BEGAN TO ECHO ACROSS FROM THE OTHER SIDE OF THE ISLAND.
What *IS* that?
tum-te-tum-te-tum
Um... Locals?
Oh goodness. Oh goodness goodness me!
AND IN THE MORNING, THEY DISCOVERED THE PILOT WAS MISSING!
He still looking fer crabs?
The LOCALS took him!

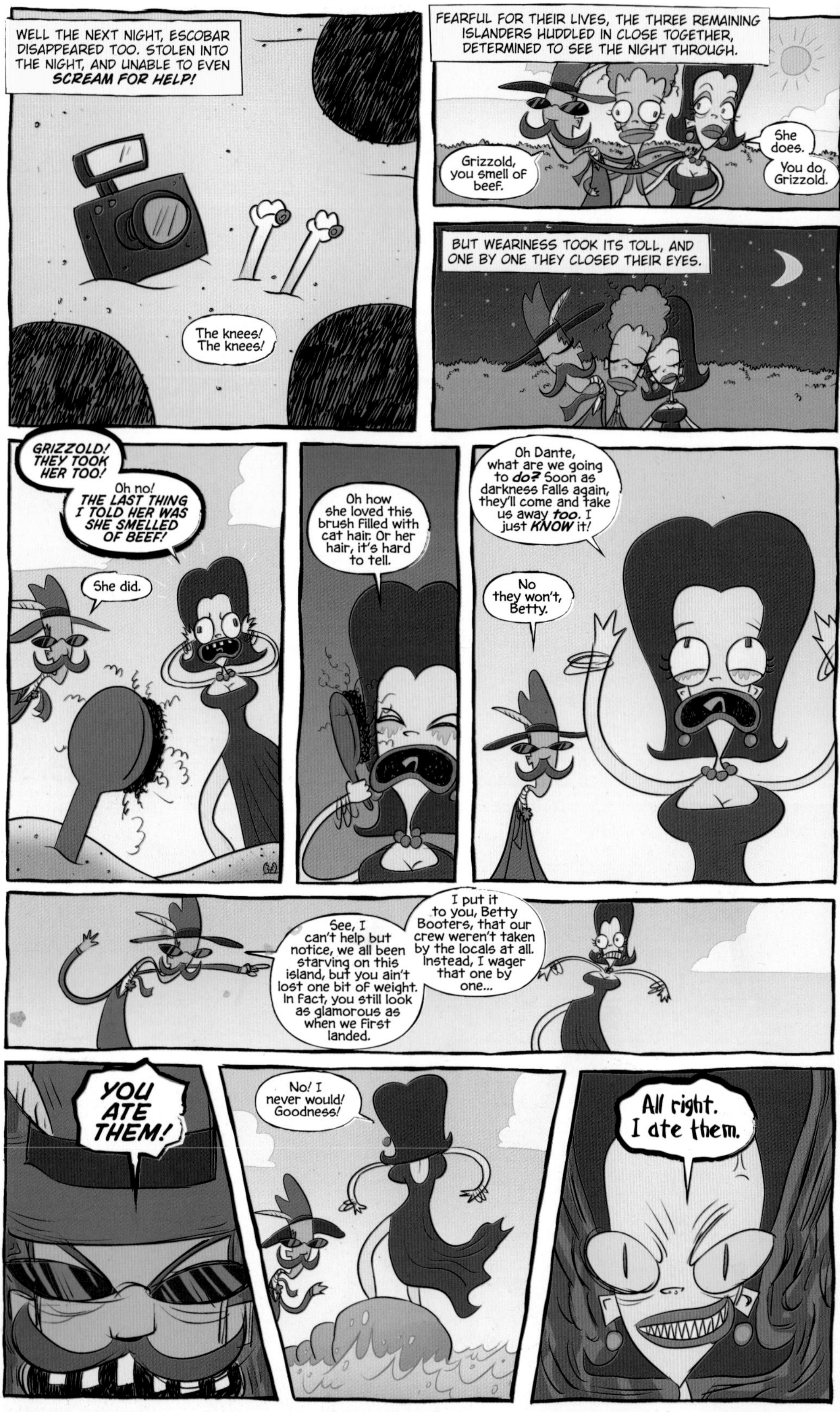
WELL THE NEXT NIGHT, ESCOBAR DISAPPEARED TOO. STOLEN INTO THE NIGHT, AND UNABLE TO EVEN SCREAM FOR HELP!
The knees! The knees!
FEARFUL FOR THEIR LIVES, THE THREE REMAINING ISLANDERS HUDDLED IN CLOSE TOGETHER, DETERMINED TO SEE THE NIGHT THROUGH.
Grizzold, you smell of beef.
She does.
You do, Grizzold.
BUT WEARINESS TOOK ITS TOLL, AND ONE BY ONE THEY CLOSED THEIR EYES.
GRIZZOLD! THEY TOOK HER TOO!
Oh no! THE LAST THING I TOLD HER WAS SHE SMELLED OF BEEF!
She did.
Oh how she loved this brush filled with cat hair. Or her hair, it's hard to tell.
Oh Dante, what are we going to do? Soon as darkness falls again, they'll come and take us away too. I just KNOW it!
No they won't, Betty.
See, I can't help but notice, we all been starving on this island, but you ain't lost one bit of weight. In fact, you still look as glamorous as when we first landed.
I put it to you, Betty Booters, that our crew weren't taken by the locals at all. Instead, I wager that one by one...
YOU ATE THEM!
No! I never would! Goodness!
All right. I ate them.

It's what my kind does! And now that you've found me out, Mr. Dante, you will never live to tell the tale!

No, I think I will.

What? Why?

Because...

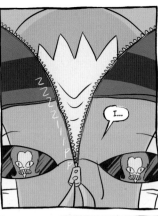

ZZZNNIIIIP

I...

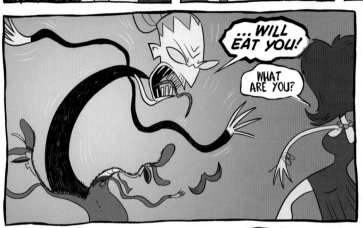

...WILL EAT YOU!

WHAT ARE YOU?

WAIT! The disguise, the plane crash, you... PLANNED all this!

OF COURSE I did. How else was I going to get a Flesh-eater alone to eat its Flesh?

NO! NO! Wait, there were probably a lot of easier ways. But... GET YOUR HANDS OFF ME!

Relax, I'm not going to use my hands...

I have a CRABBIN' FORK!

AAAAAAAA

AND THAT STORY IS TRUE AND IT IS FACT. THE END.

NO!

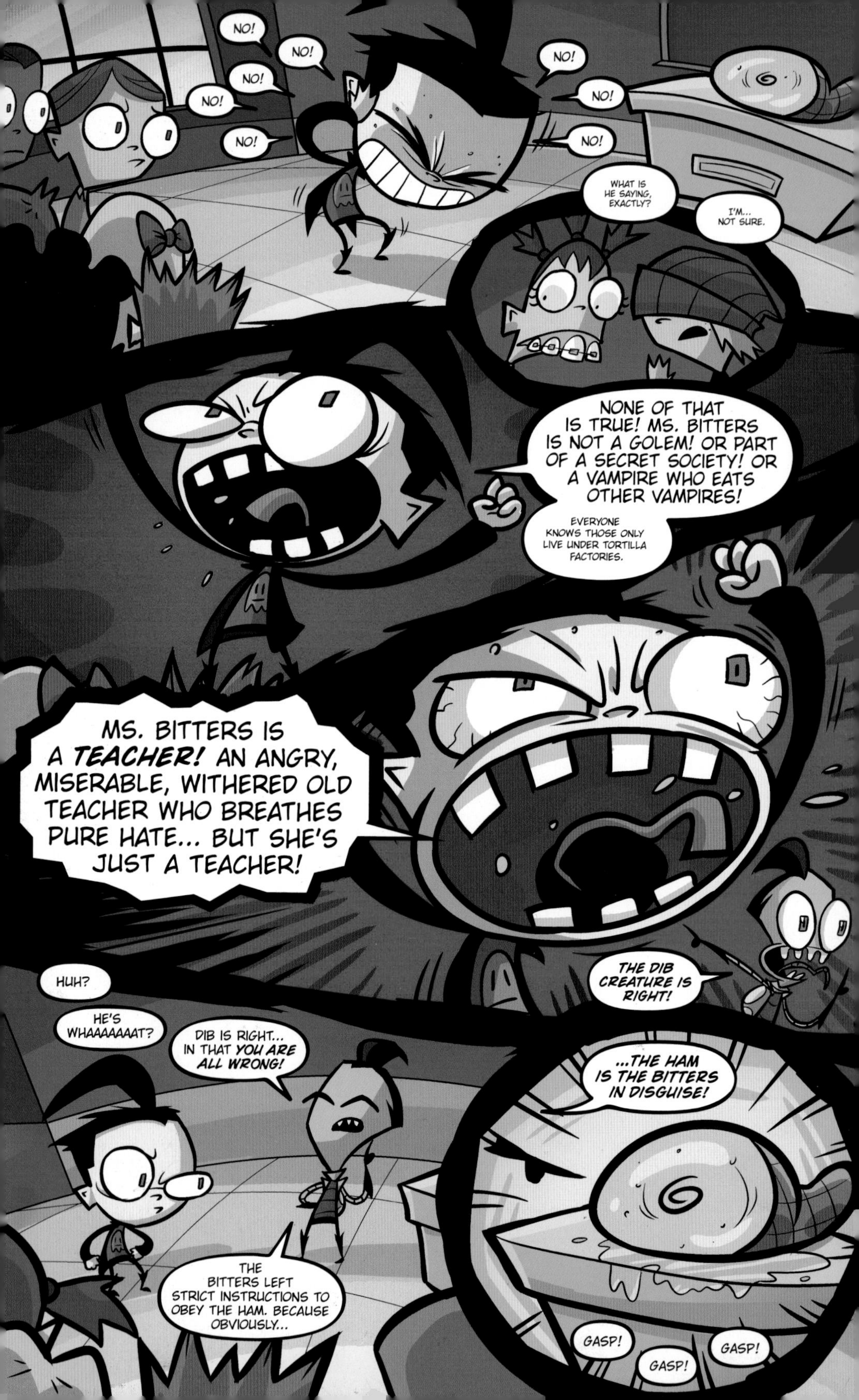
NO!
NO!
NO!
NO!
NO!
NO!
NO!
NO!
WHAT IS HE SAYING, EXACTLY?
I'M... NOT SURE.
NONE OF THAT IS TRUE! MS. BITTERS IS NOT A GOLEM! OR PART OF A SECRET SOCIETY! OR A VAMPIRE WHO EATS OTHER VAMPIRES!
EVERYONE KNOWS THOSE ONLY LIVE UNDER TORTILLA FACTORIES.
MS. BITTERS IS A TEACHER! AN ANGRY, MISERABLE, WITHERED OLD TEACHER WHO BREATHES PURE HATE... BUT SHE'S JUST A TEACHER!
THE DIB CREATURE IS RIGHT!
HUH?
HE'S WHAAAAAAAT?
DIB IS RIGHT... IN THAT YOU ARE ALL WRONG!
THE BITTERS LEFT STRICT INSTRUCTIONS TO OBEY THE HAM. BECAUSE OBVIOUSLY...
...THE HAM IS THE BITTERS IN DISGUISE!
GASP!
GASP!
GASP!

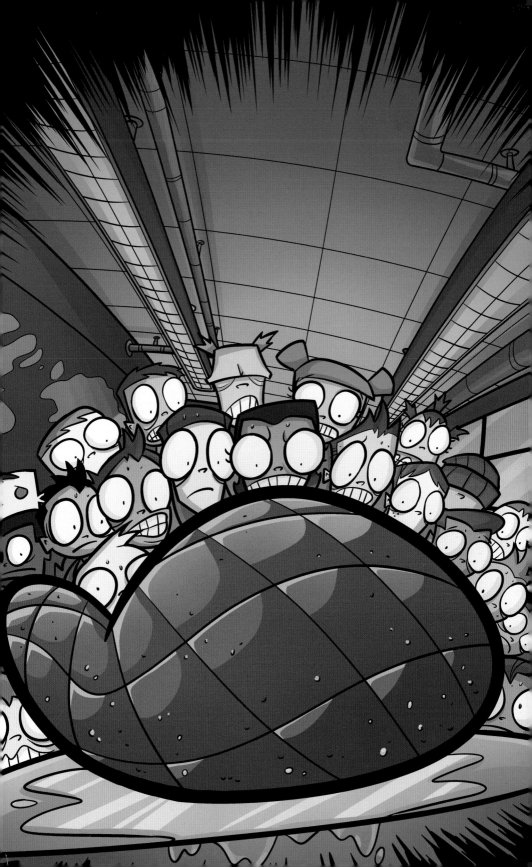

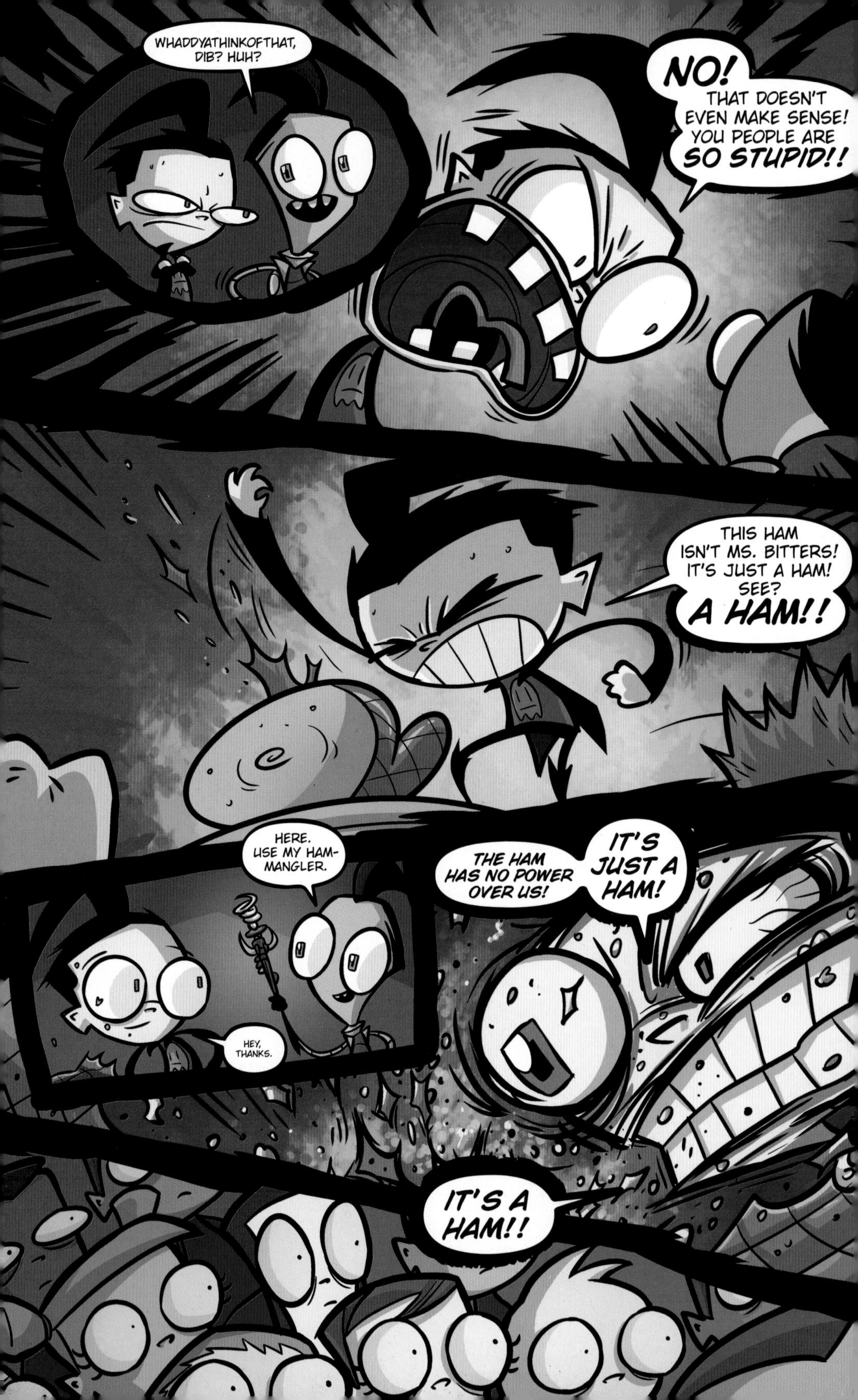

WHADDYATHINKOFTHAT, DIB? HUH?
NO! THAT DOESN'T EVEN MAKE SENSE! YOU PEOPLE ARE SO STUPID!!
THIS HAM ISN'T MS. BITTERS! IT'S JUST A HAM! SEE? A HAM!!
HERE. USE MY HAM-MANGLER.
HEY, THANKS.
THE HAM HAS NO POWER OVER US!
IT'S JUST A HAM!
IT'S A HAM!!

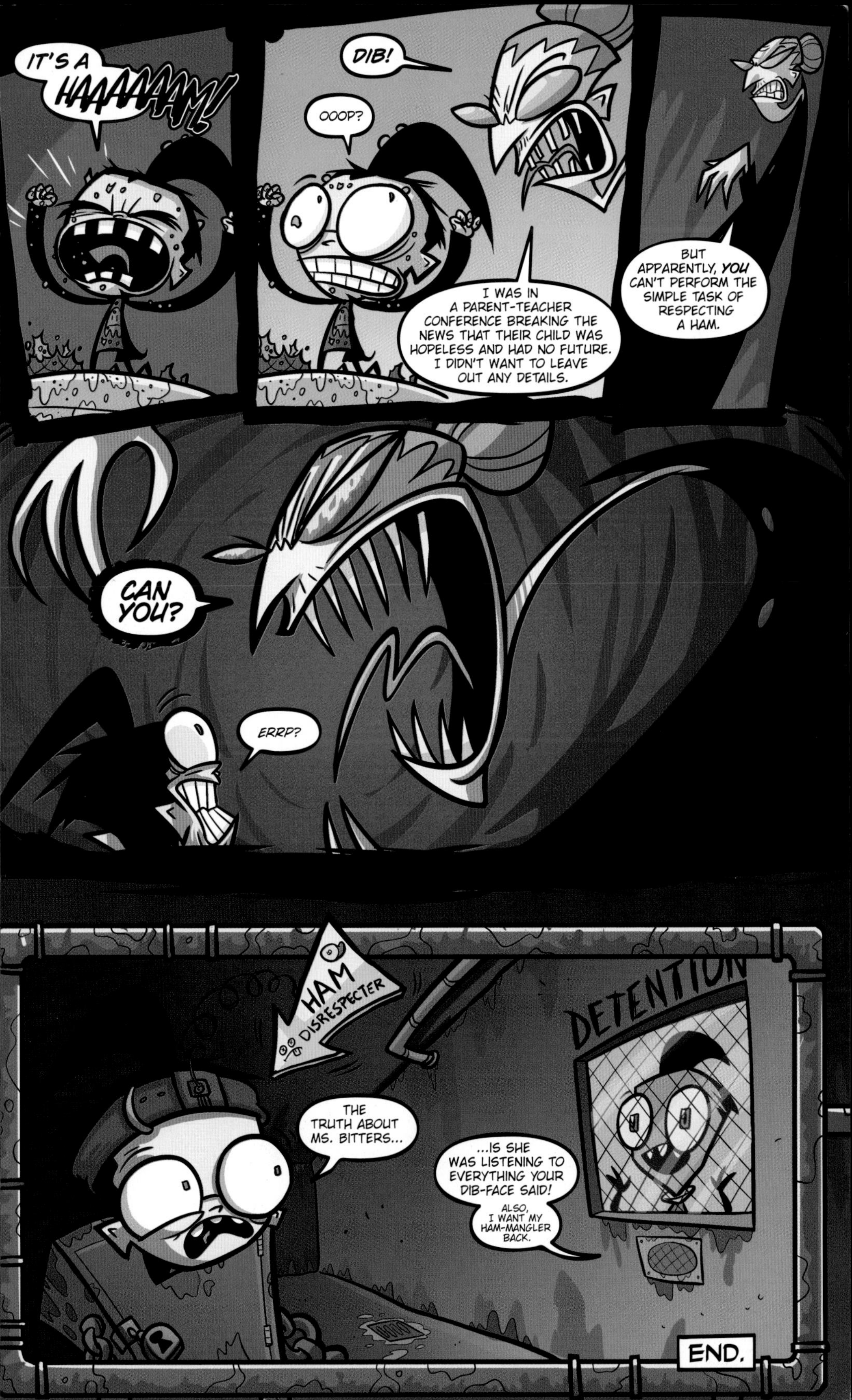

IT'S A HAAAAAAAM!
DIB!
OOOP?
I WAS IN A PARENT-TEACHER CONFERENCE BREAKING THE NEWS THAT THEIR CHILD WAS HOPELESS AND HAD NO FUTURE. I DIDN'T WANT TO LEAVE OUT ANY DETAILS.
BUT APPARENTLY, YOU CAN'T PERFORM THE SIMPLE TASK OF RESPECTING A HAM.
CAN YOU?
ERRP?
HAM DISRESPECTER
DETENTION
THE TRUTH ABOUT MS. BITTERS...
...IS SHE WAS LISTENING TO EVERYTHING YOUR DIB-FACE SAID!
ALSO, I WANT MY HAM-MANGLER BACK.
END.

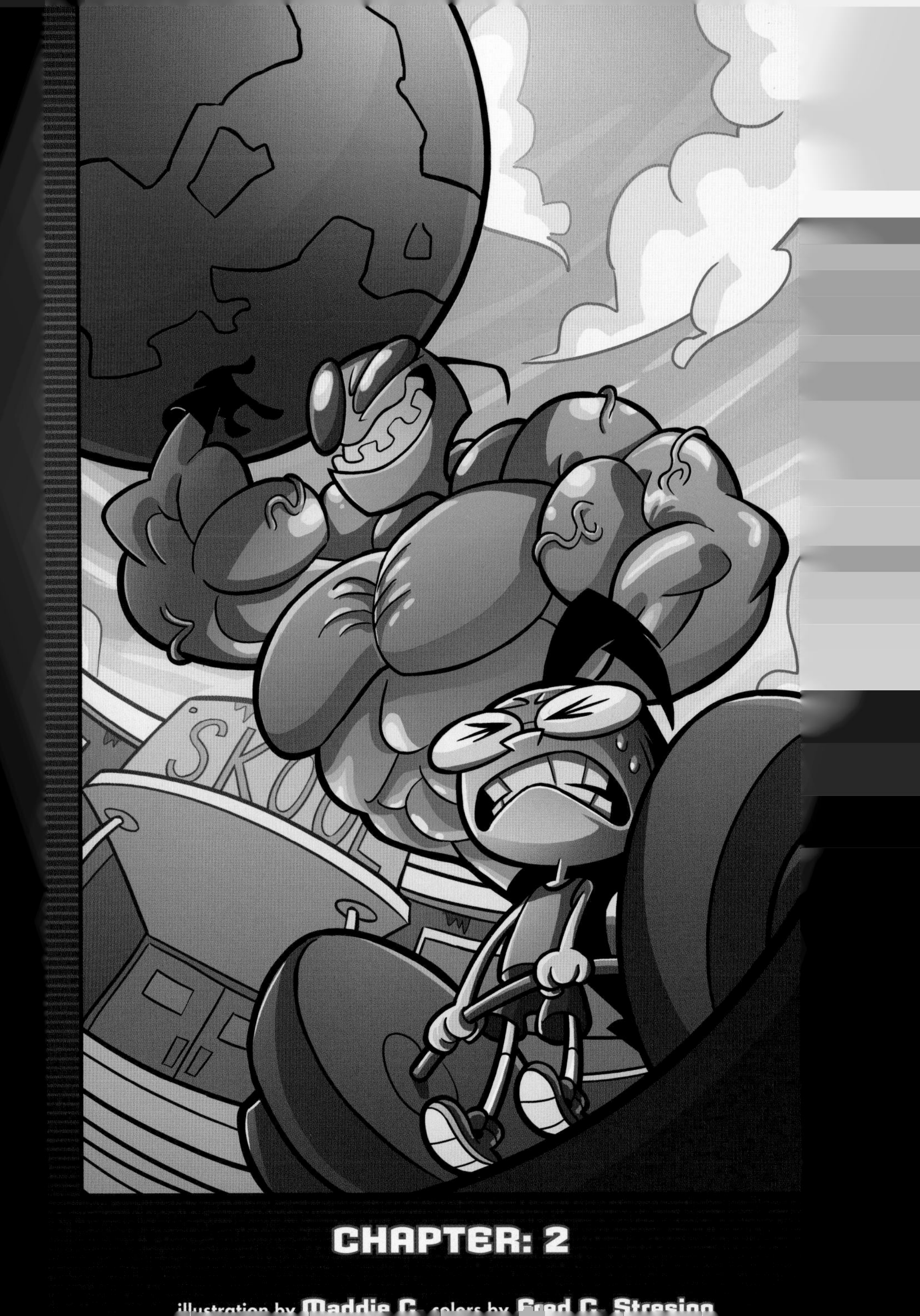
SKOOL

CHAPTER: 2

illustration by Maddie C. colors by Fred C. Stresing

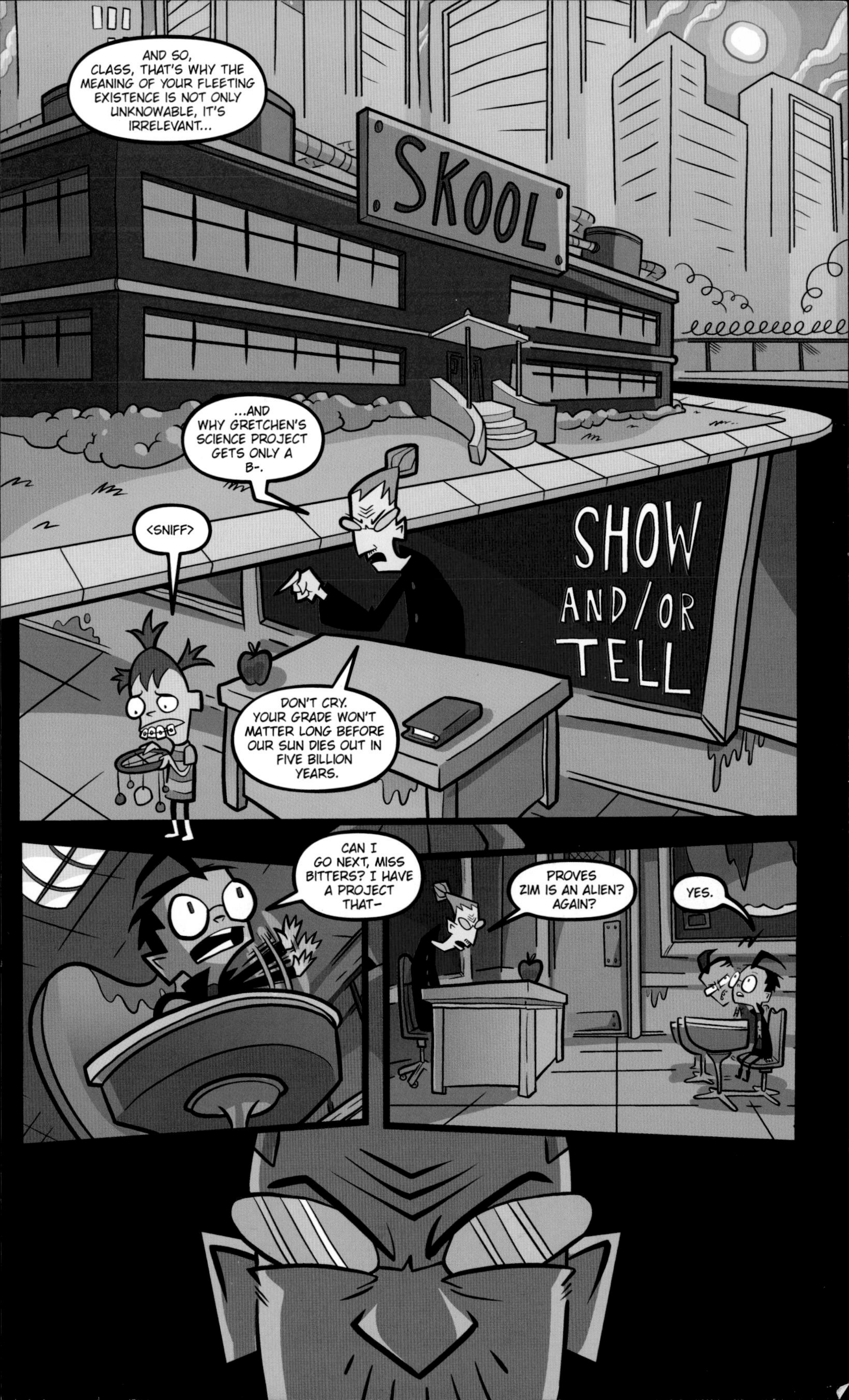
AND SO, CLASS, THAT'S WHY THE MEANING OF YOUR FLEETING EXISTENCE IS NOT ONLY UNKNOWABLE, IT'S IRRELEVANT...
SKOOL
...AND WHY GRETCHEN'S SCIENCE PROJECT GETS ONLY A B-.
<SNIFF>
SHOW AND/OR TELL
DON'T CRY. YOUR GRADE WON'T MATTER LONG BEFORE OUR SUN DIES OUT IN FIVE BILLION YEARS.
CAN I GO NEXT, MISS BITTERS? I HAVE A PROJECT THAT-
PROVES ZIM IS AN ALIEN? AGAIN?
YES.

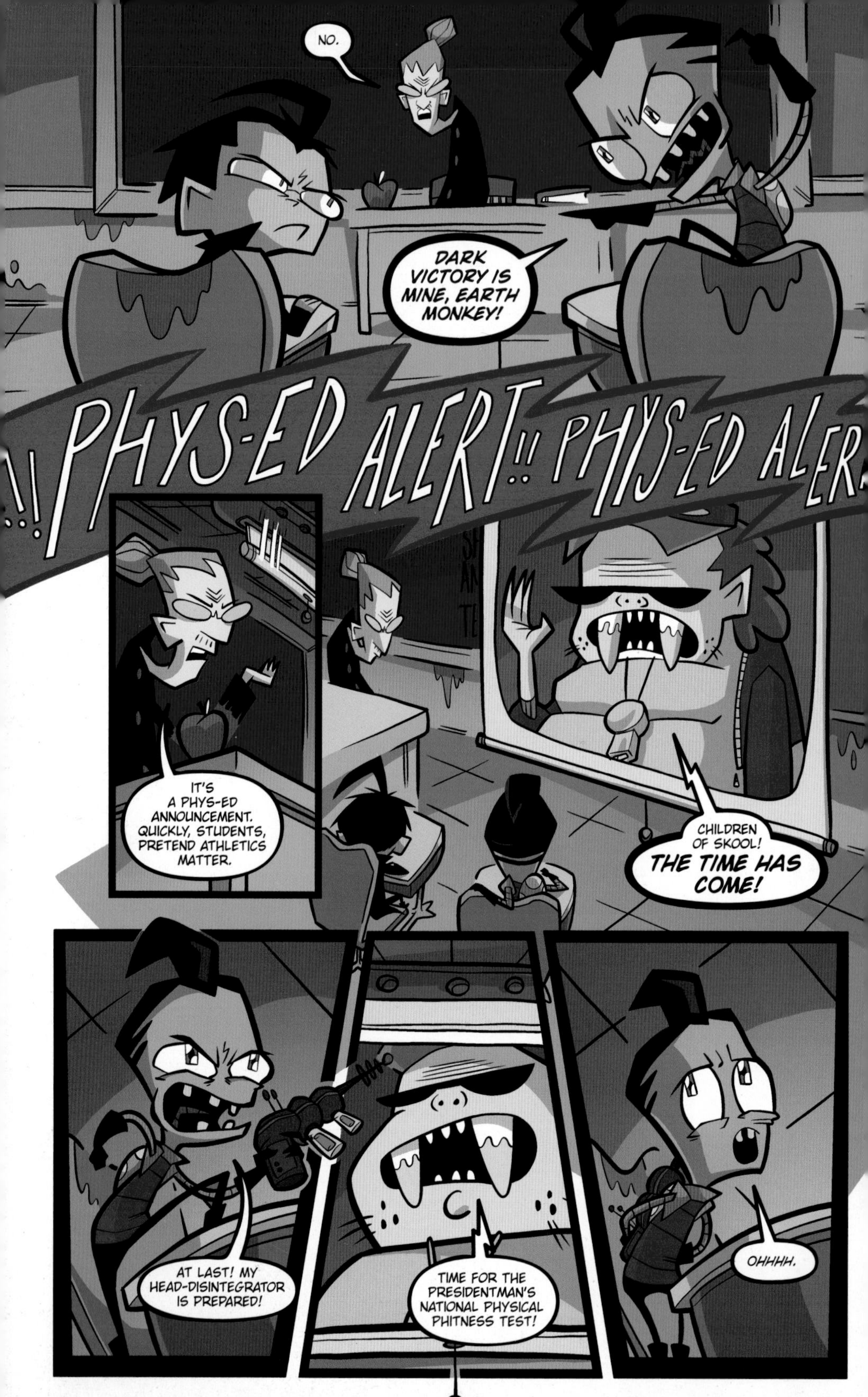
NO.
DARK VICTORY IS MINE, EARTH MONKEY!
!!PHYS-ED ALERT!! PHYS-ED ALER
IT'S A PHYS-ED ANNOUNCEMENT. QUICKLY, STUDENTS, PRETEND ATHLETICS MATTER.
CHILDREN OF SKOOL! THE TIME HAS COME!
AT LAST! MY HEAD-DISINTEGRATOR IS PREPARED!
TIME FOR THE PRESIDENTMAN'S NATIONAL PHYSICAL PHITNESS TEST!
OHHHH.

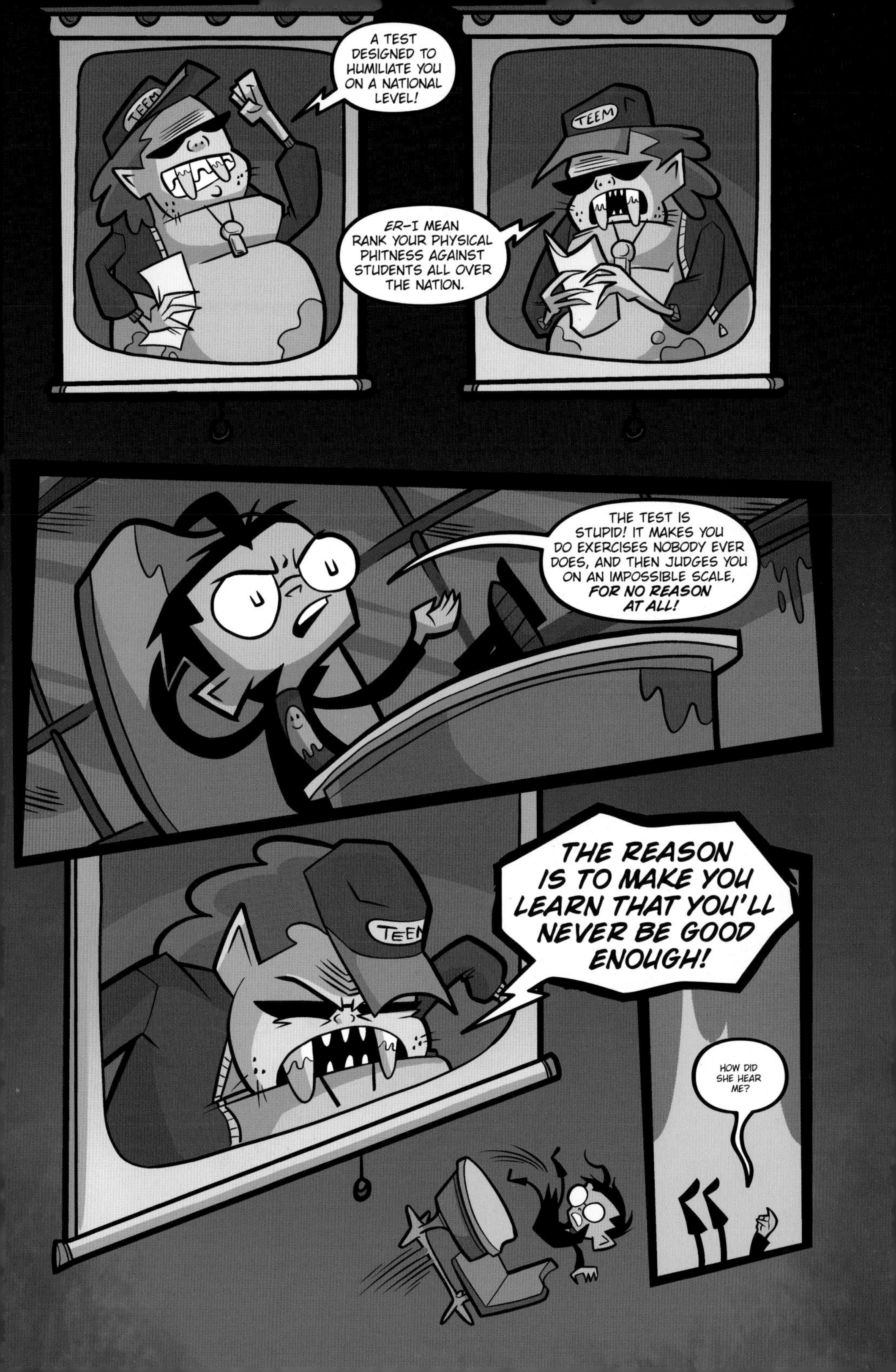
A TEST DESIGNED TO HUMILIATE YOU ON A NATIONAL LEVEL!
ER–I MEAN RANK YOUR PHYSICAL PHITNESS AGAINST STUDENTS ALL OVER THE NATION.
THE TEST IS STUPID! IT MAKES YOU DO EXERCISES NOBODY EVER DOES, AND THEN JUDGES YOU ON AN IMPOSSIBLE SCALE, FOR NO REASON AT ALL!
THE REASON IS TO MAKE YOU LEARN THAT YOU'LL NEVER BE GOOD ENOUGH!
HOW DID SHE HEAR ME?

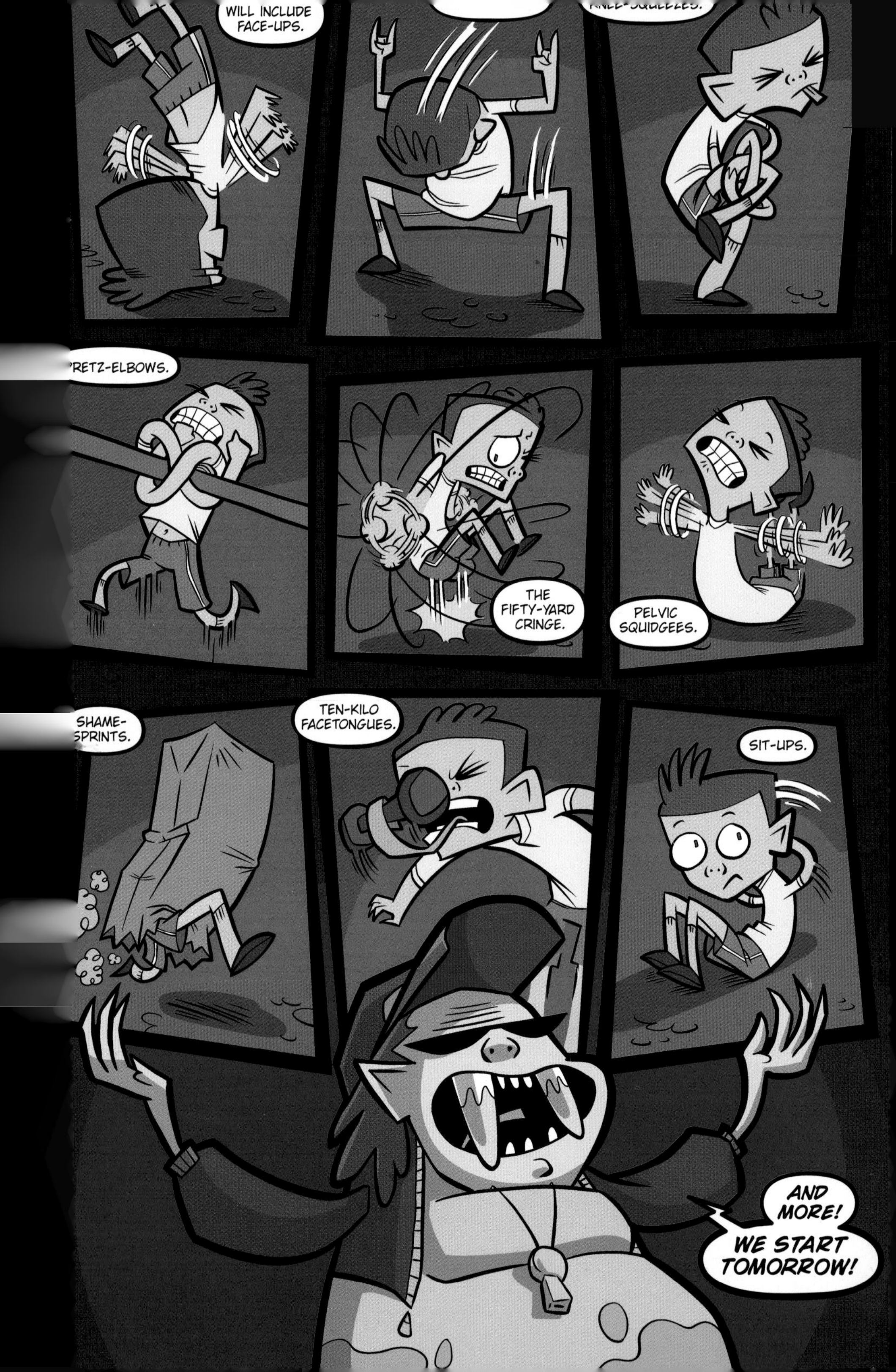
WILL INCLUDE FACE-UPS.
RETZ-ELBOWS.
THE FIFTY-YARD CRINGE.
PELVIC SQUIDGEES.
SHAME-SPRINTS.
TEN-KILO FACETONGUES.
SIT-UPS.
AND MORE!
WE START TOMORROW!

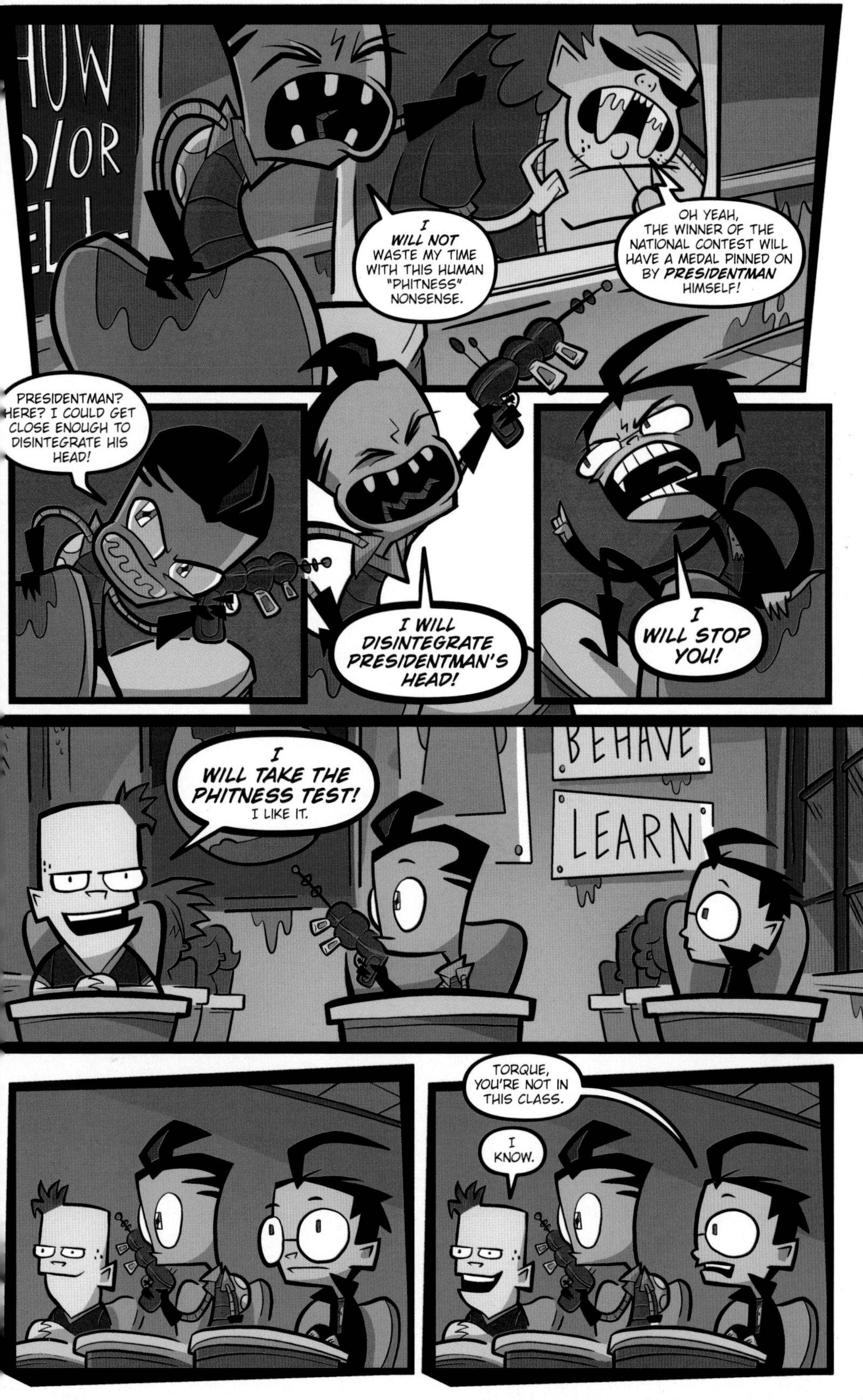
HOW
D/OR
I WILL NOT WASTE MY TIME WITH THIS HUMAN "PHITNESS" NONSENSE.
OH YEAH, THE WINNER OF THE NATIONAL CONTEST WILL HAVE A MEDAL PINNED ON BY PRESIDENTMAN HIMSELF!
PRESIDENTMAN? HERE? I COULD GET CLOSE ENOUGH TO DISINTEGRATE HIS HEAD!
I WILL DISINTEGRATE PRESIDENTMAN'S HEAD!
I WILL STOP YOU!
BEHAVE
LEARN
I WILL TAKE THE PHITNESS TEST! I LIKE IT.
TORQUE, YOU'RE NOT IN THIS CLASS.
I KNOW.

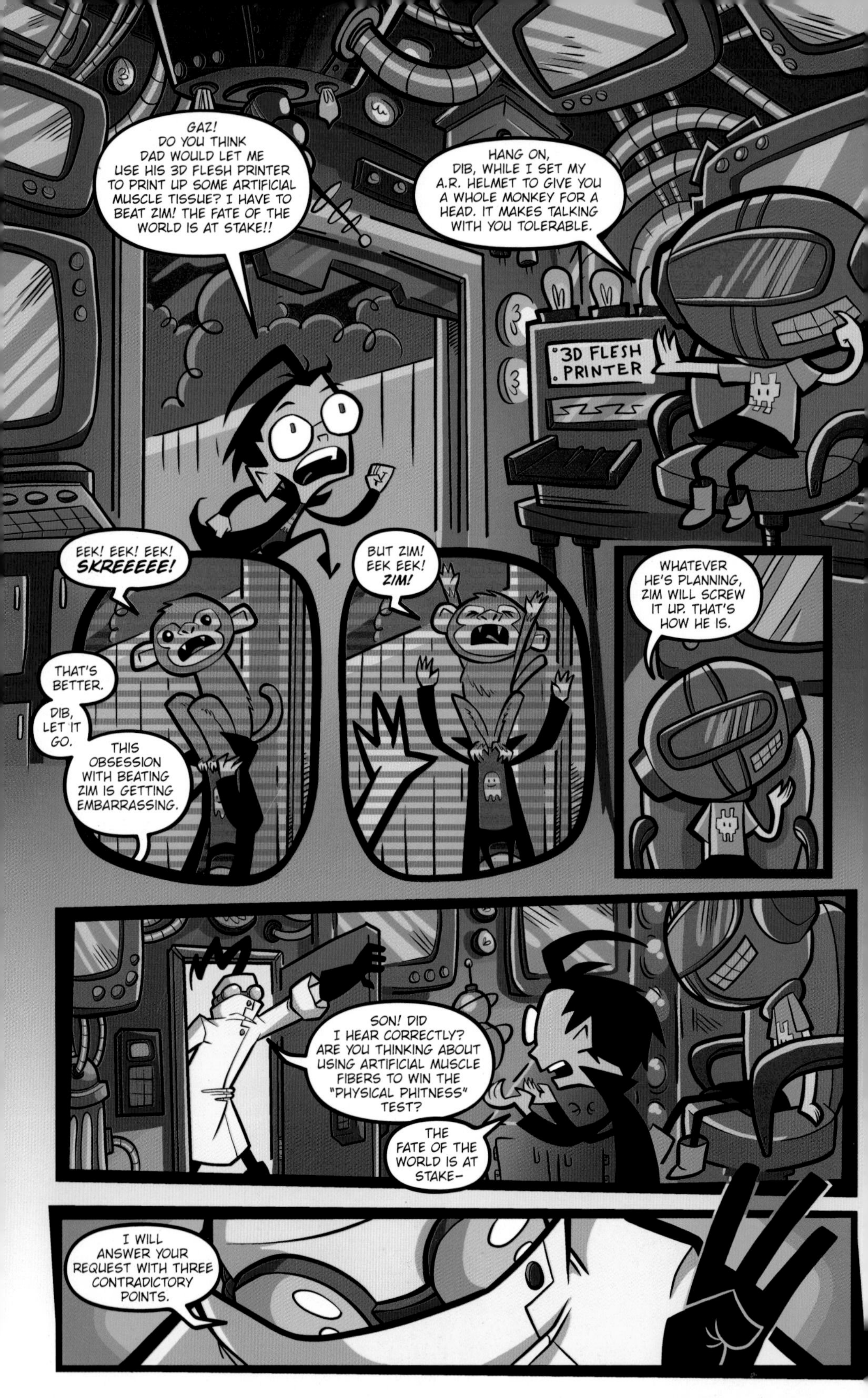
GAZ! DO YOU THINK DAD WOULD LET ME USE HIS 3D FLESH PRINTER TO PRINT UP SOME ARTIFICIAL MUSCLE TISSUE? I HAVE TO BEAT ZIM! THE FATE OF THE WORLD IS AT STAKE!!
HANG ON, DIB, WHILE I SET MY A.R. HELMET TO GIVE YOU A WHOLE MONKEY FOR A HEAD. IT MAKES TALKING WITH YOU TOLERABLE.
3D FLESH PRINTER
EEK! EEK! EEK! SKREEEEEE!
THAT'S BETTER.
DIB, LET IT GO.
THIS OBSESSION WITH BEATING ZIM IS GETTING EMBARRASSING.
BUT ZIM! EEK EEK! ZIM!
WHATEVER HE'S PLANNING, ZIM WILL SCREW IT UP. THAT'S HOW HE IS.
SON! DID I HEAR CORRECTLY? ARE YOU THINKING ABOUT USING ARTIFICIAL MUSCLE FIBERS TO WIN THE "PHYSICAL PHITNESS" TEST?
THE FATE OF THE WORLD IS AT STAKE–
I WILL ANSWER YOUR REQUEST WITH THREE CONTRADICTORY POINTS.

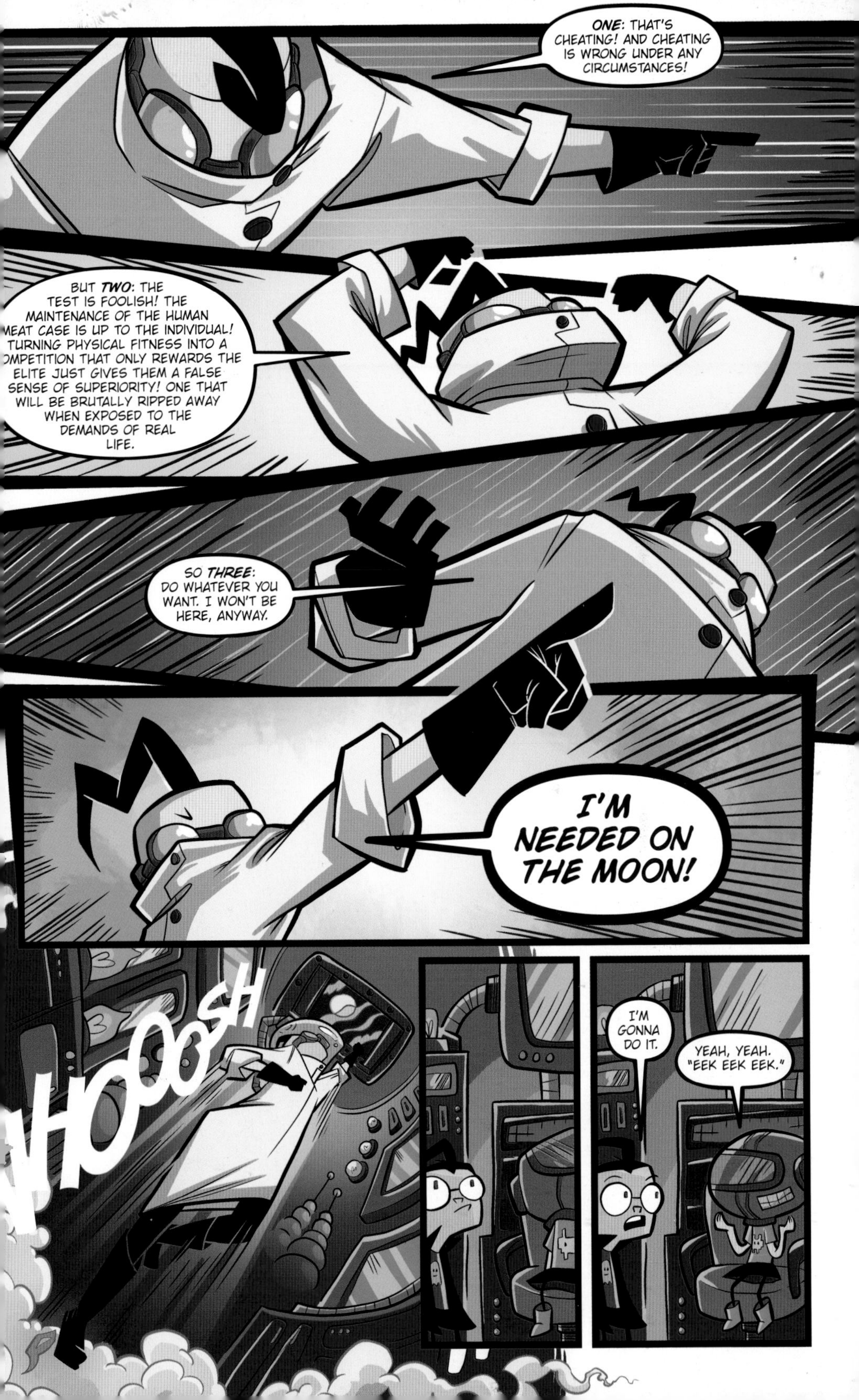
ONE: THAT'S CHEATING! AND CHEATING IS WRONG UNDER ANY CIRCUMSTANCES!
BUT TWO: THE TEST IS FOOLISH! THE MAINTENANCE OF THE HUMAN MEAT CASE IS UP TO THE INDIVIDUAL! TURNING PHYSICAL FITNESS INTO A OMPETITION THAT ONLY REWARDS THE ELITE JUST GIVES THEM A FALSE SENSE OF SUPERIORITY! ONE THAT WILL BE BRUTALLY RIPPED AWAY WHEN EXPOSED TO THE DEMANDS OF REAL LIFE.
SO THREE: DO WHATEVER YOU WANT. I WON'T BE HERE, ANYWAY.
I'M NEEDED ON THE MOON!
WHOOOSH
I'M GONNA DO IT.
YEAH, YEAH. "EEK EEK EEK."

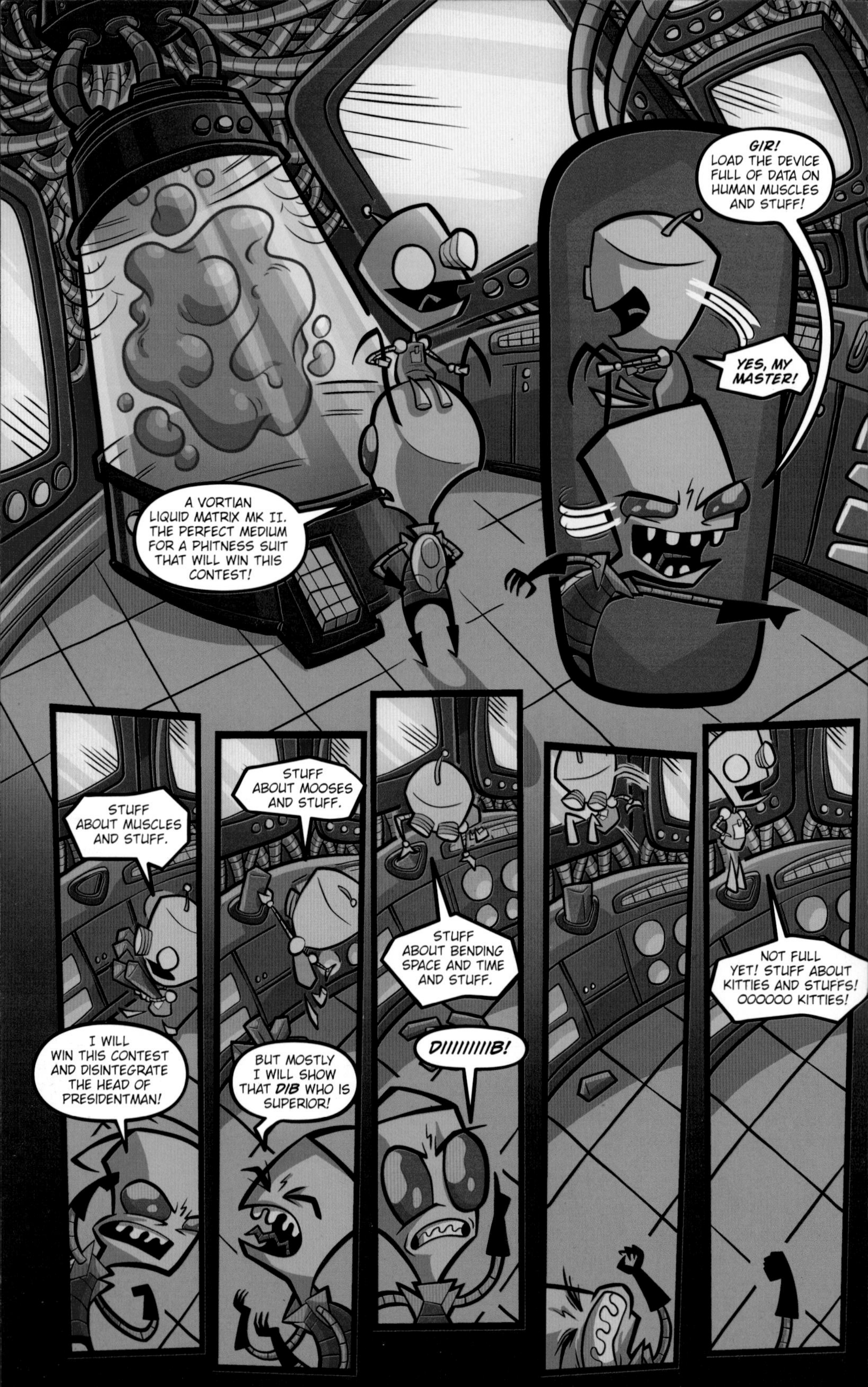
GIR! LOAD THE DEVICE FULL OF DATA ON HUMAN MUSCLES AND STUFF!
YES, MY MASTER!
A VORTIAN LIQUID MATRIX MK II. THE PERFECT MEDIUM FOR A PHITNESS SUIT THAT WILL WIN THIS CONTEST!
STUFF ABOUT MUSCLES AND STUFF.
I WILL WIN THIS CONTEST AND DISINTEGRATE THE HEAD OF PRESIDENTMAN!
STUFF ABOUT MOOSES AND STUFF.
BUT MOSTLY I WILL SHOW THAT DIB WHO IS SUPERIOR!
STUFF ABOUT BENDING SPACE AND TIME AND STUFF.
DIIIIIIIIIB!
NOT FULL YET! STUFF ABOUT KITTIES AND STUFFS! OOOOOO KITTIES!

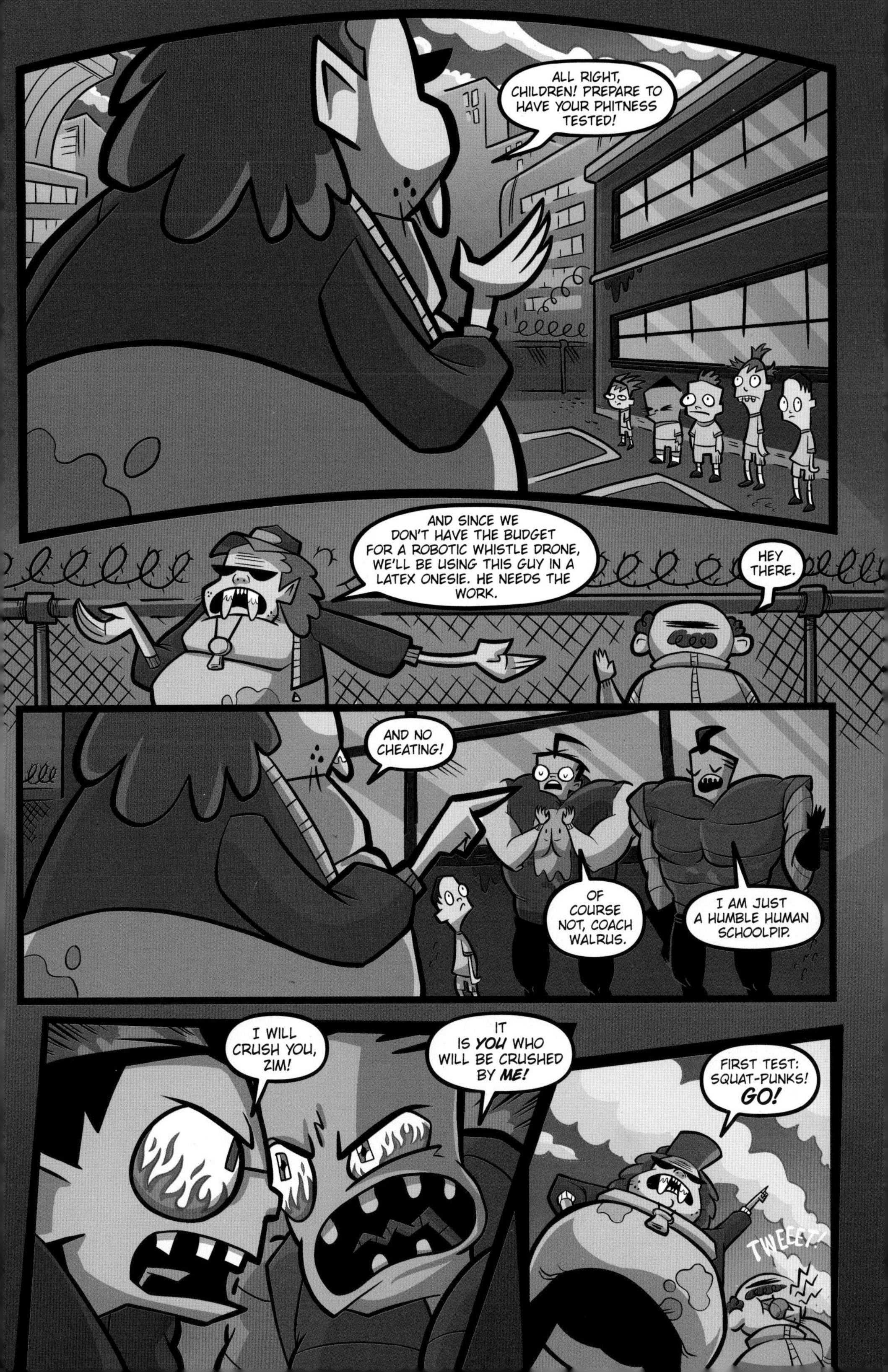
ALL RIGHT, CHILDREN! PREPARE TO HAVE YOUR PHITNESS TESTED!
AND SINCE WE DON'T HAVE THE BUDGET FOR A ROBOTIC WHISTLE DRONE, WE'LL BE USING THIS GUY IN A LATEX ONESIE. HE NEEDS THE WORK.
HEY THERE.
AND NO CHEATING!
OF COURSE NOT, COACH WALRUS.
I AM JUST A HUMBLE HUMAN SCHOOLPIP.
I WILL CRUSH YOU, ZIM!
IT IS YOU WHO WILL BE CRUSHED BY ME!
FIRST TEST: SQUAT-PUNKS! GO!
TWEEET!

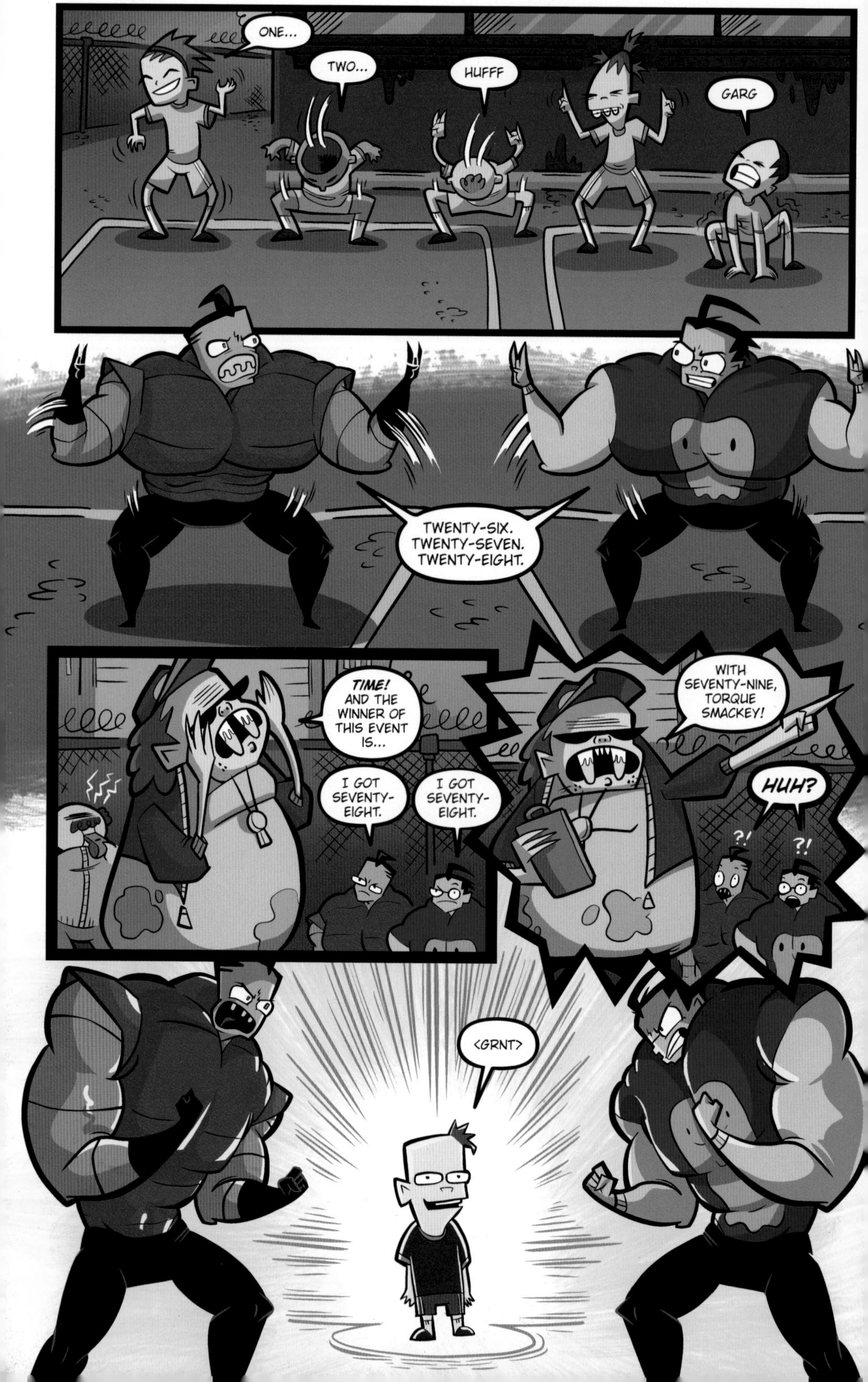
ONE...
TWO...
HUFFF
GARG
TWENTY-SIX. TWENTY-SEVEN. TWENTY-EIGHT.
TIME! AND THE WINNER OF THIS EVENT IS...
I GOT SEVENTY-EIGHT.
I GOT SEVENTY-EIGHT.
WITH SEVENTY-NINE, TORQUE SMACKEY!
HUH?
?!
?!
<GRNT>

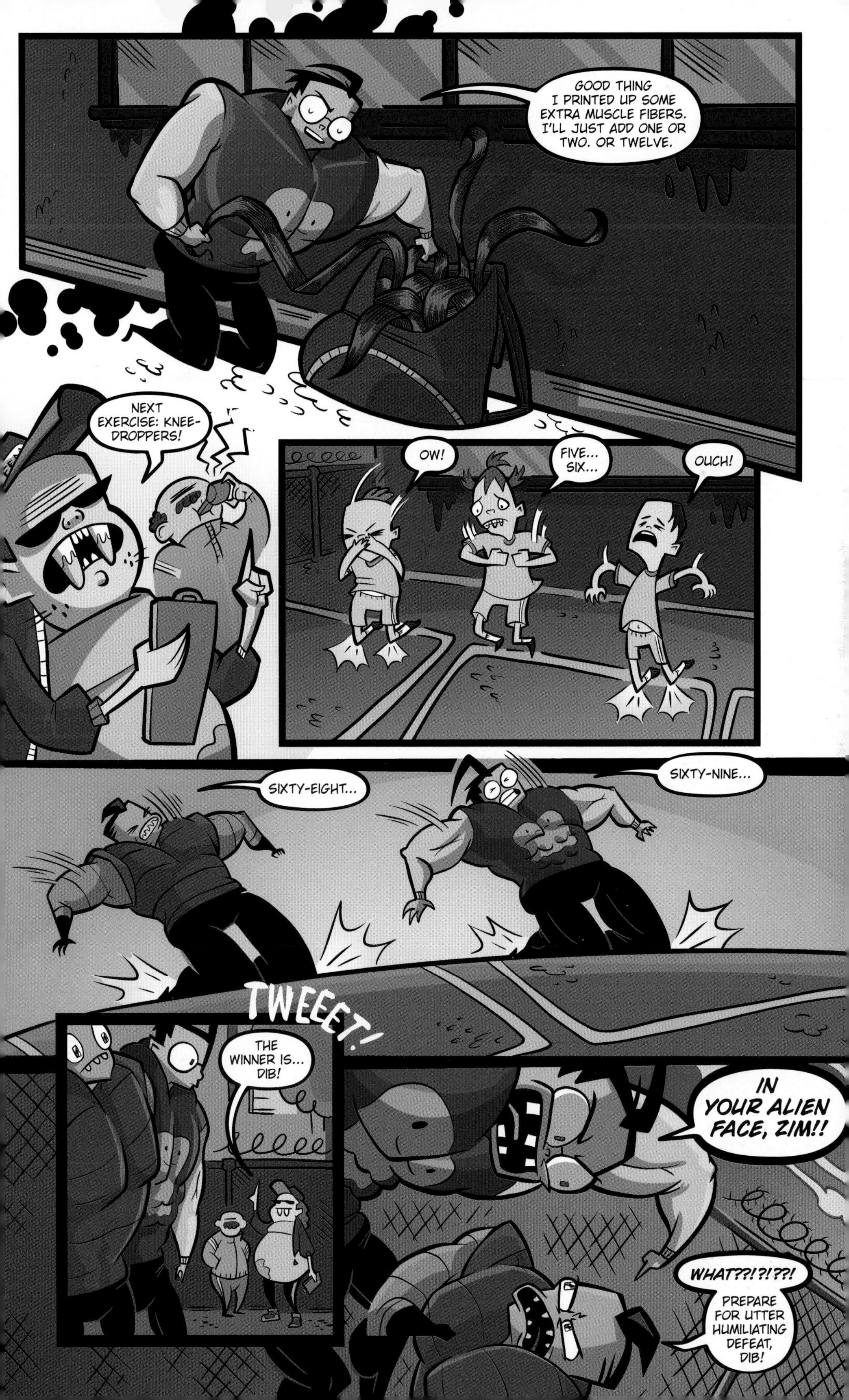
GOOD THING I PRINTED UP SOME EXTRA MUSCLE FIBERS. I'LL JUST ADD ONE OR TWO. OR TWELVE.
NEXT EXERCISE: KNEE-DROPPERS!
OW!
FIVE... SIX...
OUCH!
SIXTY-EIGHT...
SIXTY-NINE...
TWEEET!
THE WINNER IS... DIB!
IN YOUR ALIEN FACE, ZIM!!
WHAT??!?!??!
PREPARE FOR UTTER HUMILIATING DEFEAT, DIB!

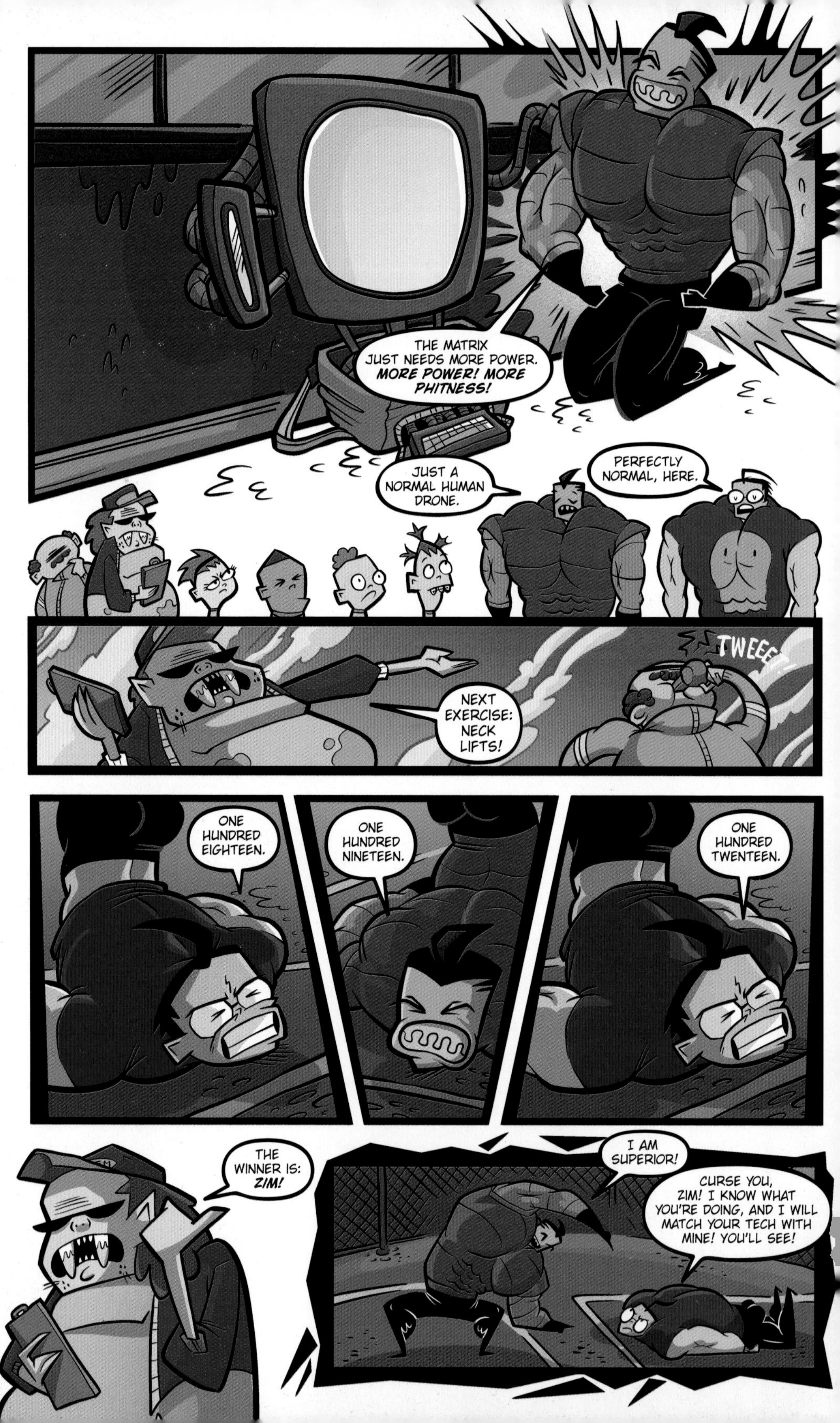
THE MATRIX JUST NEEDS MORE POWER. ***MORE POWER! MORE PHITNESS!***
JUST A NORMAL HUMAN DRONE.
PERFECTLY NORMAL, HERE.
NEXT EXERCISE: NECK LIFTS!
TWEEET!
ONE HUNDRED EIGHTEEN.
ONE HUNDRED NINETEEN.
ONE HUNDRED TWENTEEN.
THE WINNER IS: ***ZIM!***
I AM SUPERIOR!
CURSE YOU, ZIM! I KNOW WHAT YOU'RE DOING, AND I WILL MATCH YOUR TECH WITH MINE! YOU'LL SEE!

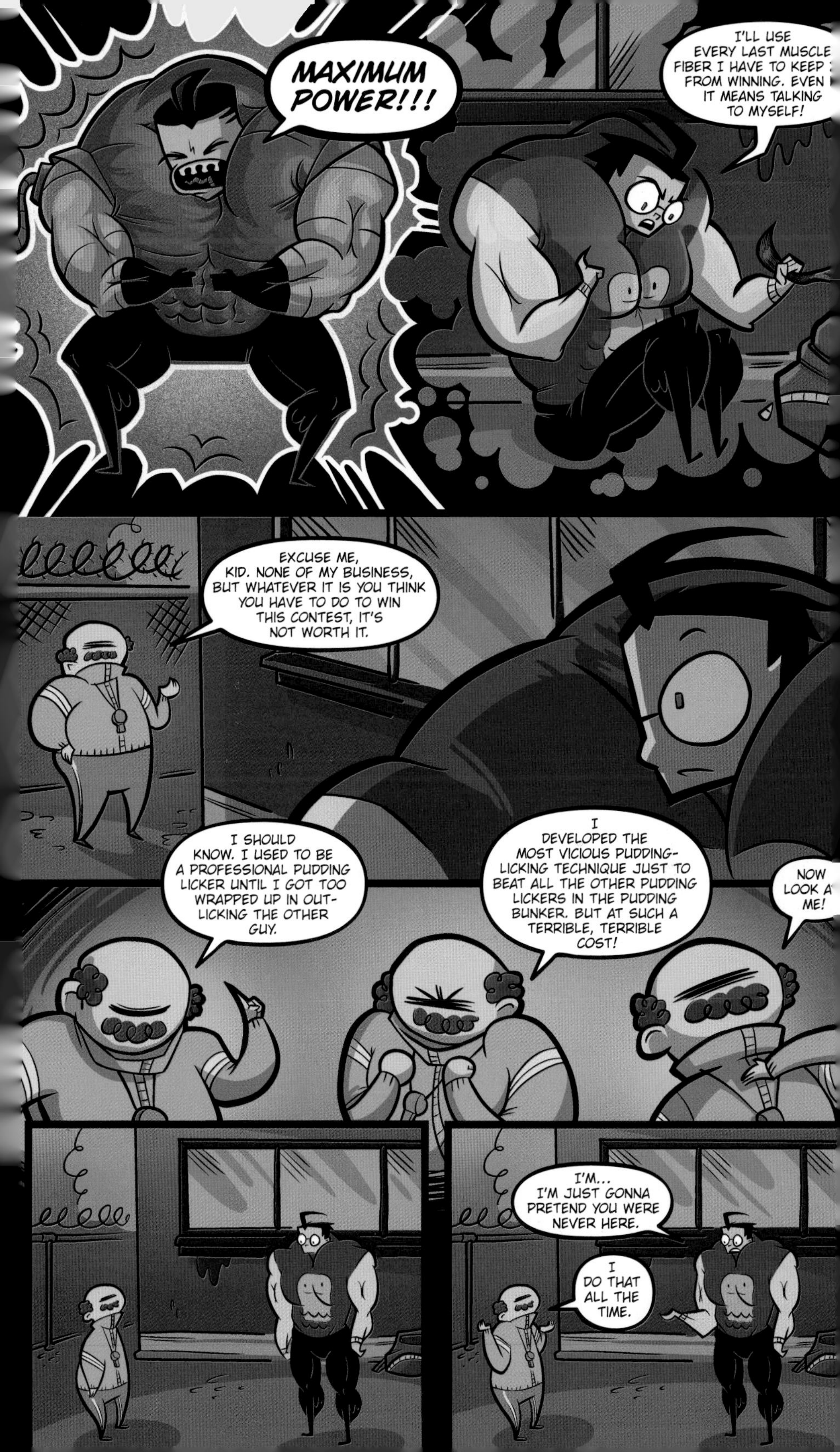
MAXIMUM POWER!!!
I'LL USE EVERY LAST MUSCLE FIBER I HAVE TO KEEP FROM WINNING. EVEN IT MEANS TALKING TO MYSELF!
EXCUSE ME, KID. NONE OF MY BUSINESS, BUT WHATEVER IT IS YOU THINK YOU HAVE TO DO TO WIN THIS CONTEST, IT'S NOT WORTH IT.
I SHOULD KNOW. I USED TO BE A PROFESSIONAL PUDDING LICKER UNTIL I GOT TOO WRAPPED UP IN OUT-LICKING THE OTHER GUY.
I DEVELOPED THE MOST VICIOUS PUDDING-LICKING TECHNIQUE JUST TO BEAT ALL THE OTHER PUDDING LICKERS IN THE PUDDING BUNKER. BUT AT SUCH A TERRIBLE, TERRIBLE COST!
NOW LOOK A ME!
I'M... I'M JUST GONNA PRETEND YOU WERE NEVER HERE.
I DO THAT ALL THE TIME.

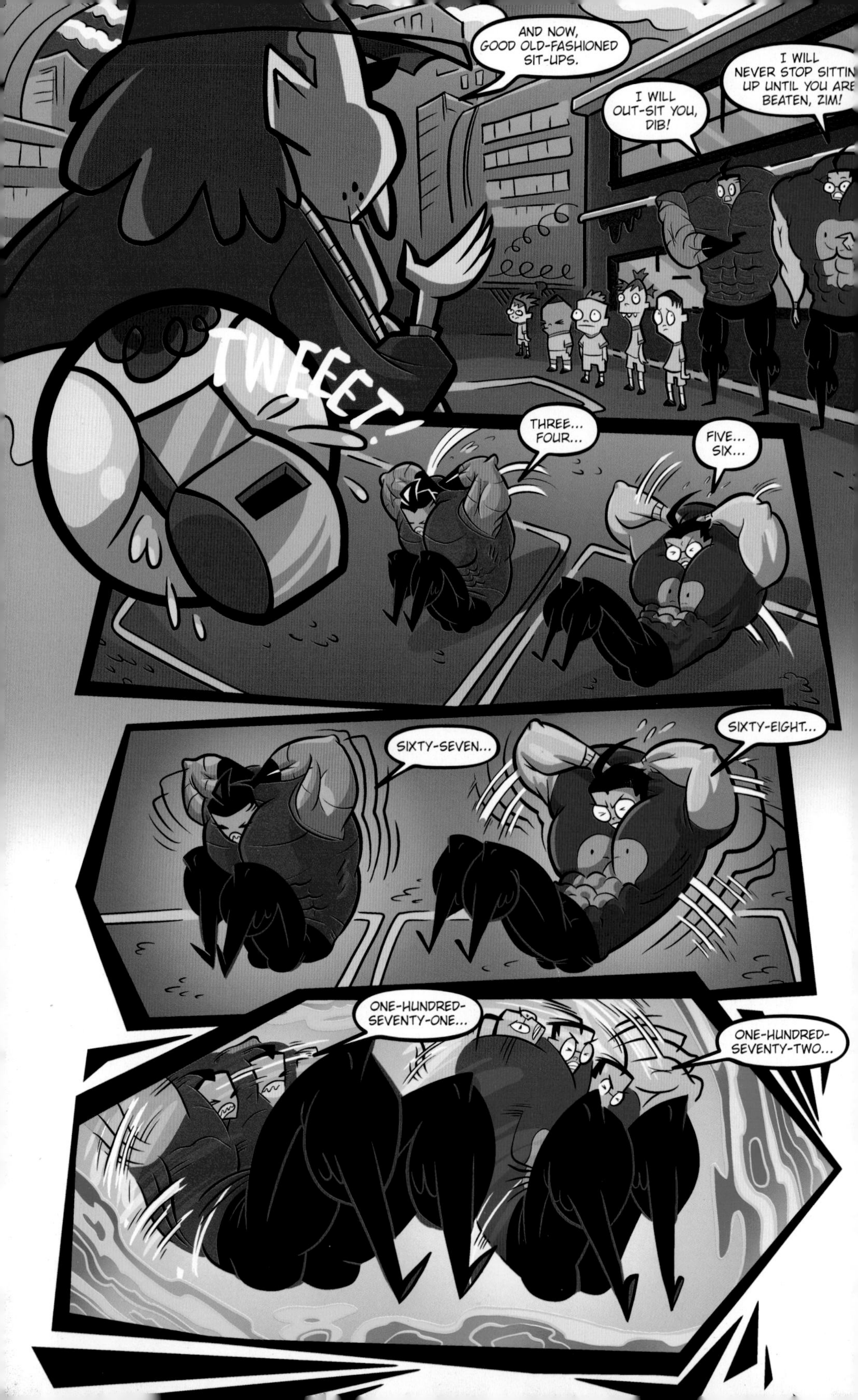
AND NOW, GOOD OLD-FASHIONED SIT-UPS.
I WILL OUT-SIT YOU, DIB!
I WILL NEVER STOP SITTIN UP UNTIL YOU ARE BEATEN, ZIM!
TWEEET!
THREE... FOUR...
FIVE... SIX...
SIXTY-SEVEN...
SIXTY-EIGHT...
ONE-HUNDRED-SEVENTY-ONE...
ONE-HUNDRED-SEVENTY-TWO...

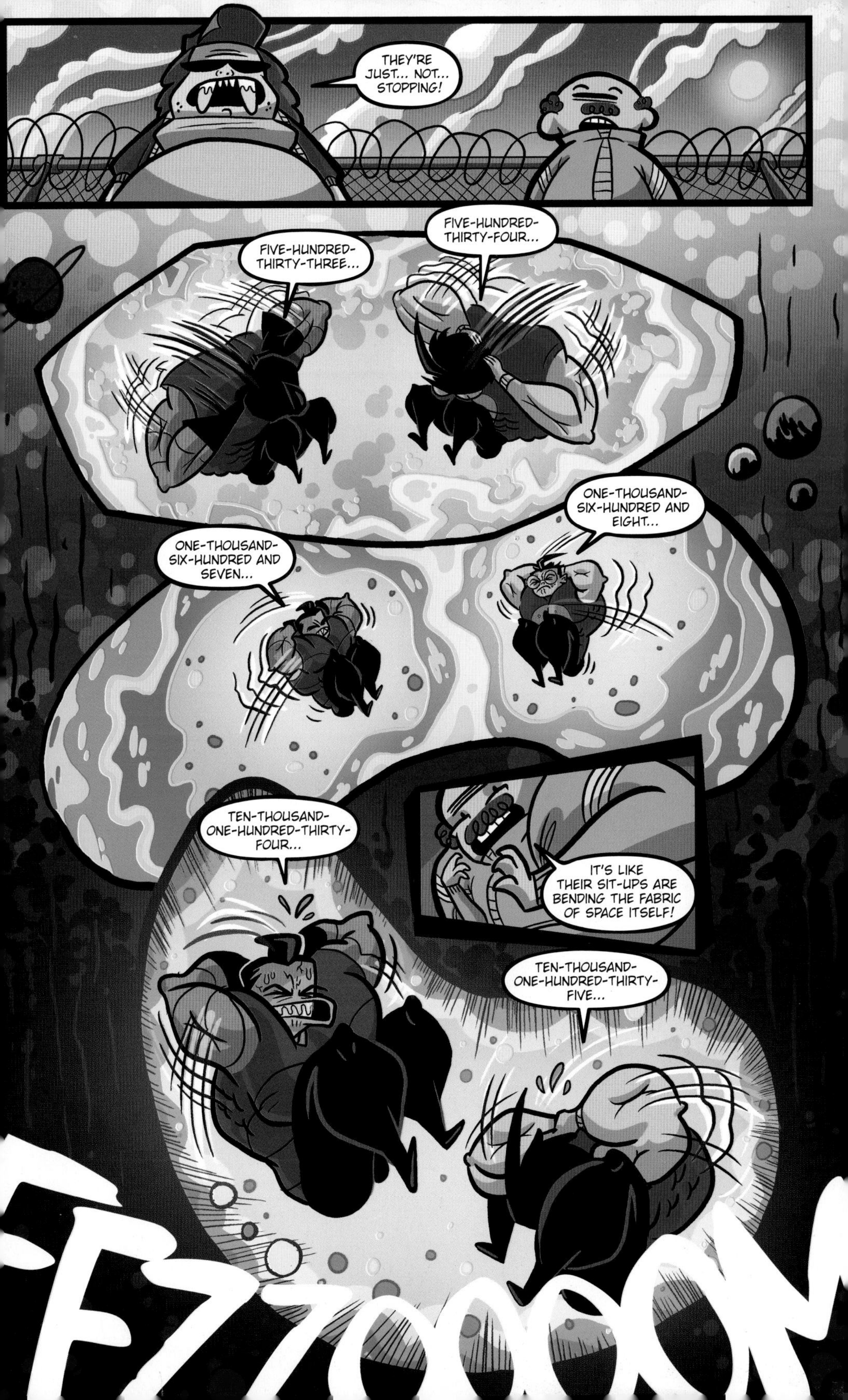
THEY'RE JUST... NOT... STOPPING!
FIVE-HUNDRED-THIRTY-THREE...
FIVE-HUNDRED-THIRTY-FOUR...
ONE-THOUSAND-SIX-HUNDRED AND SEVEN...
ONE-THOUSAND-SIX-HUNDRED AND EIGHT...
TEN-THOUSAND-ONE-HUNDRED-THIRTY-FOUR...
IT'S LIKE THEIR SIT-UPS ARE BENDING THE FABRIC OF SPACE ITSELF!
TEN-THOUSAND-ONE-HUNDRED-THIRTY-FIVE...
FZZOOOOM

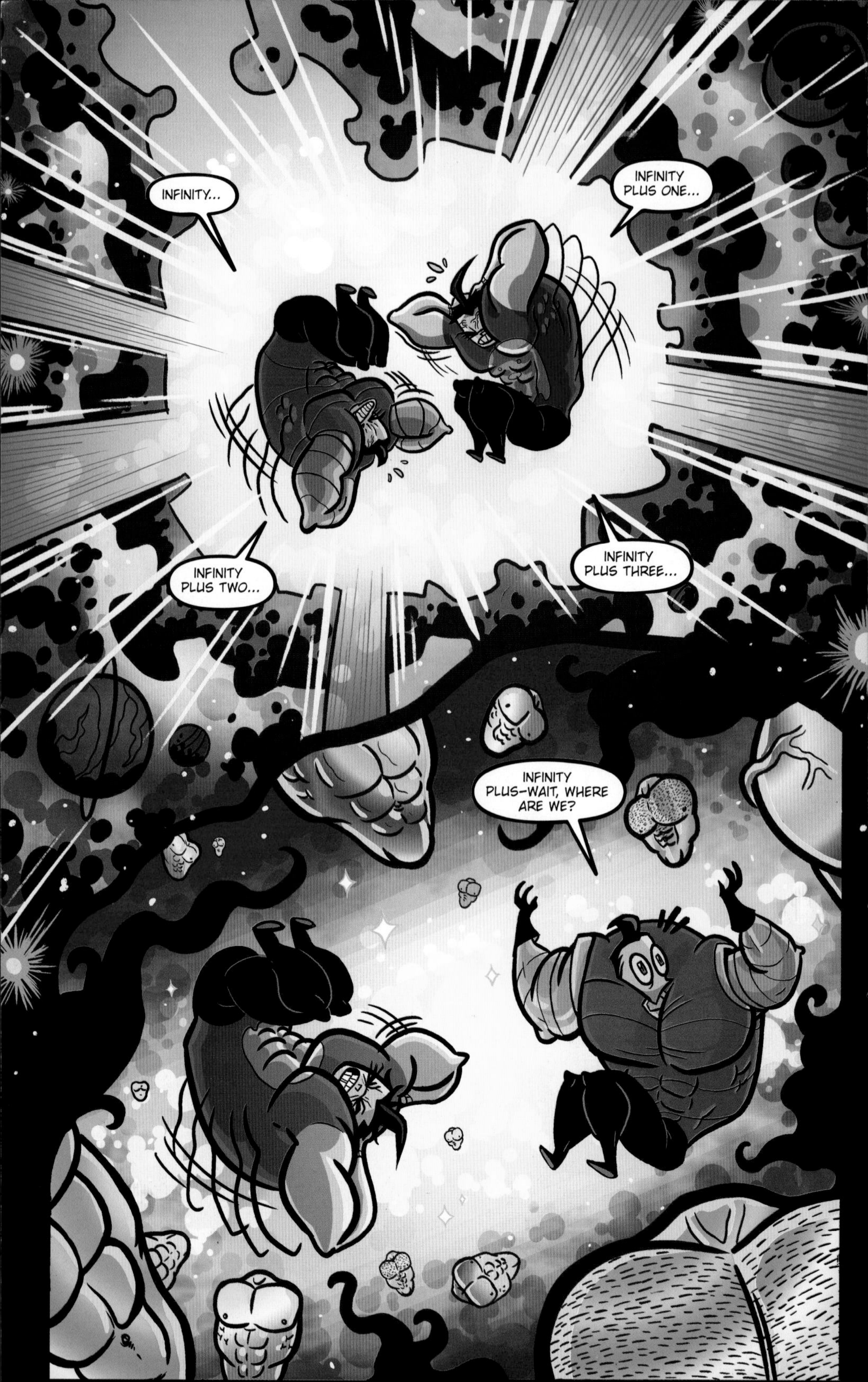
INFINITY...
INFINITY PLUS ONE...
INFINITY PLUS TWO...
INFINITY PLUS THREE...
INFINITY PLUS–WAIT, WHERE ARE WE?

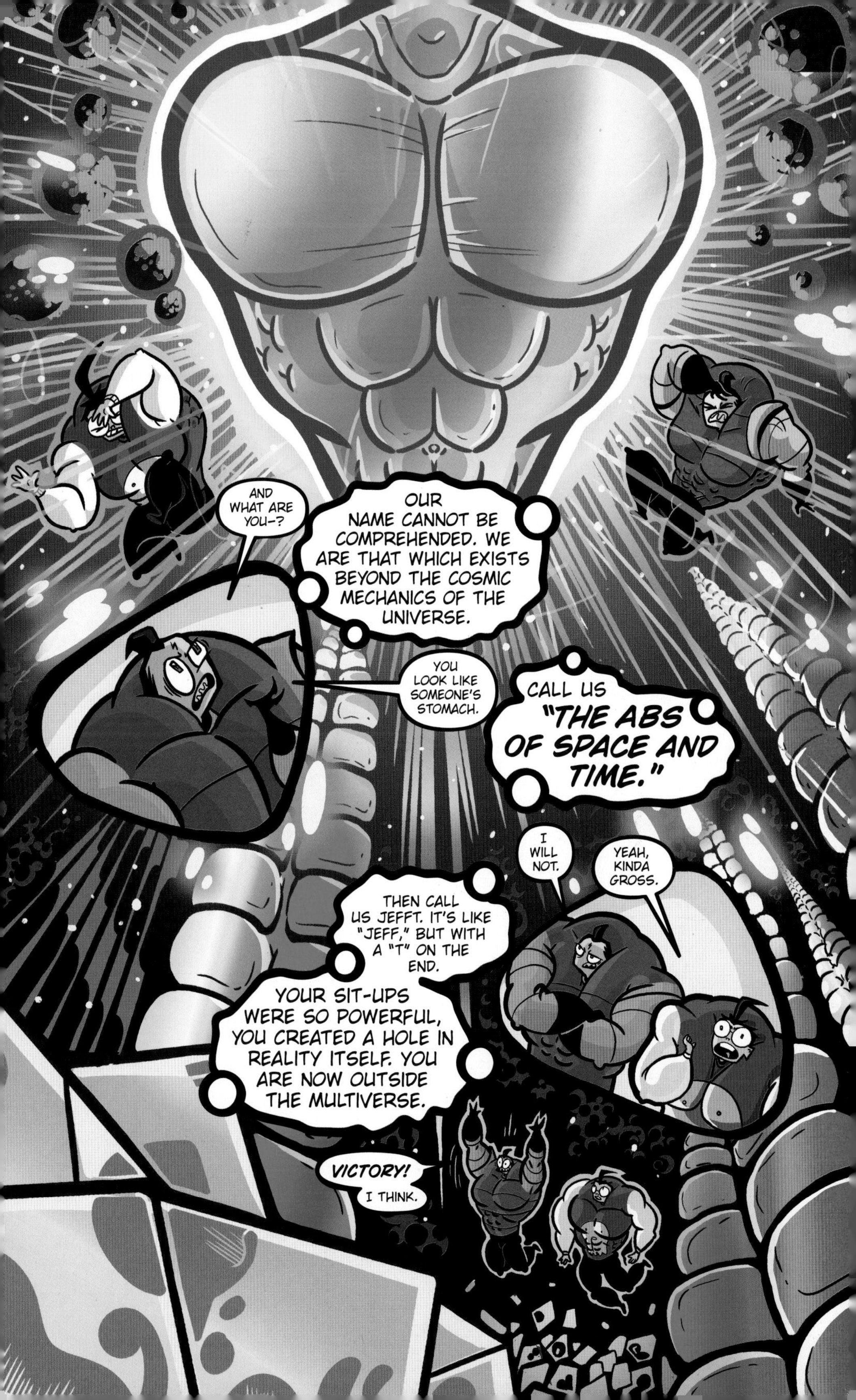
AND WHAT ARE YOU–?
OUR NAME CANNOT BE COMPREHENDED. WE ARE THAT WHICH EXISTS BEYOND THE COSMIC MECHANICS OF THE UNIVERSE.
YOU LOOK LIKE SOMEONE'S STOMACH.
CALL US "THE ABS OF SPACE AND TIME."
I WILL NOT.
YEAH, KINDA GROSS.
THEN CALL US JEFFT. IT'S LIKE "JEFF," BUT WITH A "T" ON THE END.
YOUR SIT-UPS WERE SO POWERFUL, YOU CREATED A HOLE IN REALITY ITSELF. YOU ARE NOW OUTSIDE THE MULTIVERSE.
VICTORY!
I THINK.

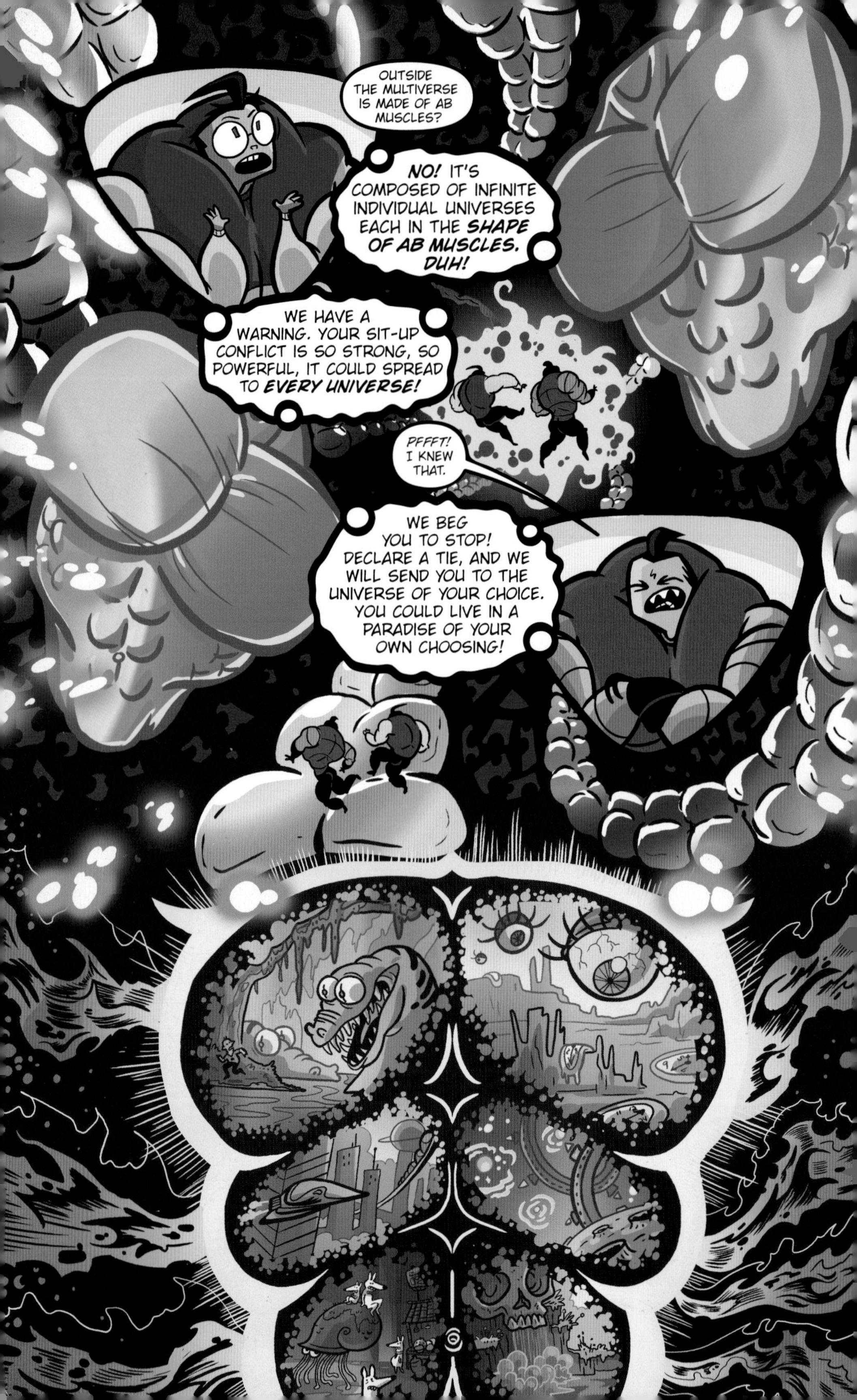
OUTSIDE THE MULTIVERSE IS MADE OF AB MUSCLES?
NO! IT'S COMPOSED OF INFINITE INDIVIDUAL UNIVERSES EACH IN THE SHAPE OF AB MUSCLES. DUH!
WE HAVE A WARNING. YOUR SIT-UP CONFLICT IS SO STRONG, SO POWERFUL, IT COULD SPREAD TO EVERY UNIVERSE!
PFFFT! I KNEW THAT.
WE BEG YOU TO STOP! DECLARE A TIE, AND WE WILL SEND YOU TO THE UNIVERSE OF YOUR CHOICE. YOU COULD LIVE IN A PARADISE OF YOUR OWN CHOOSING!

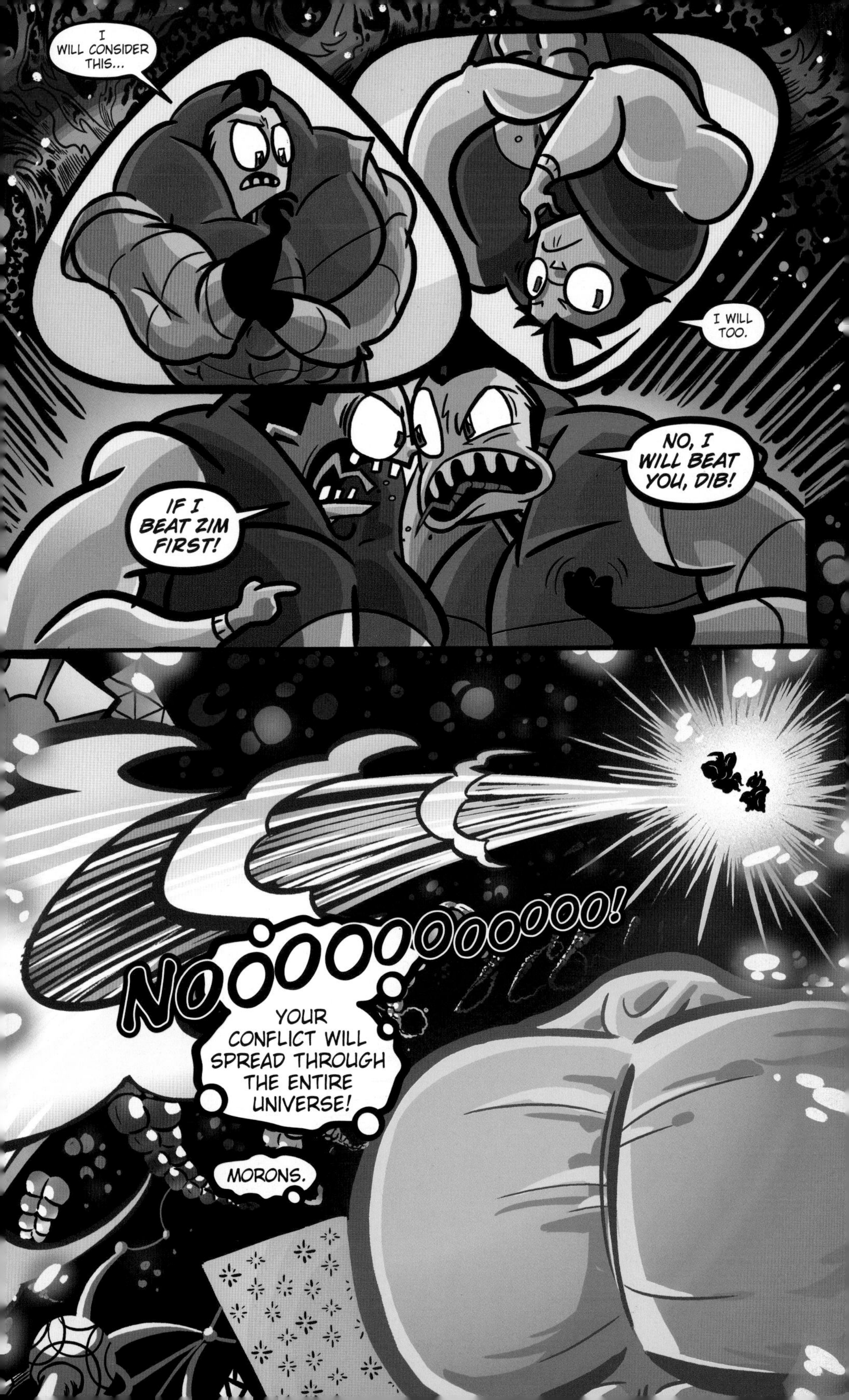
I WILL CONSIDER THIS...
I WILL TOO.
IF I BEAT ZIM FIRST!
NO, I WILL BEAT YOU, DIB!
NOOOOOOOOOOOOO!
YOUR CONFLICT WILL SPREAD THROUGH THE ENTIRE UNIVERSE!
MORONS.

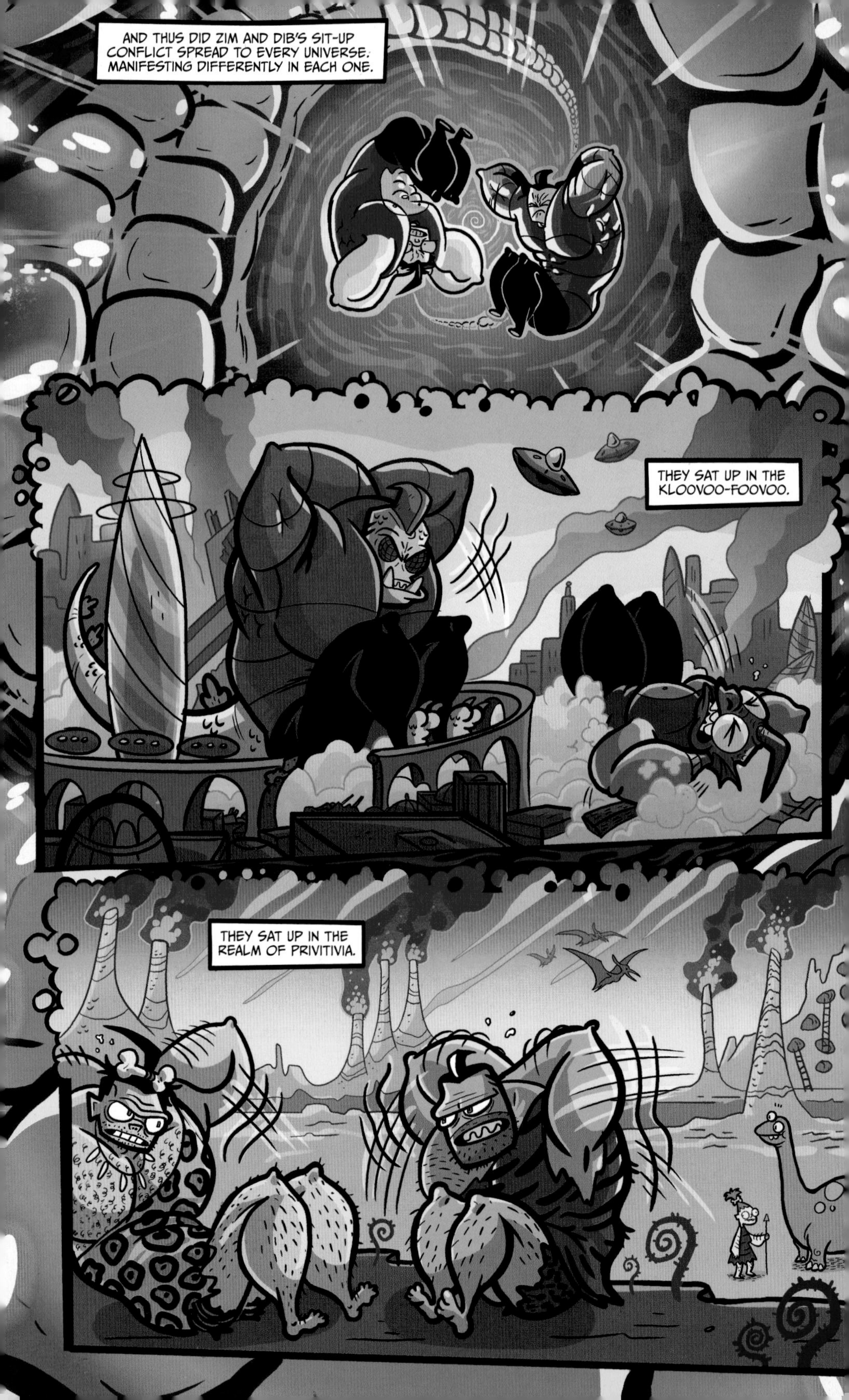
AND THUS DID ZIM AND DIB'S SIT-UP CONFLICT SPREAD TO EVERY UNIVERSE. MANIFESTING DIFFERENTLY IN EACH ONE.
THEY SAT UP IN THE KLOOVOO-FOOVOO.
THEY SAT UP IN THE REALM OF PRIVITIVIA.

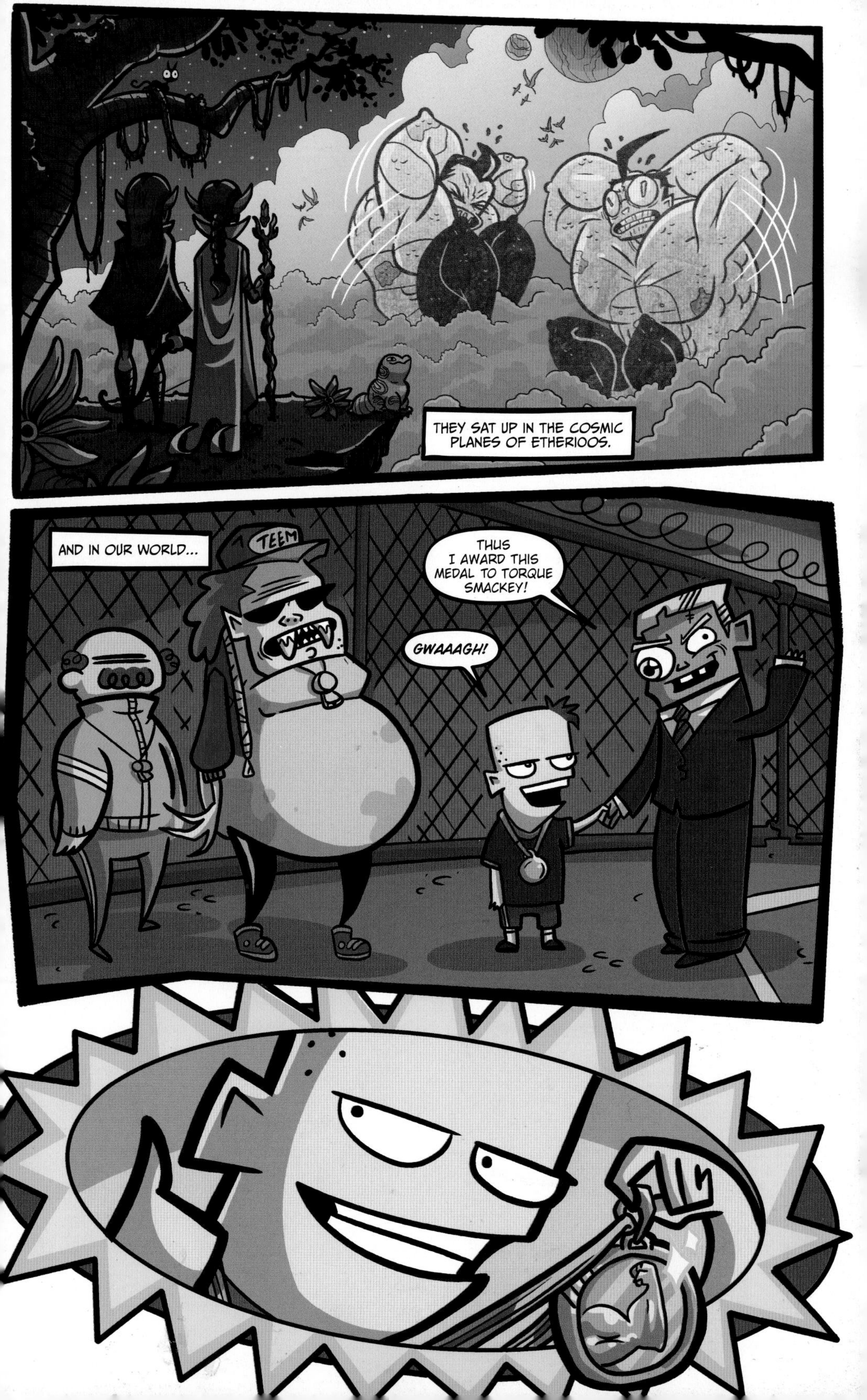
THEY SAT UP IN THE COSMIC PLANES OF ETHERIOOS.
AND IN OUR WORLD...
TEEM
THUS I AWARD THIS MEDAL TO TORQUE SMACKEY!
GWAAAGH!

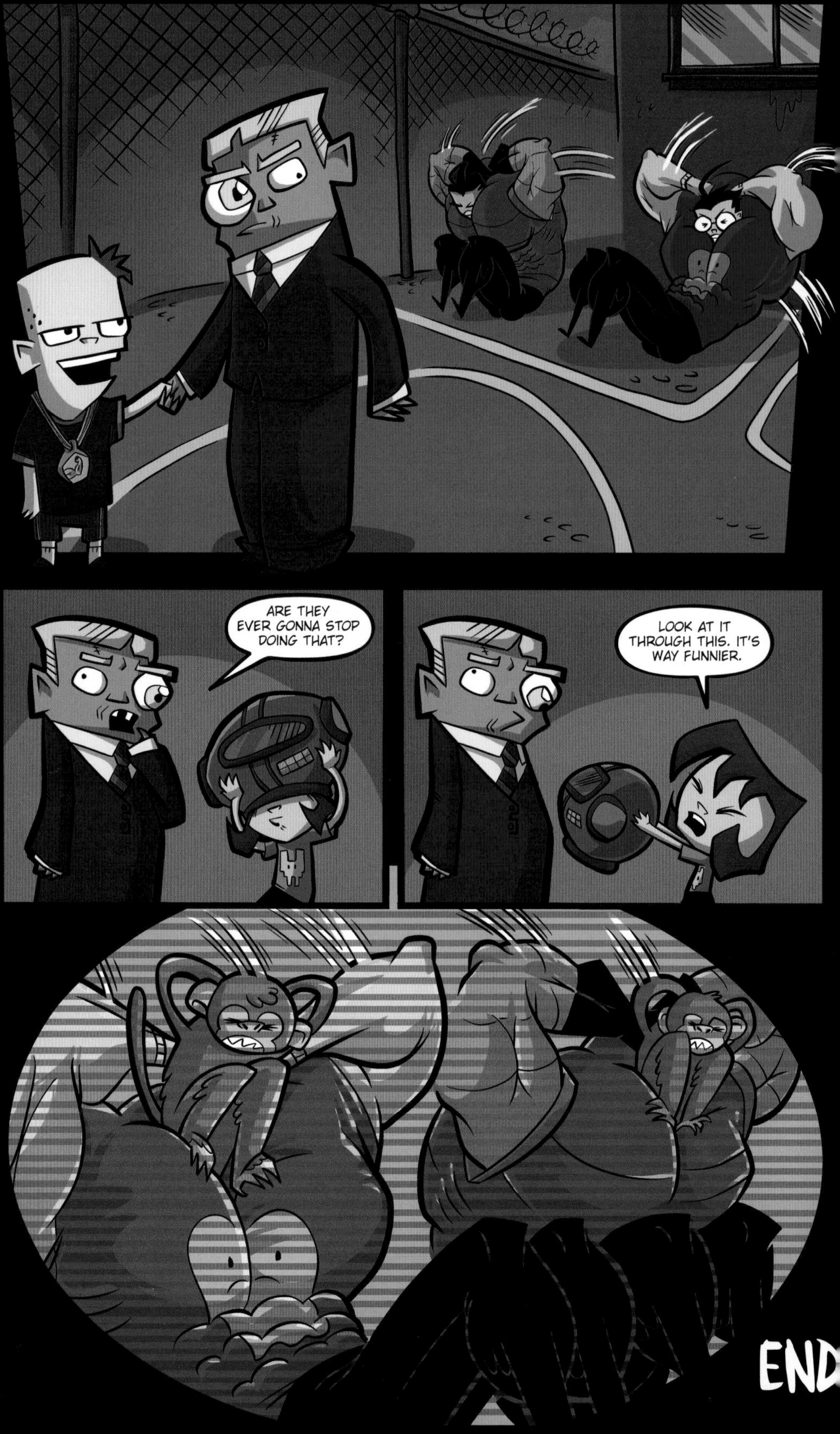
ARE THEY EVER GONNA STOP DOING THAT?
LOOK AT IT THROUGH THIS. IT'S WAY FUNNIER.
END

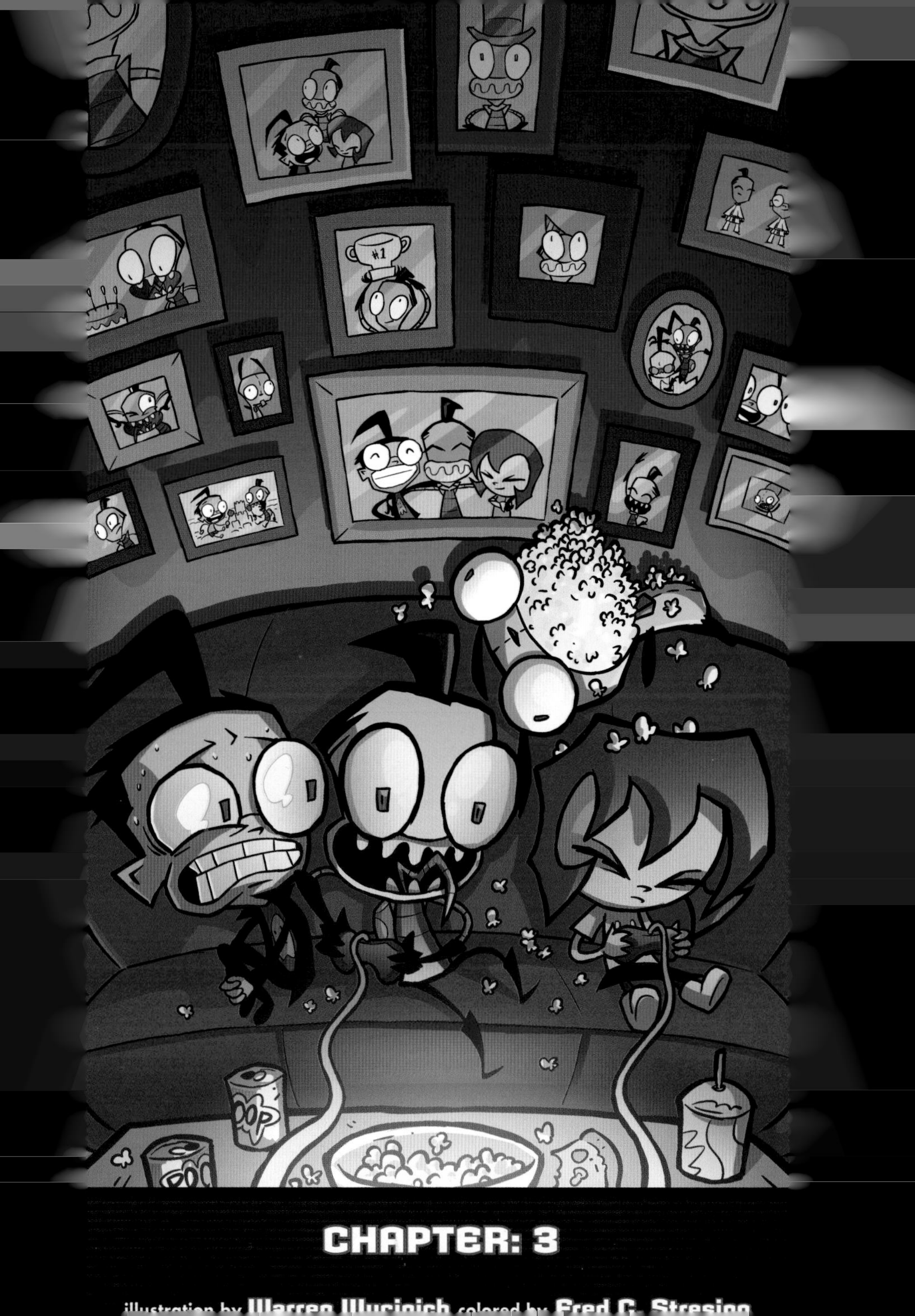
#1

CHAPTER: 3

illustration by Warren Wucinich colored by Fred C. Stresing

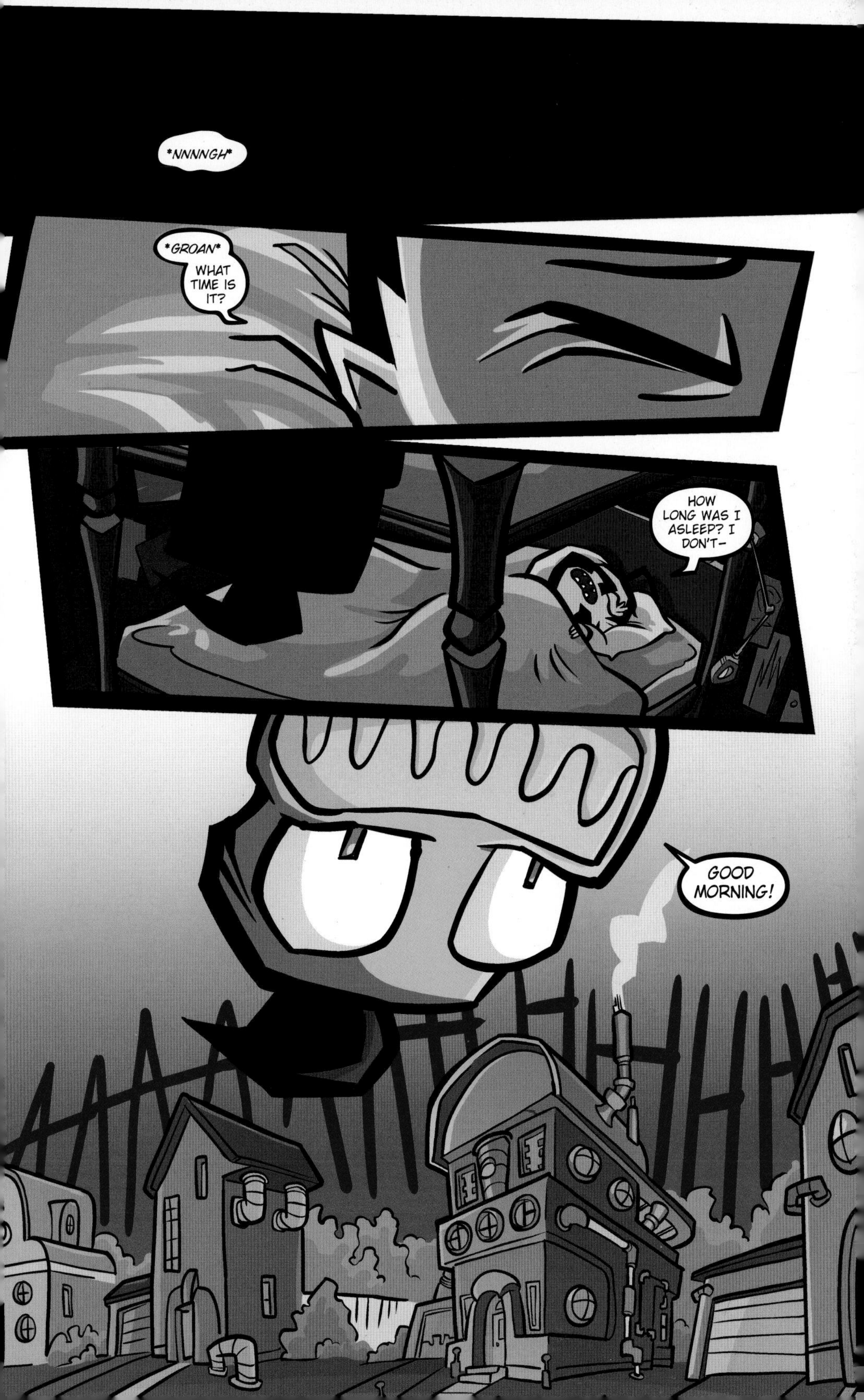
NNNNGH
GROAN WHAT TIME IS IT?
HOW LONG WAS I ASLEEP? I DON'T–
GOOD MORNING!

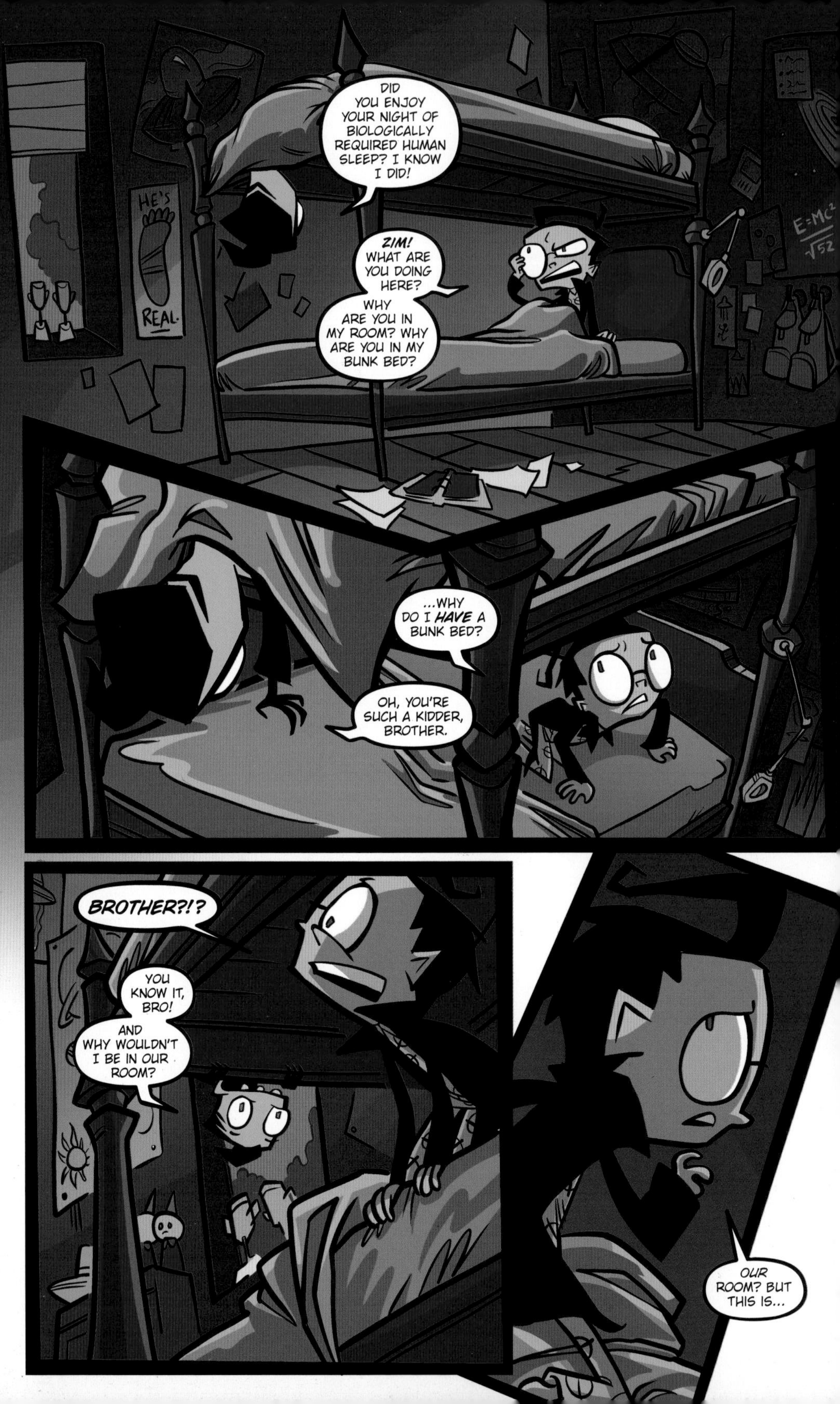
DID YOU ENJOY YOUR NIGHT OF BIOLOGICALLY REQUIRED HUMAN SLEEP? I KNOW I DID!
HE'S REAL.
ZIM! WHAT ARE YOU DOING HERE?
WHY ARE YOU IN MY ROOM? WHY ARE YOU IN MY BUNK BED?
E=MC²
...WHY DO I HAVE A BUNK BED?
OH, YOU'RE SUCH A KIDDER, BROTHER.
BROTHER?!?
YOU KNOW IT, BRO!
AND WHY WOULDN'T I BE IN OUR ROOM?
OUR ROOM? BUT THIS IS...

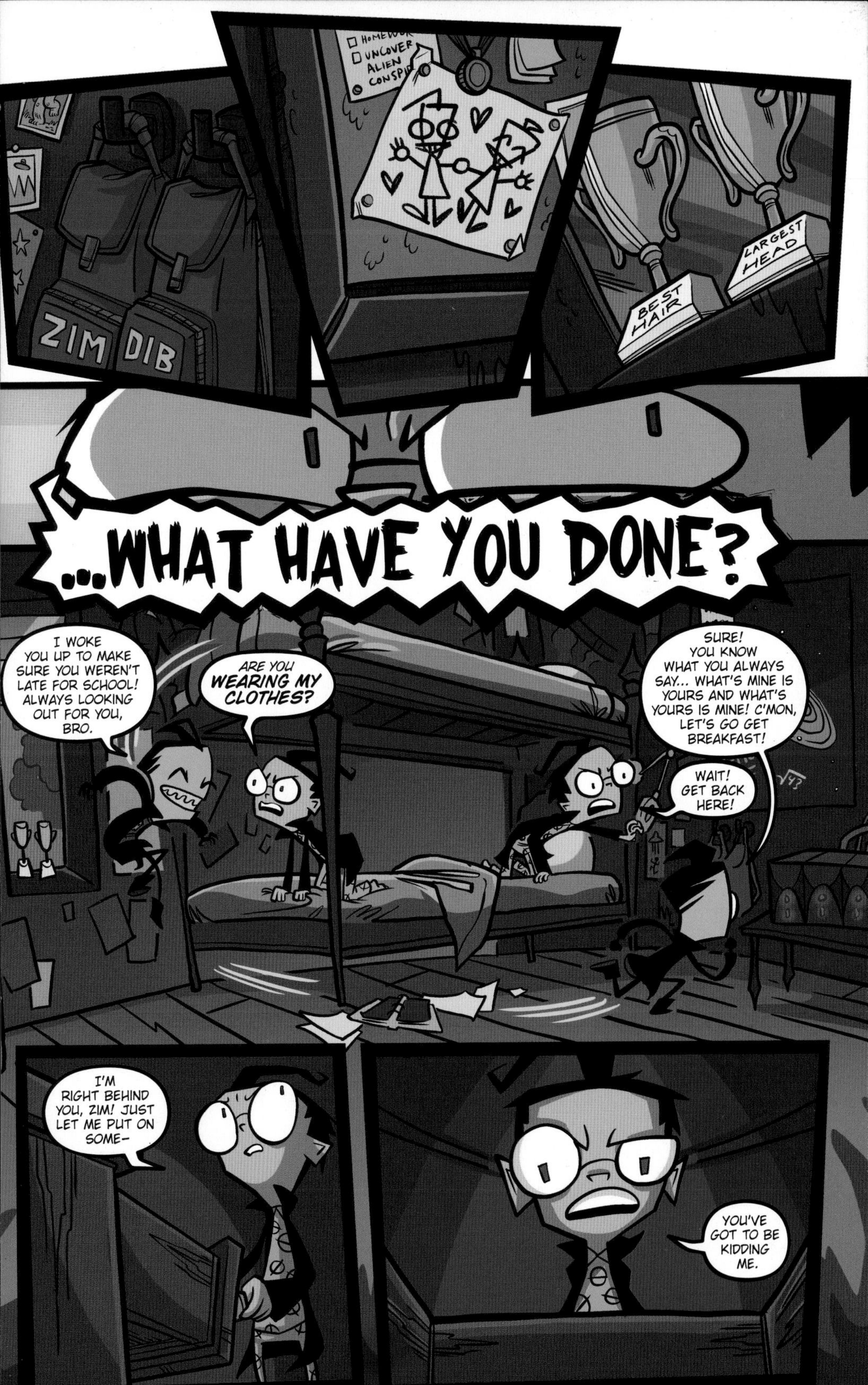
HOMEWOR
UNCOVER ALIEN CONSPI
ZIM
DIB
BEST HAIR
LARGEST HEAD
...WHAT HAVE YOU DONE?
I WOKE YOU UP TO MAKE SURE YOU WEREN'T LATE FOR SCHOOL! ALWAYS LOOKING OUT FOR YOU, BRO.
ARE YOU WEARING MY CLOTHES?
SURE! YOU KNOW WHAT YOU ALWAYS SAY... WHAT'S MINE IS YOURS AND WHAT'S YOURS IS MINE! C'MON, LET'S GO GET BREAKFAST!
WAIT! GET BACK HERE!
I'M RIGHT BEHIND YOU, ZIM! JUST LET ME PUT ON SOME-
YOU'VE GOT TO BE KIDDING ME.

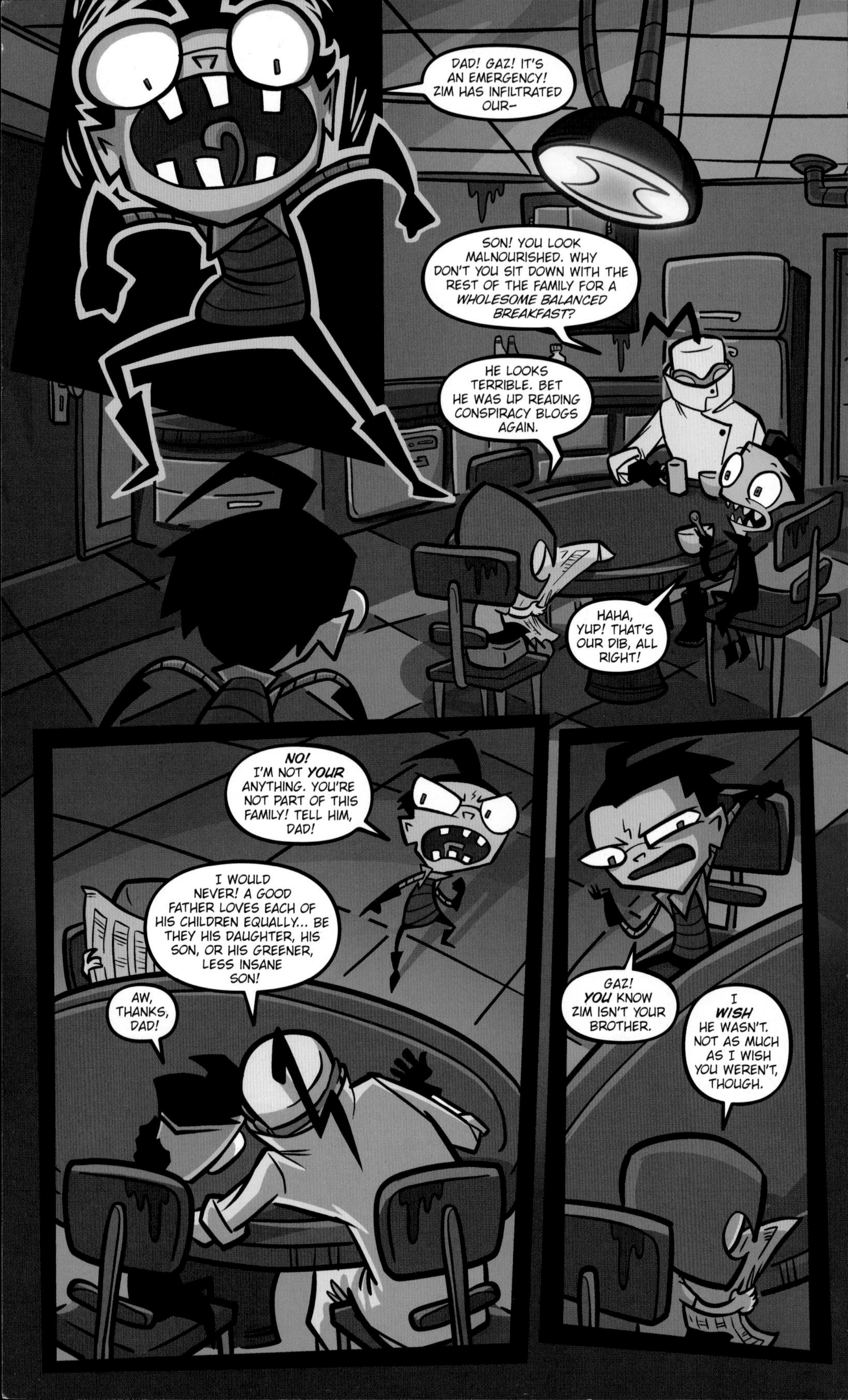
DAD! GAZ! IT'S AN EMERGENCY! ZIM HAS INFILTRATED OUR-
SON! YOU LOOK MALNOURISHED. WHY DON'T YOU SIT DOWN WITH THE REST OF THE FAMILY FOR A *WHOLESOME BALANCED BREAKFAST?*
HE LOOKS TERRIBLE. BET HE WAS UP READING CONSPIRACY BLOGS AGAIN.
HAHA, YUP! THAT'S OUR DIB, ALL RIGHT!
NO! I'M NOT ***YOUR*** ANYTHING. YOU'RE NOT PART OF THIS FAMILY! TELL HIM, DAD!
I WOULD NEVER! A GOOD FATHER LOVES EACH OF HIS CHILDREN EQUALLY... BE THEY HIS DAUGHTER, HIS SON, OR HIS GREENER, LESS INSANE SON!
AW, THANKS, DAD!
GAZ! ***YOU*** KNOW ZIM ISN'T YOUR BROTHER.
I ***WISH*** HE WASN'T. NOT AS MUCH AS I WISH YOU WEREN'T, THOUGH.

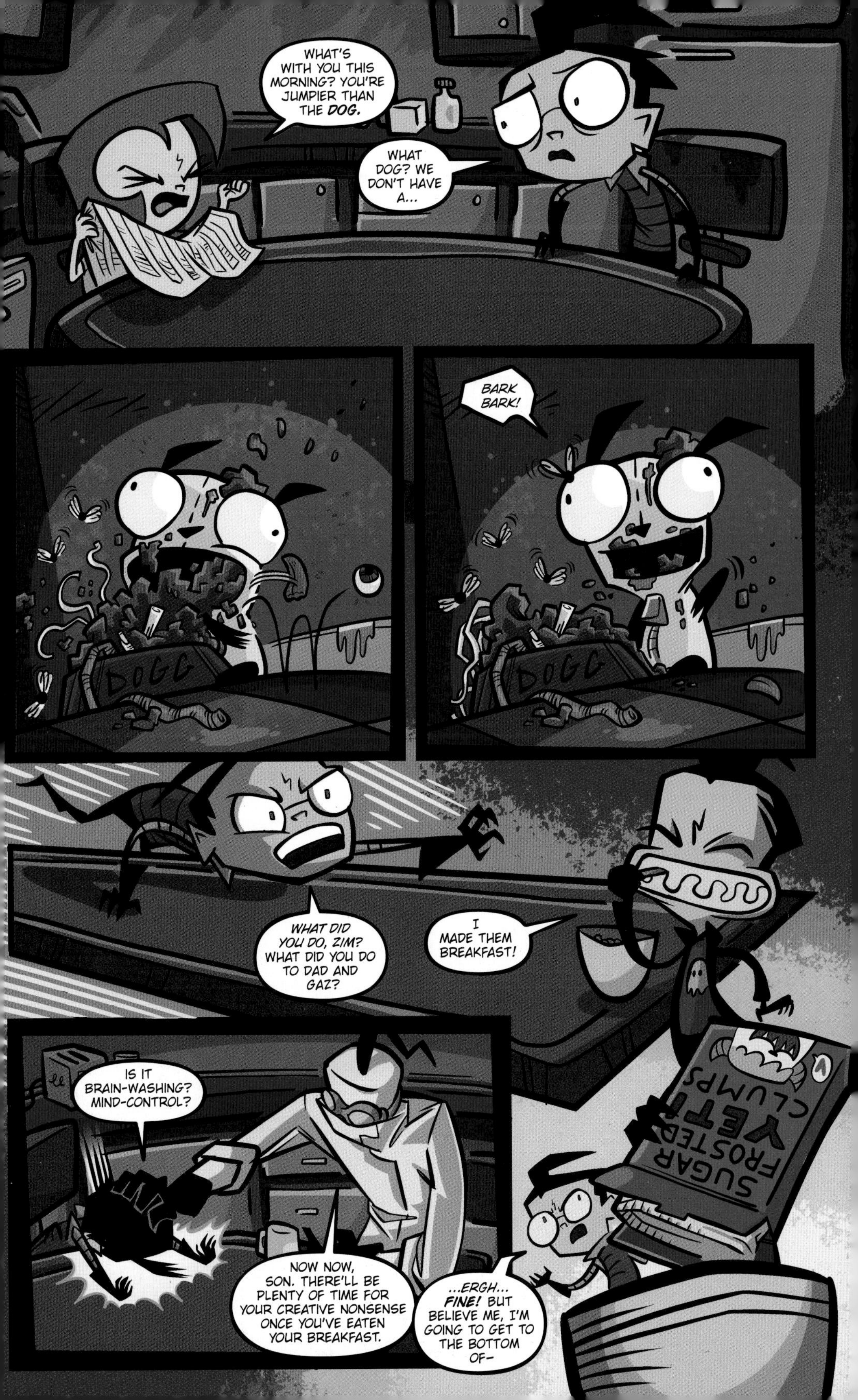

WHAT'S WITH YOU THIS MORNING? YOU'RE JUMPIER THAN THE DOG.
WHAT DOG? WE DON'T HAVE A...
DOGG
BARK BARK!
DOGG
WHAT DID YOU DO, ZIM? WHAT DID YOU DO TO DAD AND GAZ?
I MADE THEM BREAKFAST!
IS IT BRAIN-WASHING? MIND-CONTROL?
SUGAR FROSTED YETI CLUMPS
NOW NOW, SON. THERE'LL BE PLENTY OF TIME FOR YOUR CREATIVE NONSENSE ONCE YOU'VE EATEN YOUR BREAKFAST.
...ERGH... FINE! BUT BELIEVE ME, I'M GOING TO GET TO THE BOTTOM OF-

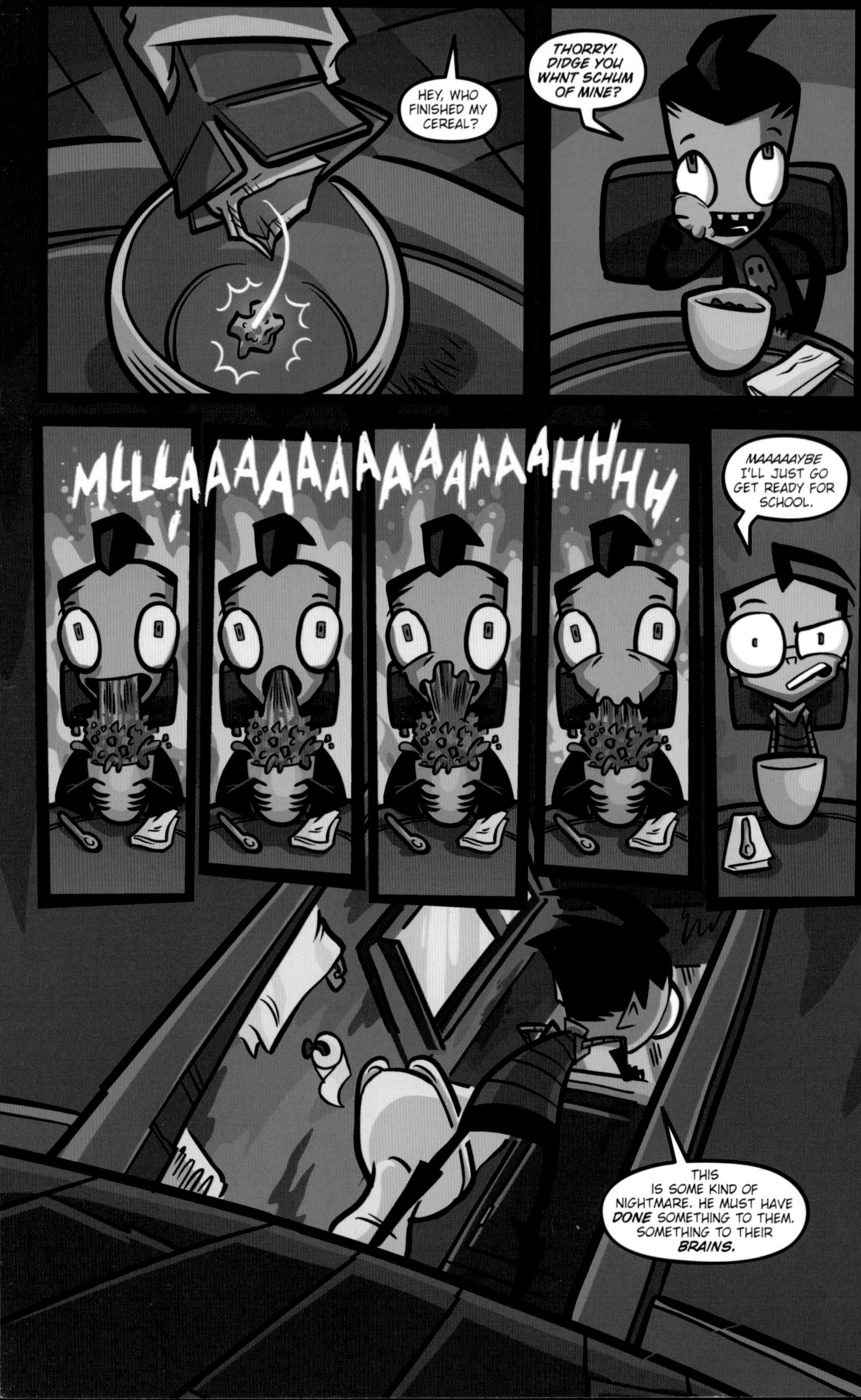
HEY, WHO FINISHED MY CEREAL?
THORRY! DIDGE YOU WHNT SCHUM OF MINE?
MLLLAAAAAAAAAAAAAAHHHH
MAAAAAYBE I'LL JUST GO GET READY FOR SCHOOL.
THIS IS SOME KIND OF NIGHTMARE. HE MUST HAVE DONE SOMETHING TO THEM. SOMETHING TO THEIR BRAINS.

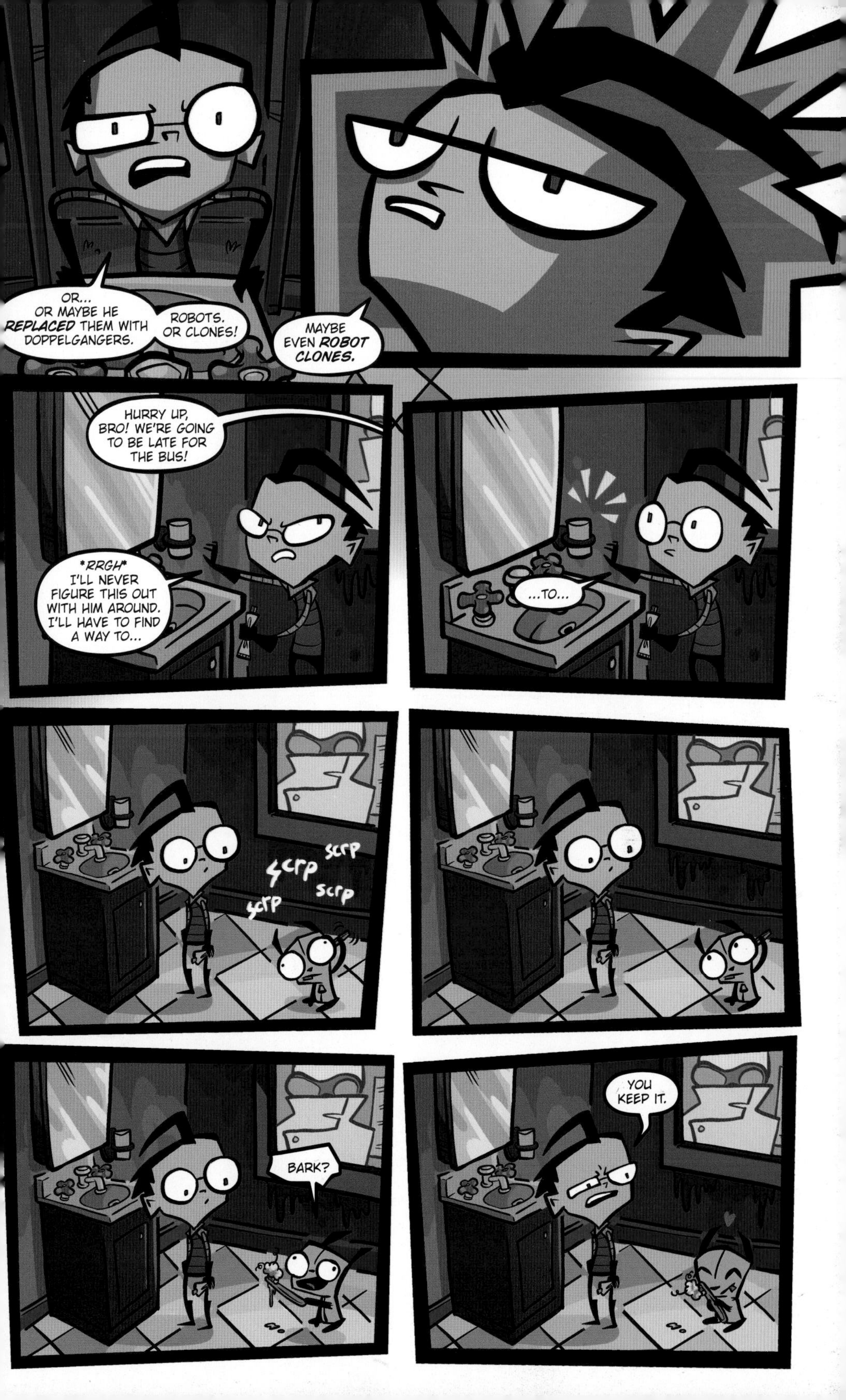

OR... OR MAYBE HE REPLACED THEM WITH DOPPELGANGERS.
ROBOTS. OR CLONES!
MAYBE EVEN ROBOT CLONES.
HURRY UP, BRO! WE'RE GOING TO BE LATE FOR THE BUS!
RRGH I'LL NEVER FIGURE THIS OUT WITH HIM AROUND. I'LL HAVE TO FIND A WAY TO...
...TO...
SCRP
SCRP
SCRP
SCRP
BARK?
YOU KEEP IT.

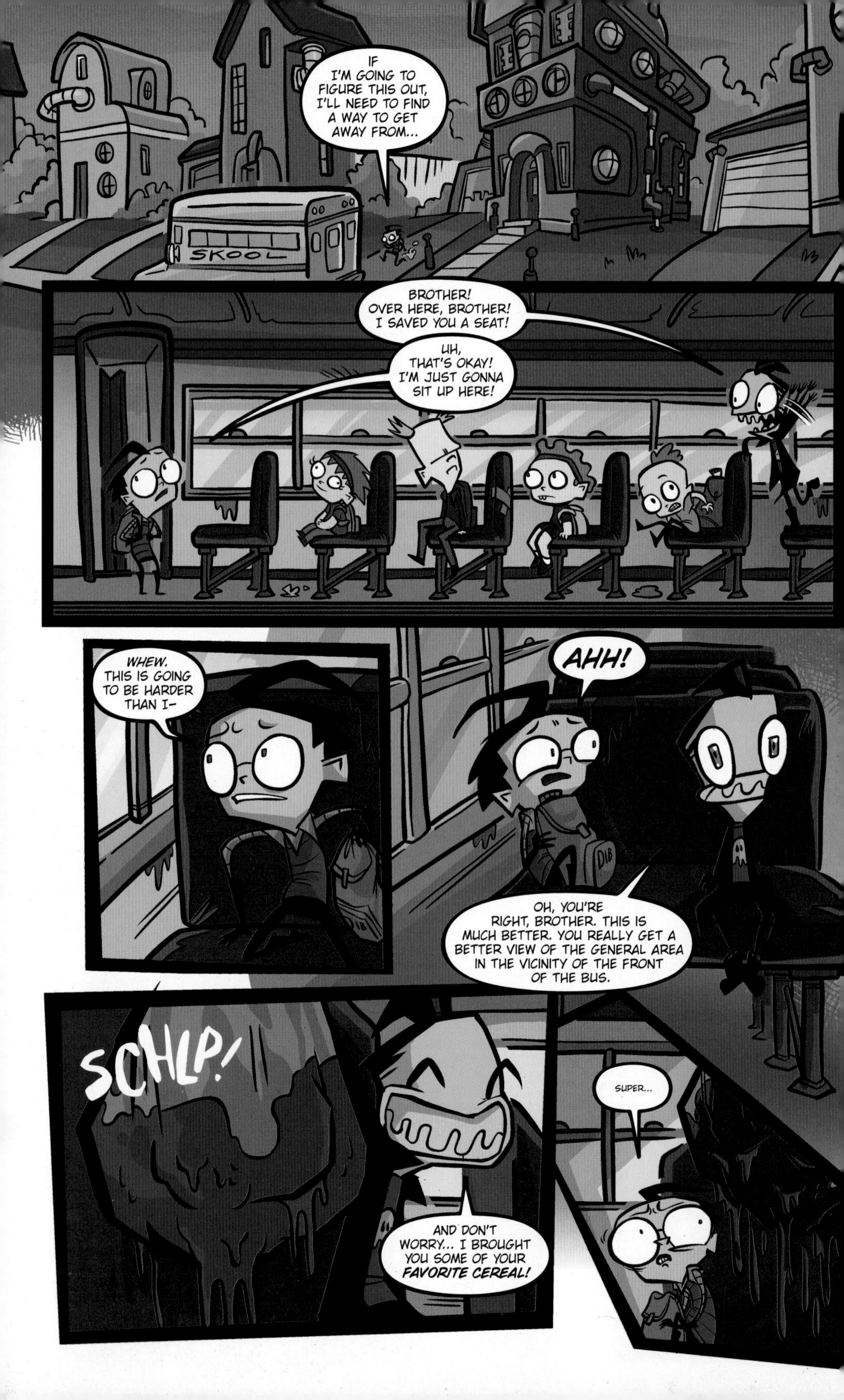
IF I'M GOING TO FIGURE THIS OUT, I'LL NEED TO FIND A WAY TO GET AWAY FROM...
SKOOL
BROTHER! OVER HERE, BROTHER! I SAVED YOU A SEAT!
UH, THAT'S OKAY! I'M JUST GONNA SIT UP HERE!
WHEW. THIS IS GOING TO BE HARDER THAN I-
AHH!
OH, YOU'RE RIGHT, BROTHER. THIS IS MUCH BETTER. YOU REALLY GET A BETTER VIEW OF THE GENERAL AREA IN THE VICINITY OF THE FRONT OF THE BUS.
SCHLP!
AND DON'T WORRY... I BROUGHT YOU SOME OF YOUR *FAVORITE CEREAL!*
SUPER...

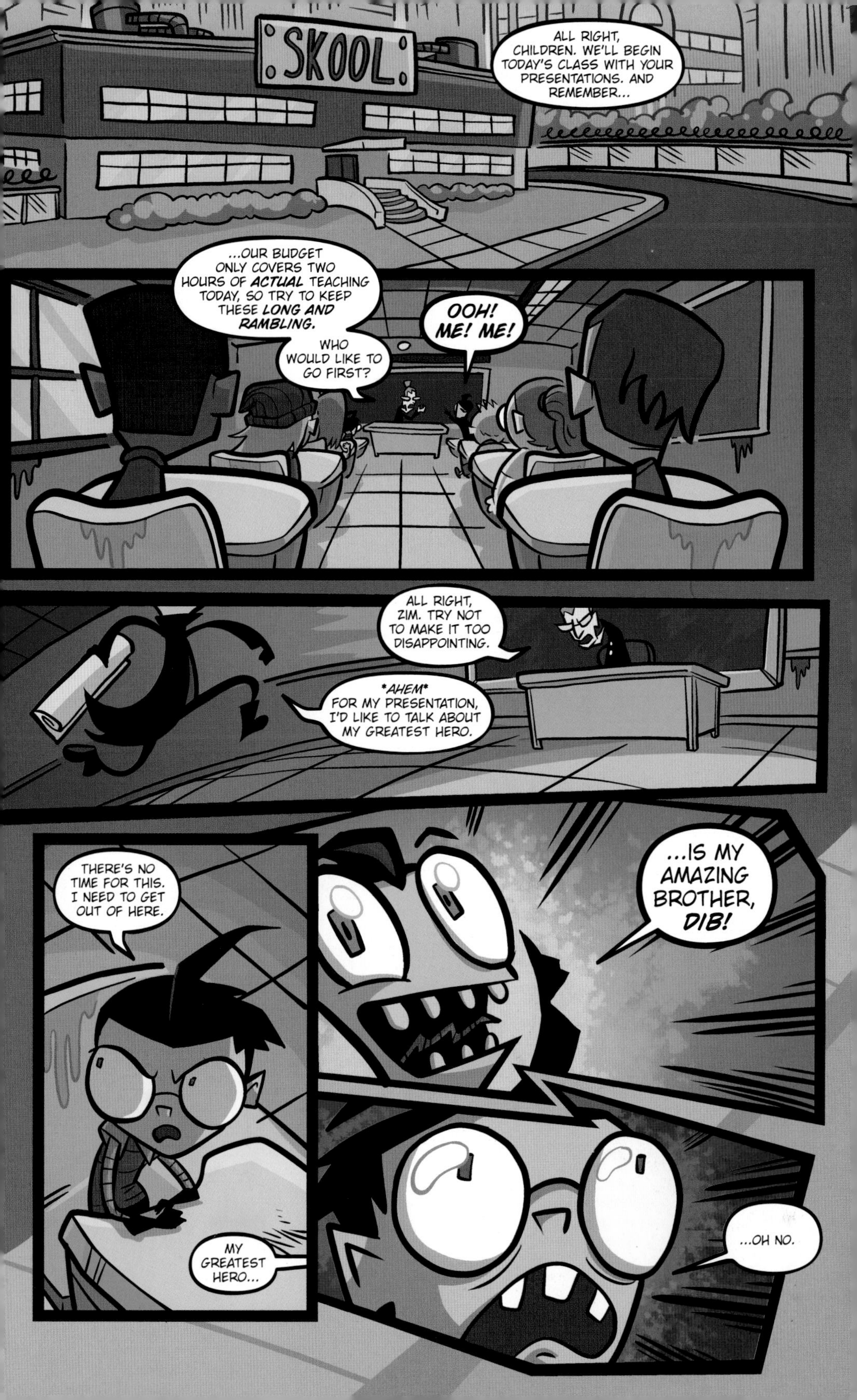
SKOOL
ALL RIGHT, CHILDREN. WE'LL BEGIN TODAY'S CLASS WITH YOUR PRESENTATIONS. AND REMEMBER...
...OUR BUDGET ONLY COVERS TWO HOURS OF ACTUAL TEACHING TODAY, SO TRY TO KEEP THESE LONG AND RAMBLING.
WHO WOULD LIKE TO GO FIRST?
OOH! ME! ME!
ALL RIGHT, ZIM. TRY NOT TO MAKE IT TOO DISAPPOINTING.
AHEM FOR MY PRESENTATION, I'D LIKE TO TALK ABOUT MY GREATEST HERO.
THERE'S NO TIME FOR THIS. I NEED TO GET OUT OF HERE.
MY GREATEST HERO...
...IS MY AMAZING BROTHER, DIB!
...OH NO.

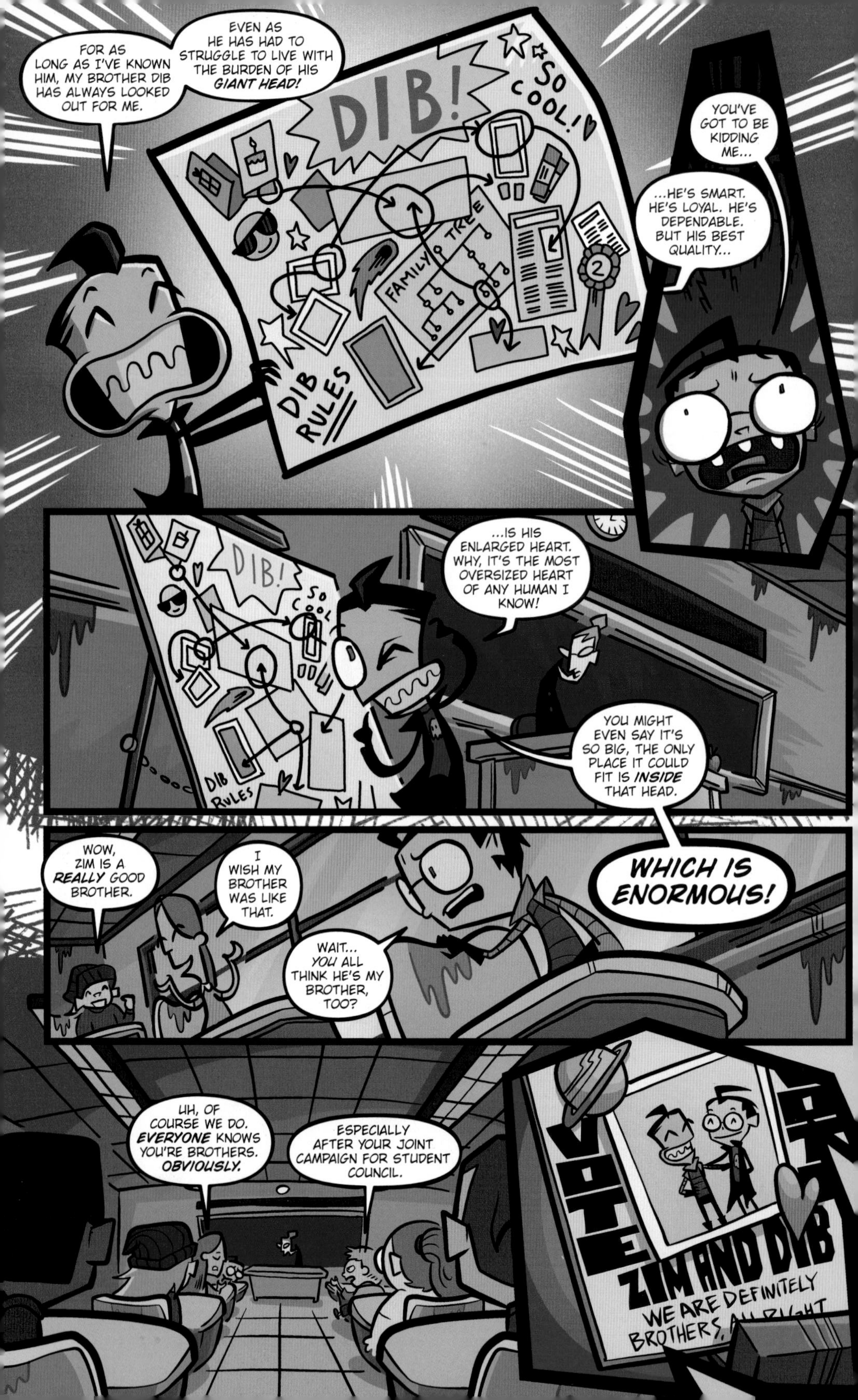
FOR AS LONG AS I'VE KNOWN HIM, MY BROTHER DIB HAS ALWAYS LOOKED OUT FOR ME.
EVEN AS HE HAS HAD TO STRUGGLE TO LIVE WITH THE BURDEN OF HIS *GIANT HEAD!*
DIB!
SO COOL!
FAMILY TREE
DIB RULES
YOU'VE GOT TO BE KIDDING ME...
...HE'S SMART. HE'S LOYAL. HE'S DEPENDABLE. BUT HIS BEST QUALITY...
DIB!
SO COOL
DIB RULES
...IS HIS ENLARGED HEART. WHY, IT'S THE MOST OVERSIZED HEART OF ANY HUMAN I KNOW!
YOU MIGHT EVEN SAY IT'S SO BIG, THE ONLY PLACE IT COULD FIT IS *INSIDE* THAT HEAD.
WHICH IS ENORMOUS!
WOW, ZIM IS A ***REALLY*** GOOD BROTHER.
I WISH MY BROTHER WAS LIKE THAT.
WAIT... *YOU* ALL THINK HE'S MY BROTHER, TOO?
UH, OF COURSE WE DO. ***EVERYONE*** KNOWS YOU'RE BROTHERS. ***OBVIOUSLY.***
ESPECIALLY AFTER YOUR JOINT CAMPAIGN FOR STUDENT COUNCIL.
VOTE
ZIM AND DIB
WE ARE DEFINITELY BROTHERS

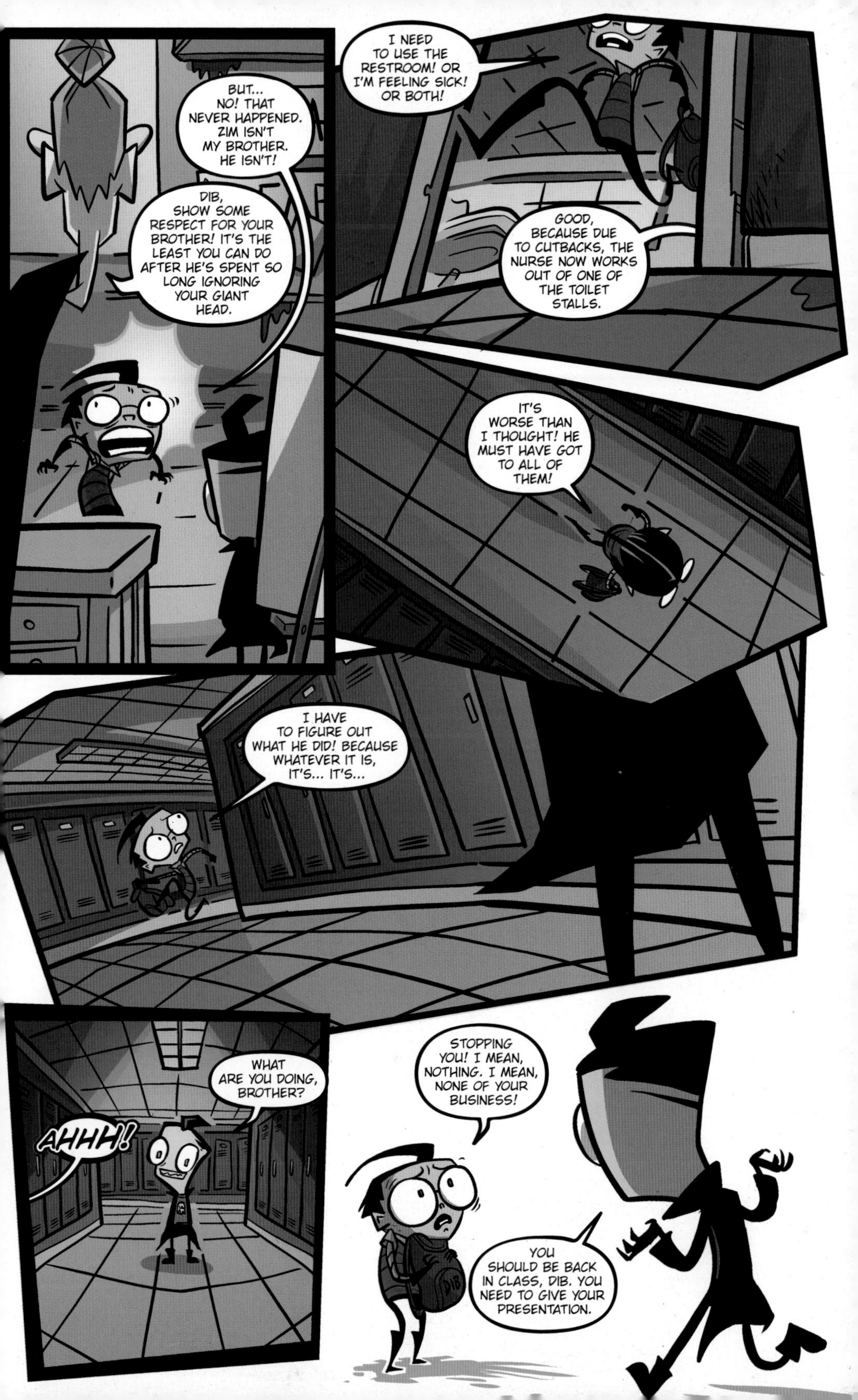
BUT... NO! THAT NEVER HAPPENED. ZIM ISN'T MY BROTHER. HE ISN'T!
DIB, SHOW SOME RESPECT FOR YOUR BROTHER! IT'S THE LEAST YOU CAN DO AFTER HE'S SPENT SO LONG IGNORING YOUR GIANT HEAD.
I NEED TO USE THE RESTROOM! OR I'M FEELING SICK! OR BOTH!
GOOD, BECAUSE DUE TO CUTBACKS, THE NURSE NOW WORKS OUT OF ONE OF THE TOILET STALLS.
IT'S WORSE THAN I THOUGHT! HE MUST HAVE GOT TO ALL OF THEM!
I HAVE TO FIGURE OUT WHAT HE DID! BECAUSE WHATEVER IT IS, IT'S... IT'S...
WHAT ARE YOU DOING, BROTHER?
AHHH!
STOPPING YOU! I MEAN, NOTHING. I MEAN, NONE OF YOUR BUSINESS!
YOU SHOULD BE BACK IN CLASS, DIB. YOU NEED TO GIVE YOUR PRESENTATION.
DIB

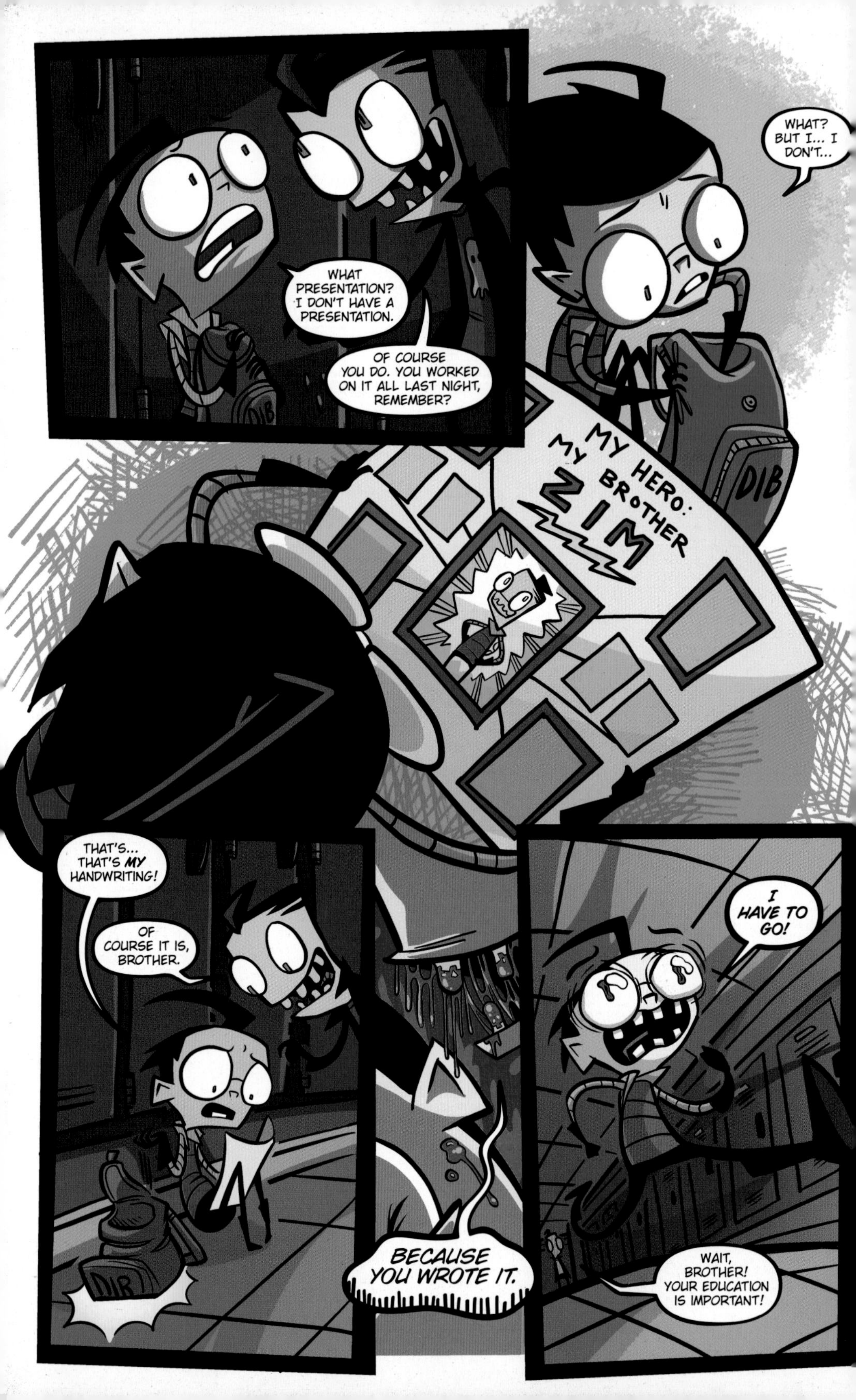
WHAT PRESENTATION? I DON'T HAVE A PRESENTATION.
OF COURSE YOU DO. YOU WORKED ON IT ALL LAST NIGHT, REMEMBER?
WHAT? BUT I... I DON'T...
MY HERO: MY BROTHER ZIM
DIB
THAT'S... THAT'S MY HANDWRITING!
OF COURSE IT IS, BROTHER.
BECAUSE YOU WROTE IT.
I HAVE TO GO!
WAIT, BROTHER! YOUR EDUCATION IS IMPORTANT!

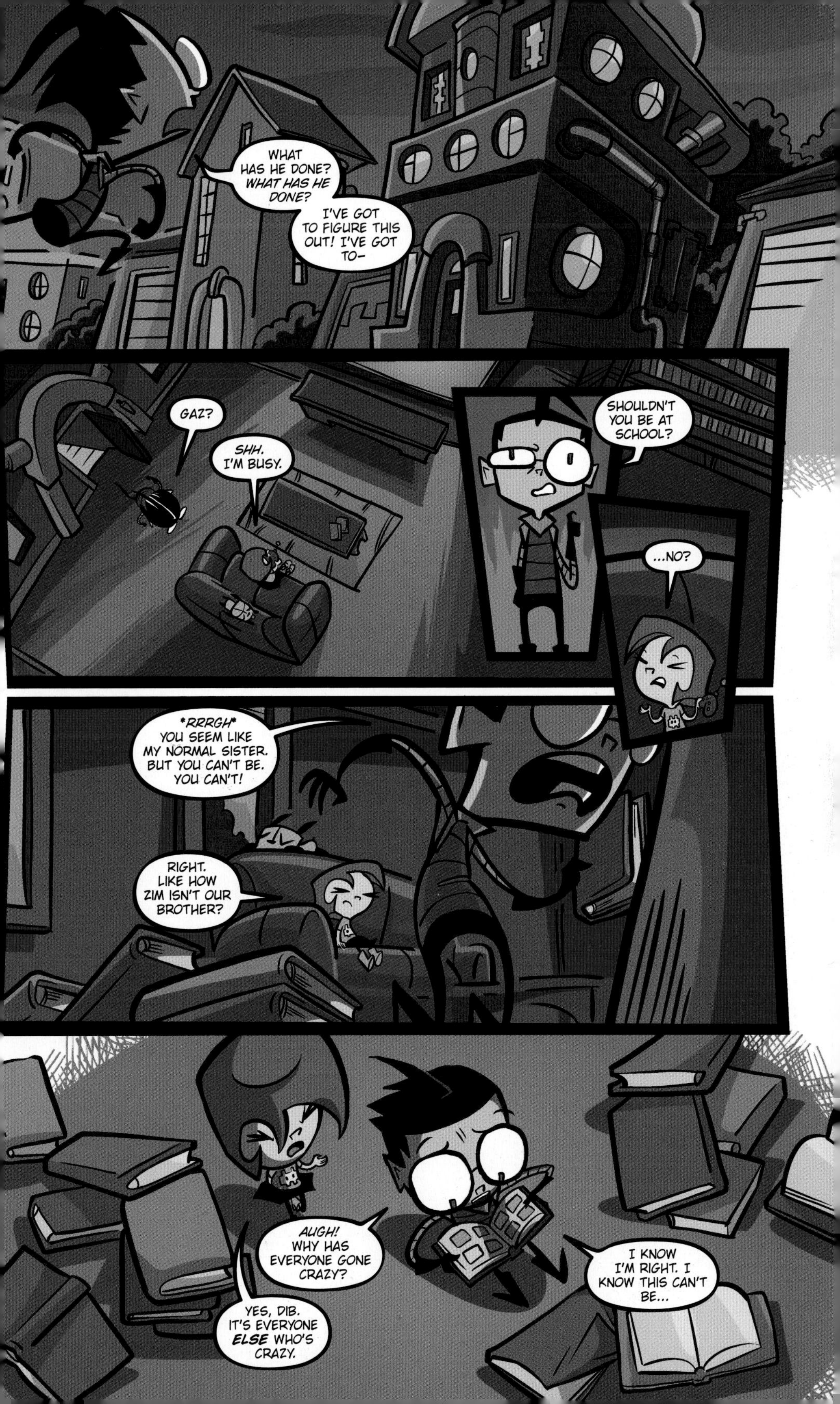

WHAT HAS HE DONE? WHAT HAS HE DONE?
I'VE GOT TO FIGURE THIS OUT! I'VE GOT TO-
GAZ?
SHH. I'M BUSY.
SHOULDN'T YOU BE AT SCHOOL?
...NO?
RRRGH YOU SEEM LIKE MY NORMAL SISTER. BUT YOU CAN'T BE. YOU CAN'T!
RIGHT. LIKE HOW ZIM ISN'T OUR BROTHER?
AUGH! WHY HAS EVERYONE GONE CRAZY?
YES, DIB. IT'S EVERYONE ELSE WHO'S CRAZY.
I KNOW I'M RIGHT. I KNOW THIS CAN'T BE...

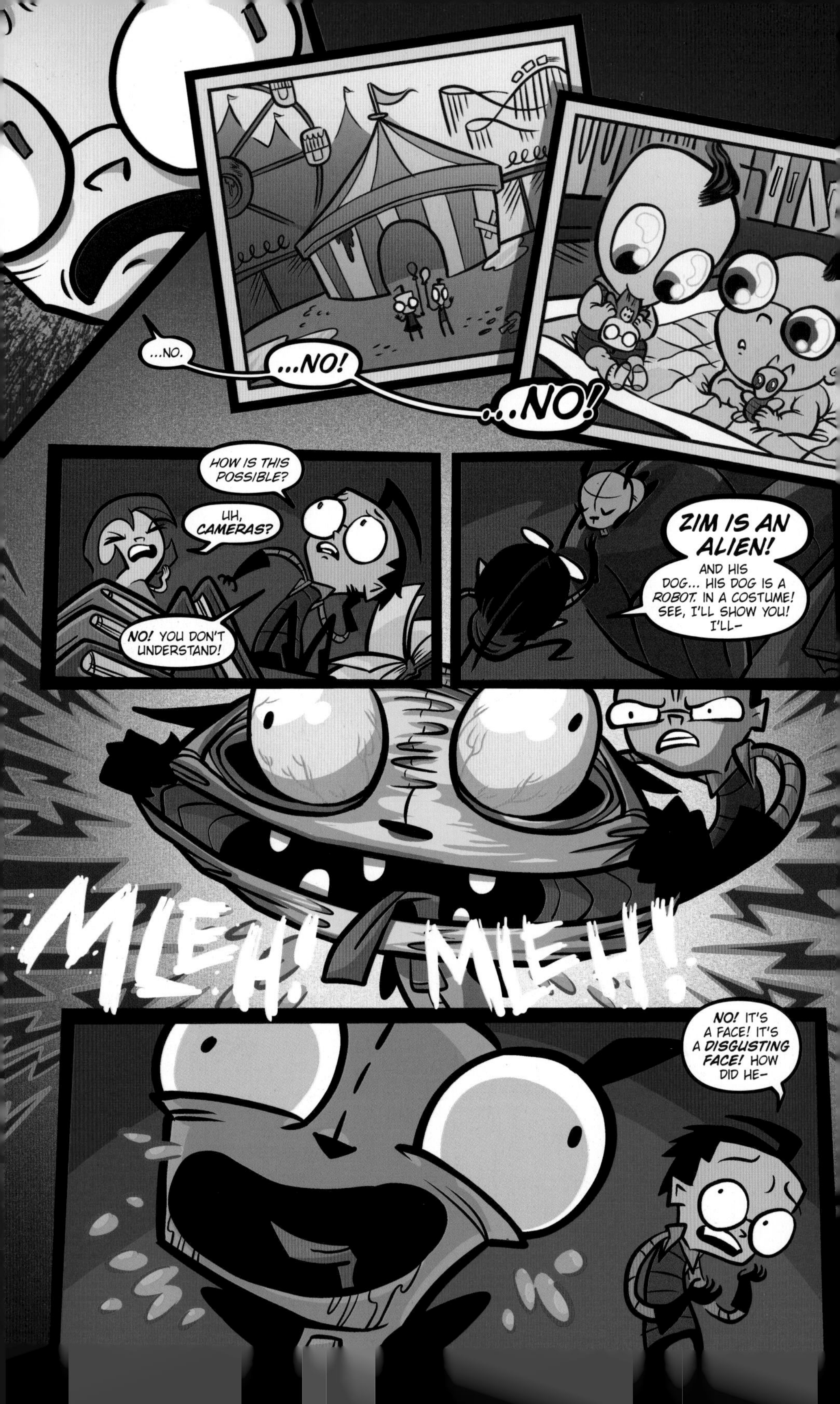

...NO.
...NO!
...NO!
HOW IS THIS POSSIBLE?
UH, CAMERAS?
NO! YOU DON'T UNDERSTAND!
ZIM IS AN ALIEN!
AND HIS DOG... HIS DOG IS A ROBOT. IN A COSTUME! SEE, I'LL SHOW YOU! I'LL–
MLEH! MLEH!
NO! IT'S A FACE! IT'S A DISGUSTING FACE! HOW DID HE–

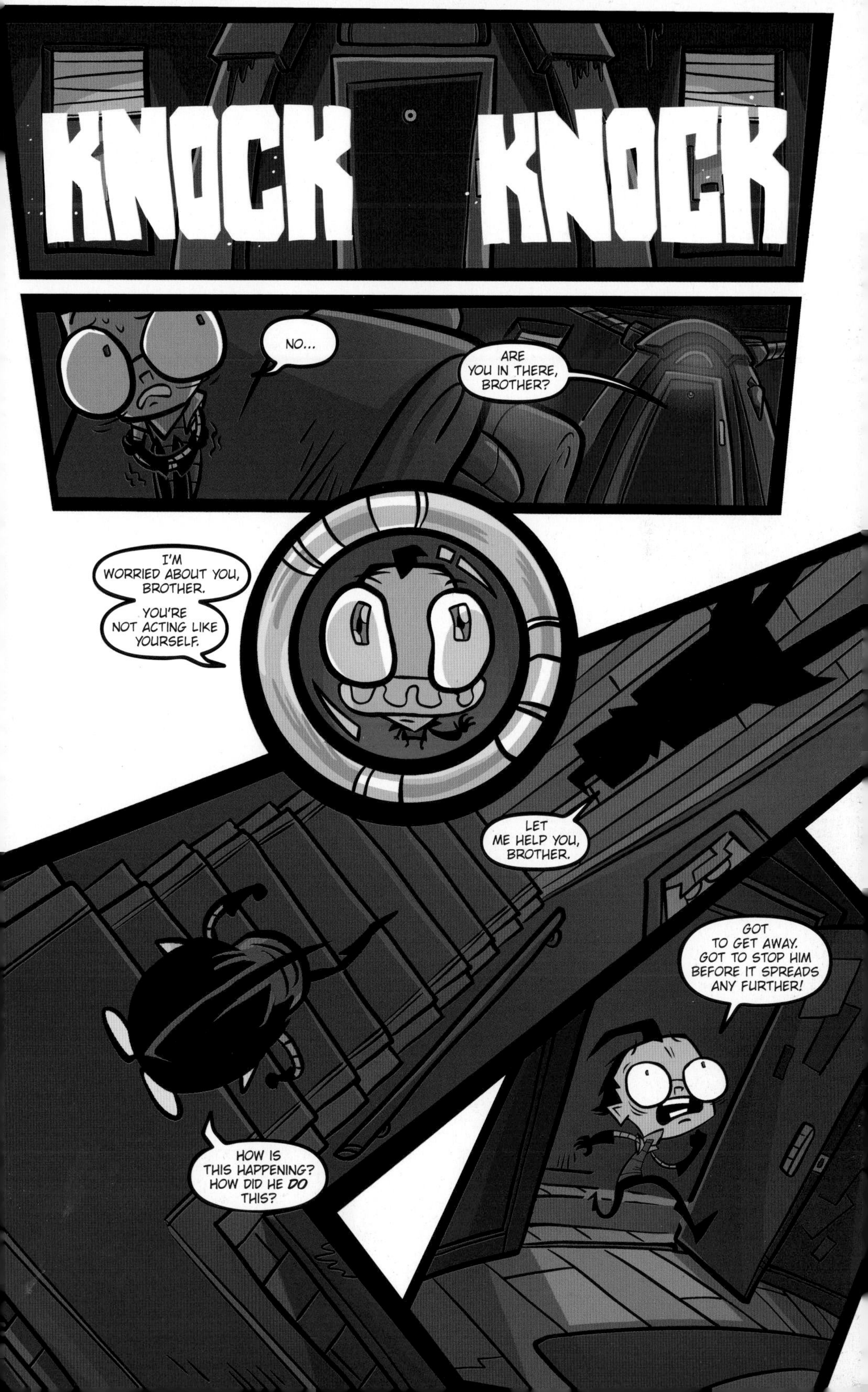
KNOCK KNOCK
NO...
ARE YOU IN THERE, BROTHER?
I'M WORRIED ABOUT YOU, BROTHER.
YOU'RE NOT ACTING LIKE YOURSELF.
LET ME HELP YOU, BROTHER.
GOT TO GET AWAY. GOT TO STOP HIM BEFORE IT SPREADS ANY FURTHER!
HOW IS THIS HAPPENING? HOW DID HE *DO* THIS?

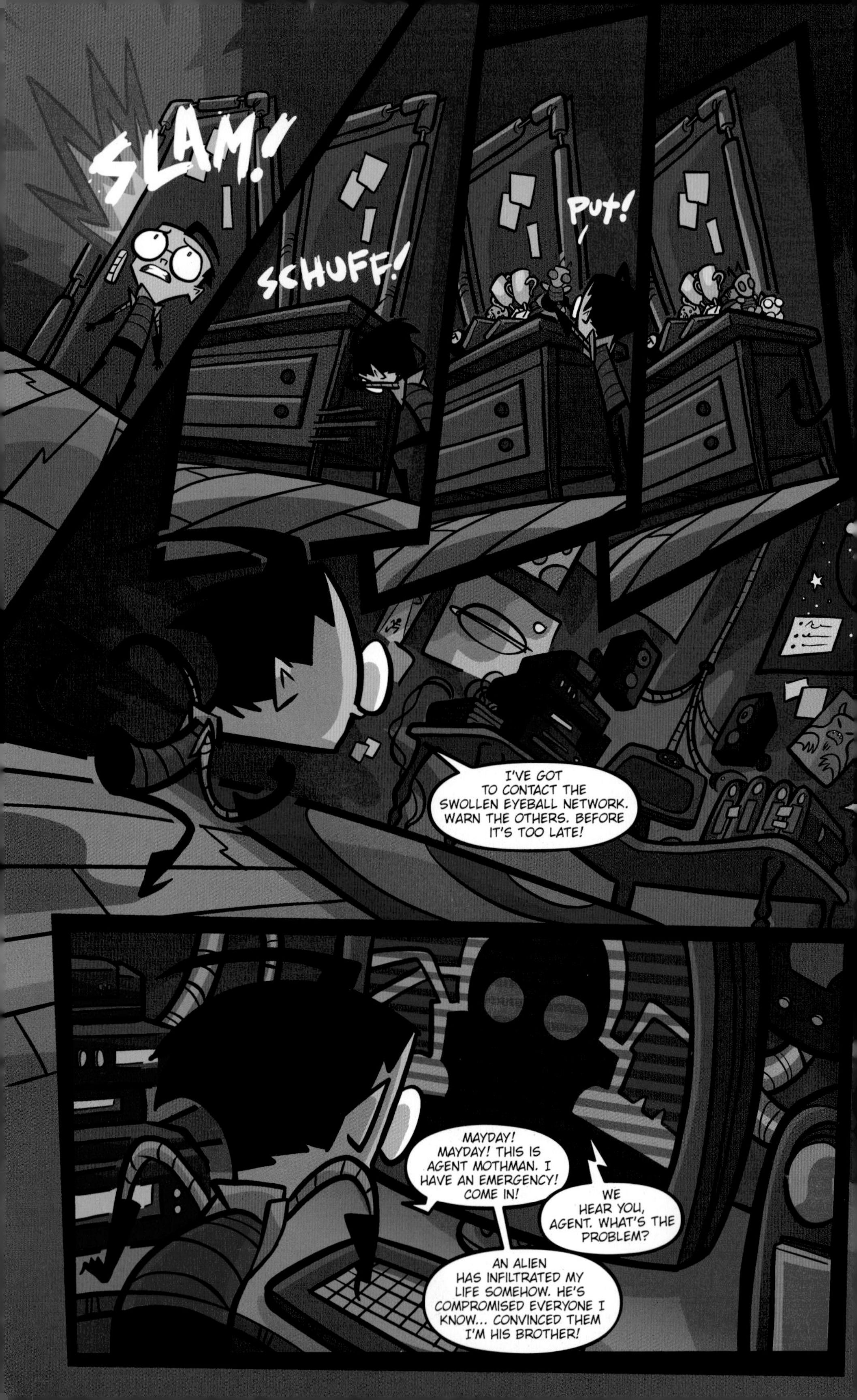
SLAM!
SCHUFF!
PUT!
I'VE GOT TO CONTACT THE SWOLLEN EYEBALL NETWORK. WARN THE OTHERS. BEFORE IT'S TOO LATE!
MAYDAY! MAYDAY! THIS IS AGENT MOTHMAN. I HAVE AN EMERGENCY! COME IN!
WE HEAR YOU, AGENT. WHAT'S THE PROBLEM?
AN ALIEN HAS INFILTRATED MY LIFE SOMEHOW. HE'S COMPROMISED EVERYONE I KNOW... CONVINCED THEM I'M HIS BROTHER!

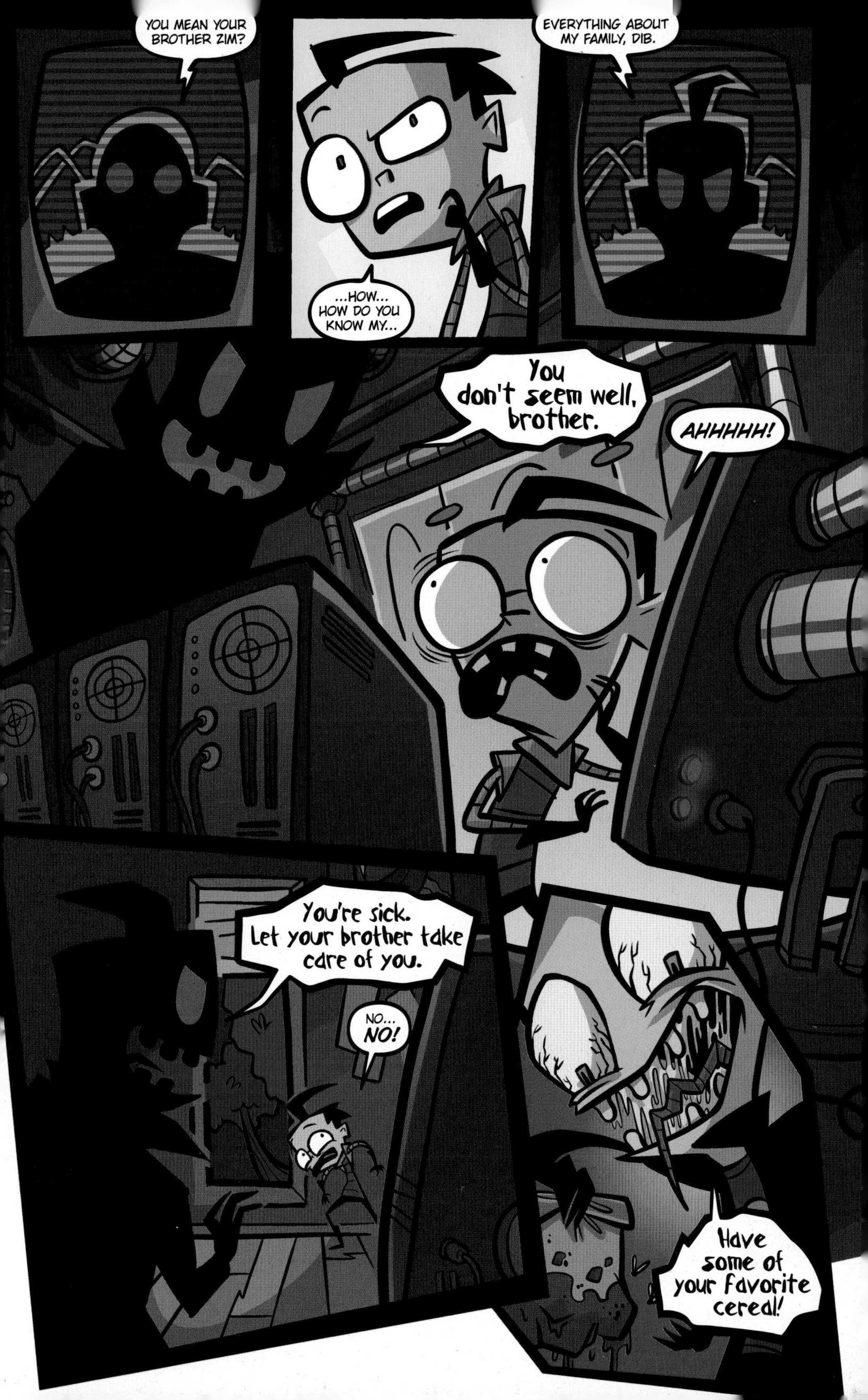
YOU MEAN YOUR BROTHER ZIM?
...HOW... HOW DO YOU KNOW MY...
EVERYTHING ABOUT MY FAMILY, DIB.
You don't seem well, brother.
AHHHHH!
You're sick. Let your brother take care of you.
NO... NO!
Have some of your favorite cereal!

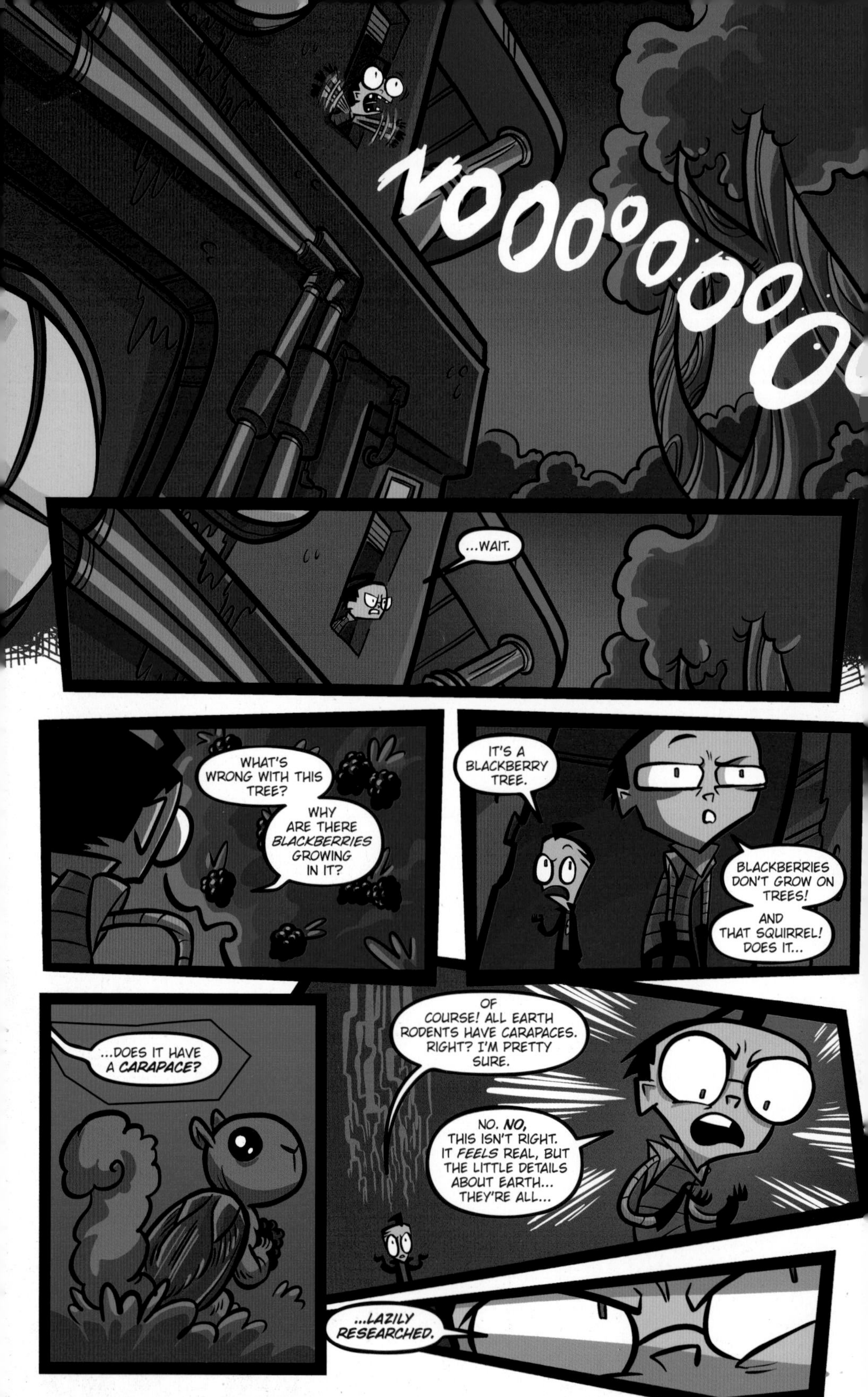
NOOOOOOOO
...WAIT.
WHAT'S WRONG WITH THIS TREE?
WHY ARE THERE BLACKBERRIES GROWING IN IT?
IT'S A BLACKBERRY TREE.
BLACKBERRIES DON'T GROW ON TREES!
AND THAT SQUIRREL! DOES IT...
...DOES IT HAVE A CARAPACE?
OF COURSE! ALL EARTH RODENTS HAVE CARAPACES. RIGHT? I'M PRETTY SURE.
NO. NO, THIS ISN'T RIGHT. IT FEELS REAL, BUT THE LITTLE DETAILS ABOUT EARTH... THEY'RE ALL...
...LAZILY RESEARCHED.

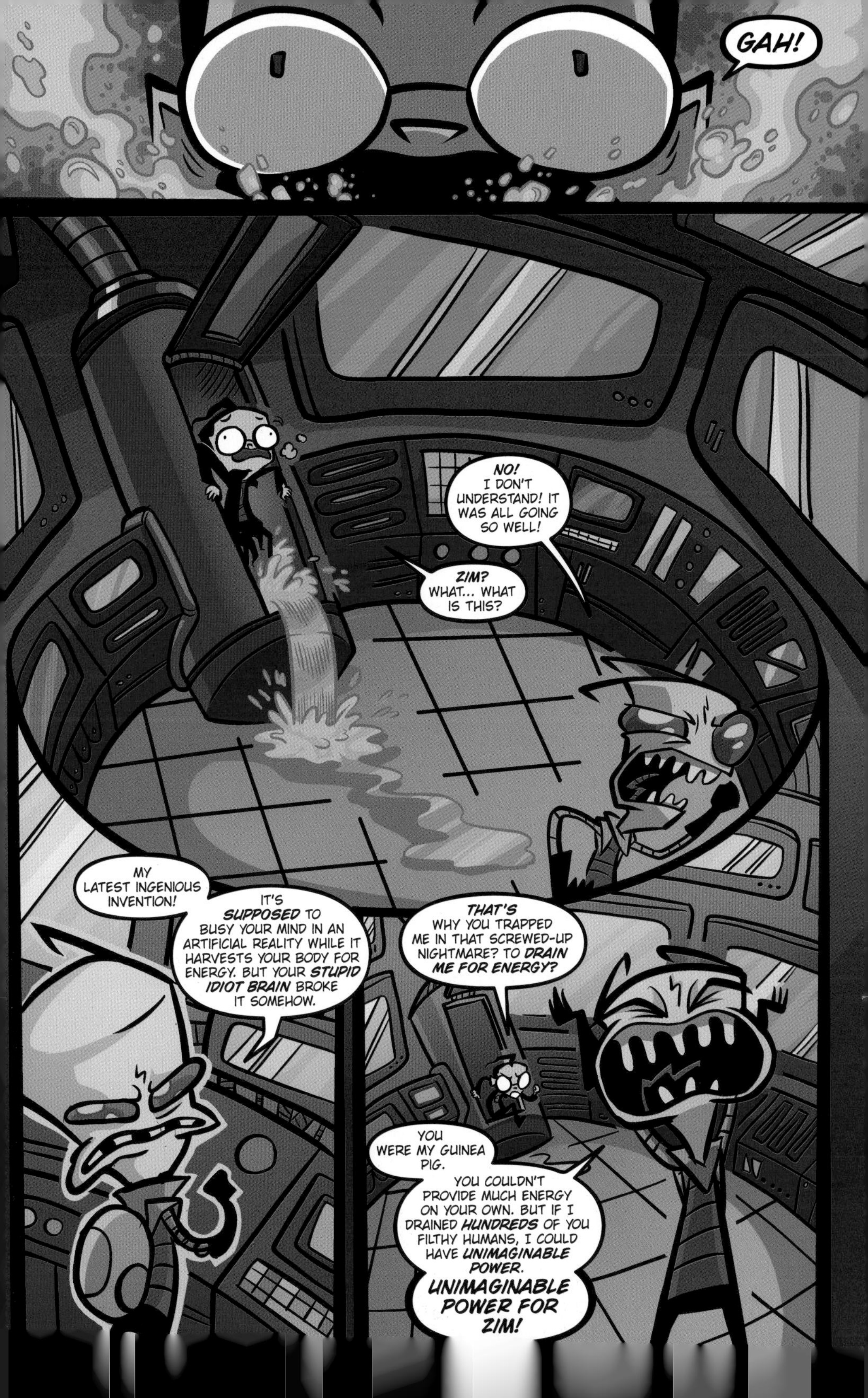
GAH!
NO! I DON'T UNDERSTAND! IT WAS ALL GOING SO WELL!
ZIM? WHAT... WHAT IS THIS?
MY LATEST INGENIOUS INVENTION!
IT'S SUPPOSED TO BUSY YOUR MIND IN AN ARTIFICIAL REALITY WHILE IT HARVESTS YOUR BODY FOR ENERGY. BUT YOUR STUPID IDIOT BRAIN BROKE IT SOMEHOW.
THAT'S WHY YOU TRAPPED ME IN THAT SCREWED-UP NIGHTMARE? TO DRAIN ME FOR ENERGY?
YOU WERE MY GUINEA PIG.
YOU COULDN'T PROVIDE MUCH ENERGY ON YOUR OWN. BUT IF I DRAINED HUNDREDS OF YOU FILTHY HUMANS, I COULD HAVE UNIMAGINABLE POWER.
UNIMAGINABLE POWER FOR ZIM!

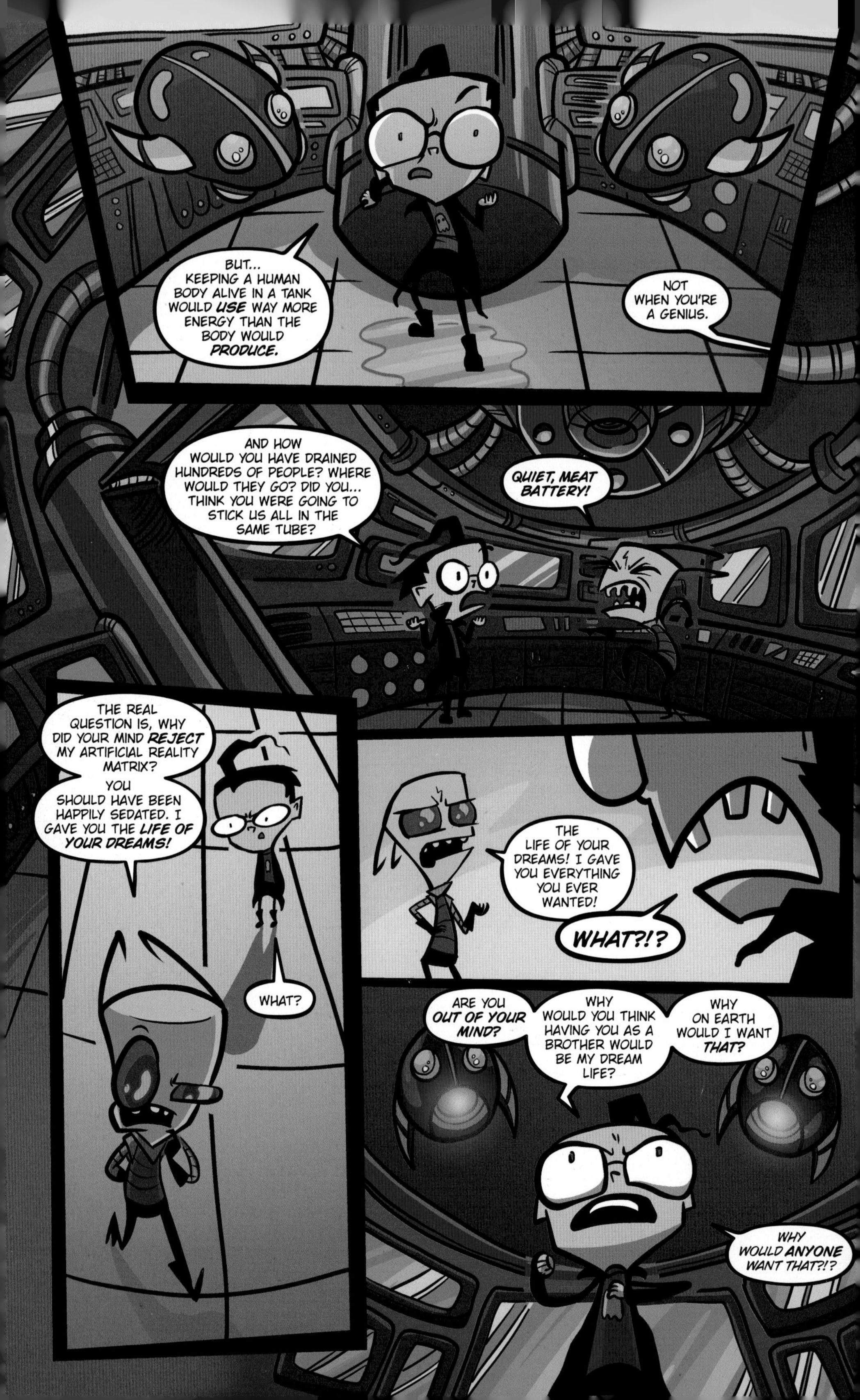
BUT... KEEPING A HUMAN BODY ALIVE IN A TANK WOULD USE WAY MORE ENERGY THAN THE BODY WOULD PRODUCE.
NOT WHEN YOU'RE A GENIUS.
AND HOW WOULD YOU HAVE DRAINED HUNDREDS OF PEOPLE? WHERE WOULD THEY GO? DID YOU... THINK YOU WERE GOING TO STICK US ALL IN THE SAME TUBE?
QUIET, MEAT BATTERY!
THE REAL QUESTION IS, WHY DID YOUR MIND REJECT MY ARTIFICIAL REALITY MATRIX?
YOU SHOULD HAVE BEEN HAPPILY SEDATED. I GAVE YOU THE LIFE OF YOUR DREAMS!
WHAT?
THE LIFE OF YOUR DREAMS! I GAVE YOU EVERYTHING YOU EVER WANTED!
WHAT?!?
ARE YOU OUT OF YOUR MIND?
WHY WOULD YOU THINK HAVING YOU AS A BROTHER WOULD BE MY DREAM LIFE?
WHY ON EARTH WOULD I WANT THAT?
WHY WOULD ANYONE WANT THAT?!?

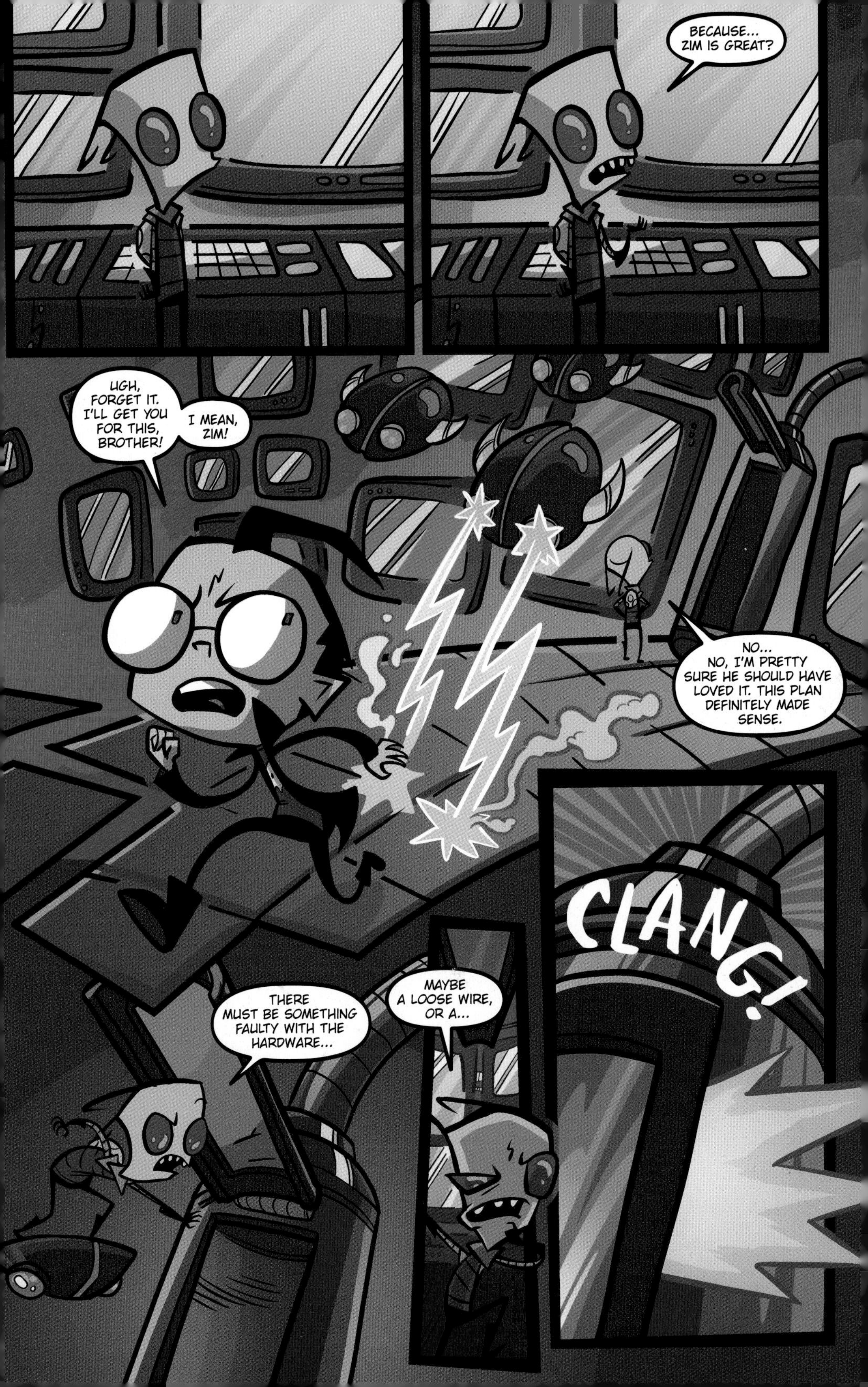
BECAUSE... ZIM IS GREAT?
UGH, FORGET IT. I'LL GET YOU FOR THIS, BROTHER!
I MEAN, ZIM!
NO... NO, I'M PRETTY SURE HE SHOULD HAVE LOVED IT. THIS PLAN DEFINITELY MADE SENSE.
THERE MUST BE SOMETHING FAULTY WITH THE HARDWARE...
MAYBE A LOOSE WIRE, OR A...
CLANG!

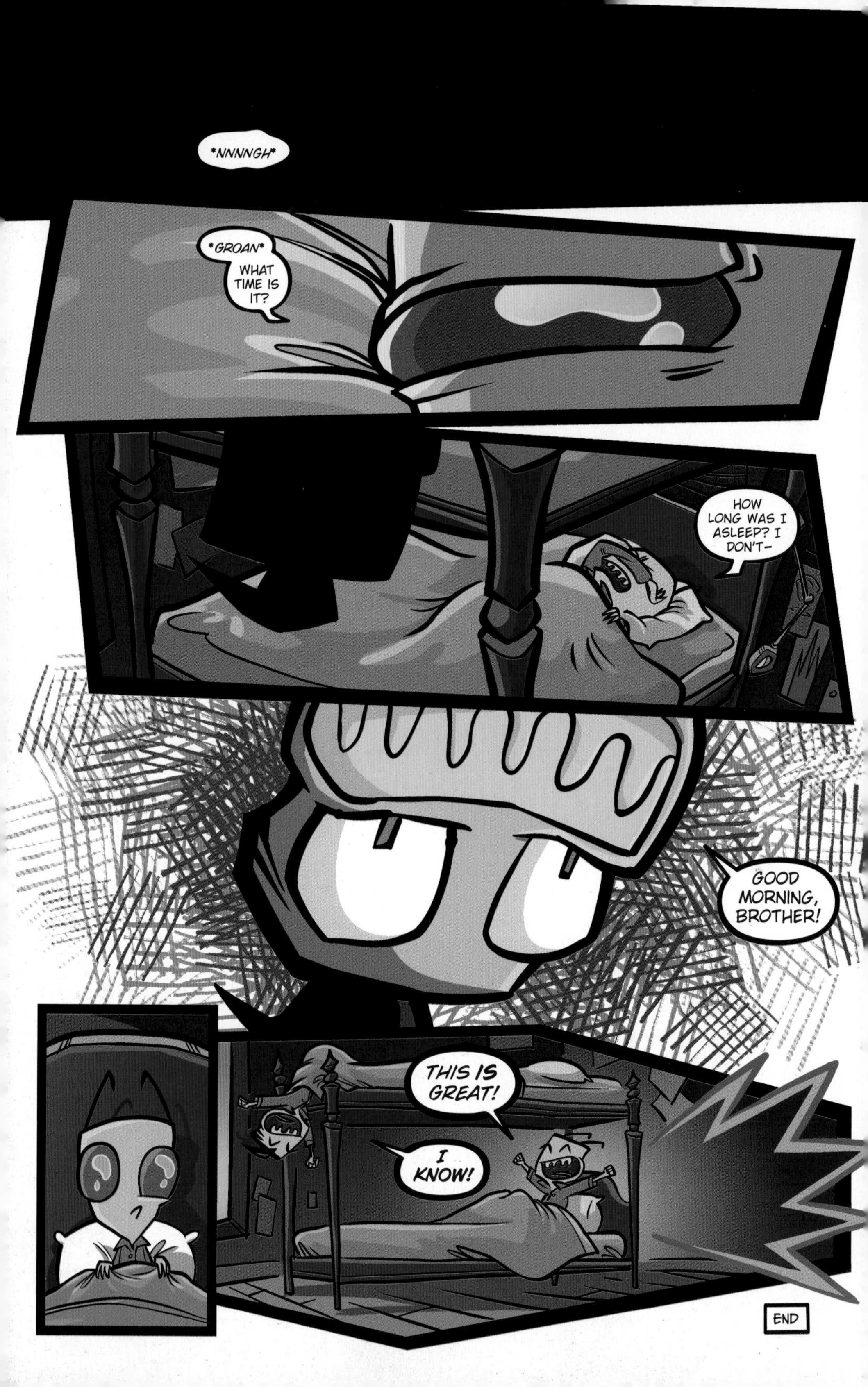
NNNNGH
GROAN WHAT TIME IS IT?
HOW LONG WAS I ASLEEP? I DON'T-
GOOD MORNING, BROTHER!
THIS IS GREAT!
I KNOW!
END

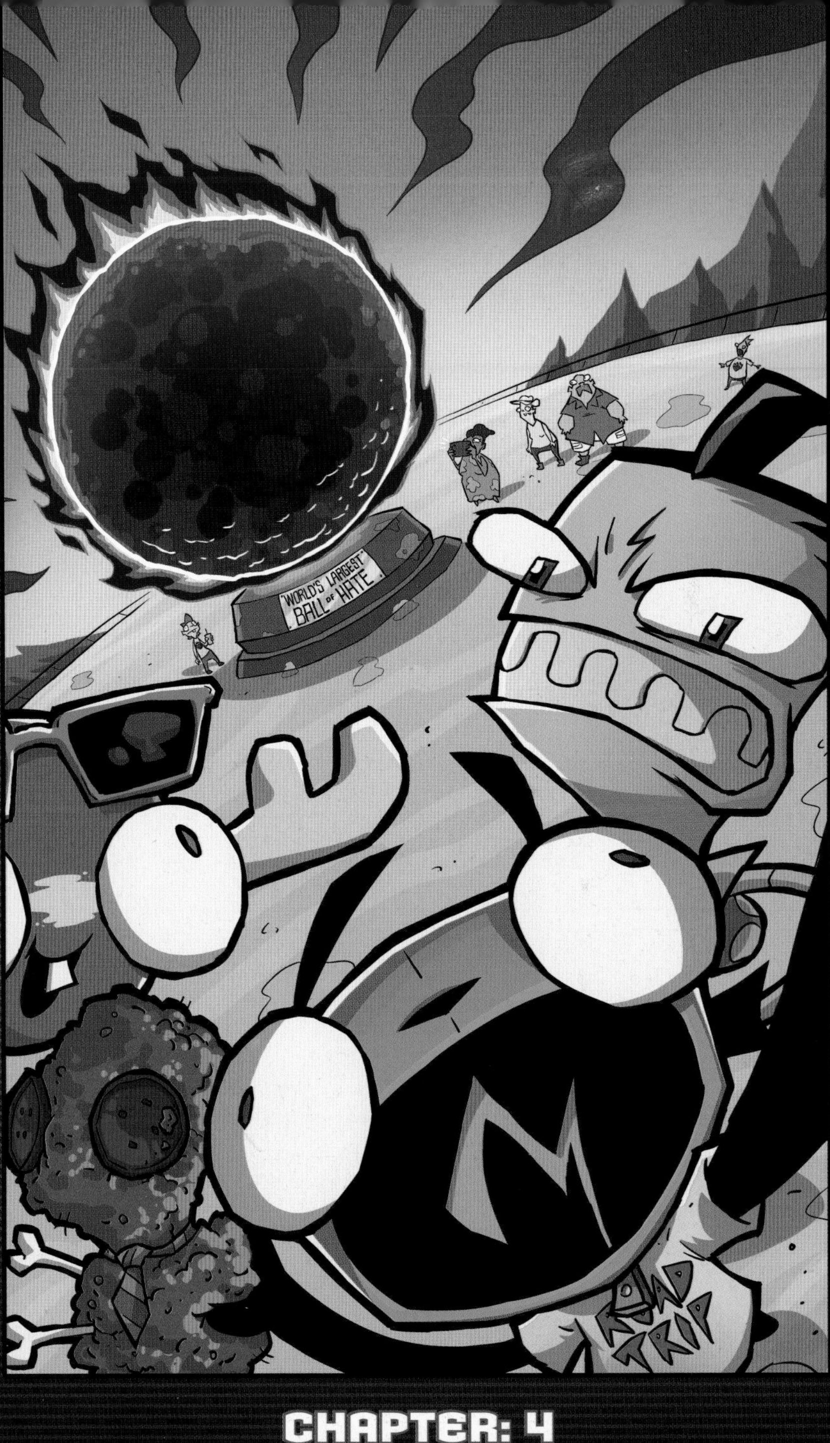
"WORLD'S LARGEST" BALL of HATE
ROAD TRIP

CHAPTER: 4

illustration by Warren Wucinich colored by Fred C. Stresing

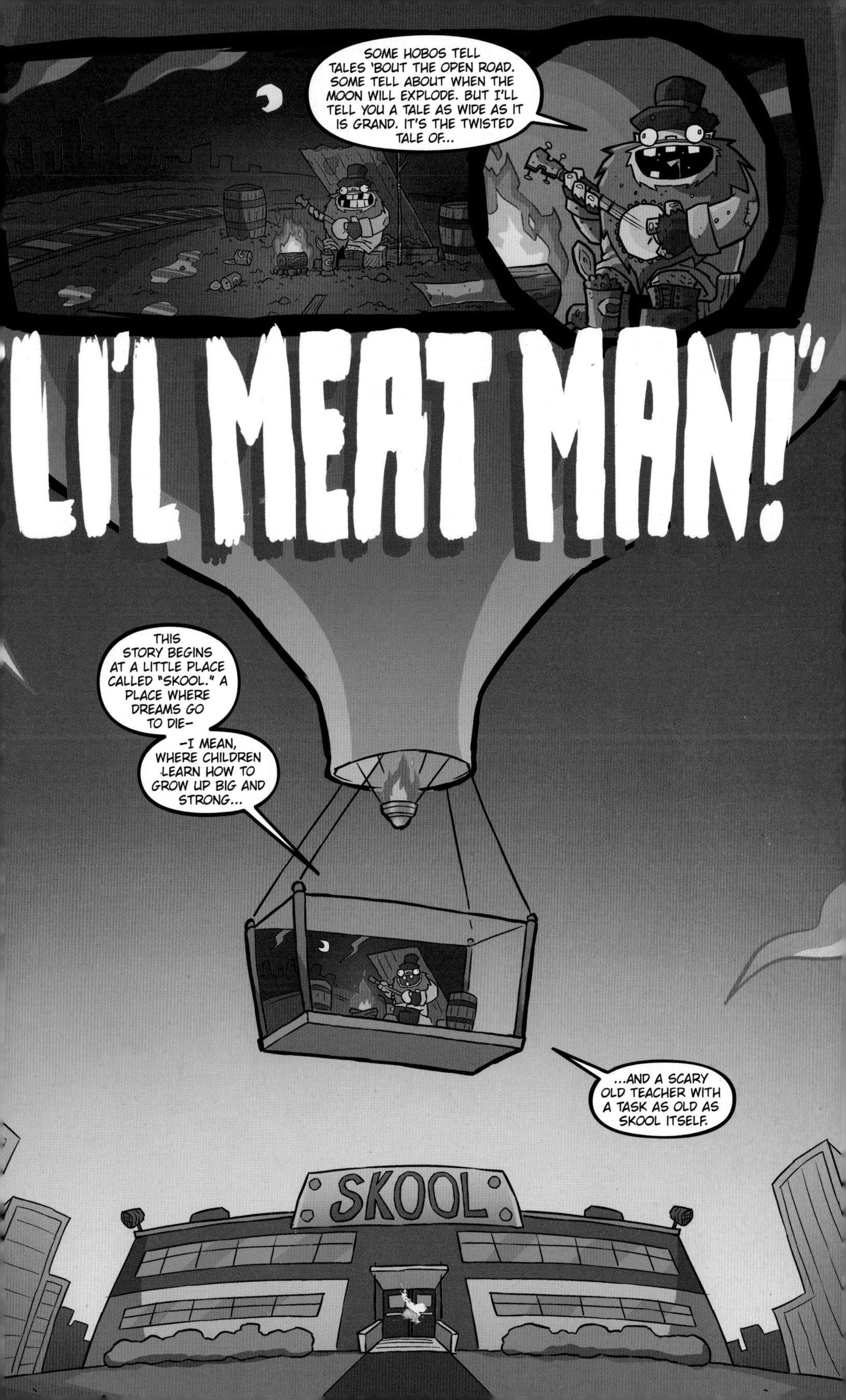
SOME HOBOS TELL TALES 'BOUT THE OPEN ROAD. SOME TELL ABOUT WHEN THE MOON WILL EXPLODE. BUT I'LL TELL YOU A TALE AS WIDE AS IT IS GRAND. IT'S THE TWISTED TALE OF...
LI'L MEAT MAN!"
THIS STORY BEGINS AT A LITTLE PLACE CALLED "SKOOL." A PLACE WHERE DREAMS GO TO DIE–
–I MEAN, WHERE CHILDREN LEARN HOW TO GROW UP BIG AND STRONG...
...AND A SCARY OLD TEACHER WITH A TASK AS OLD AS SKOOL ITSELF.
SKOOL

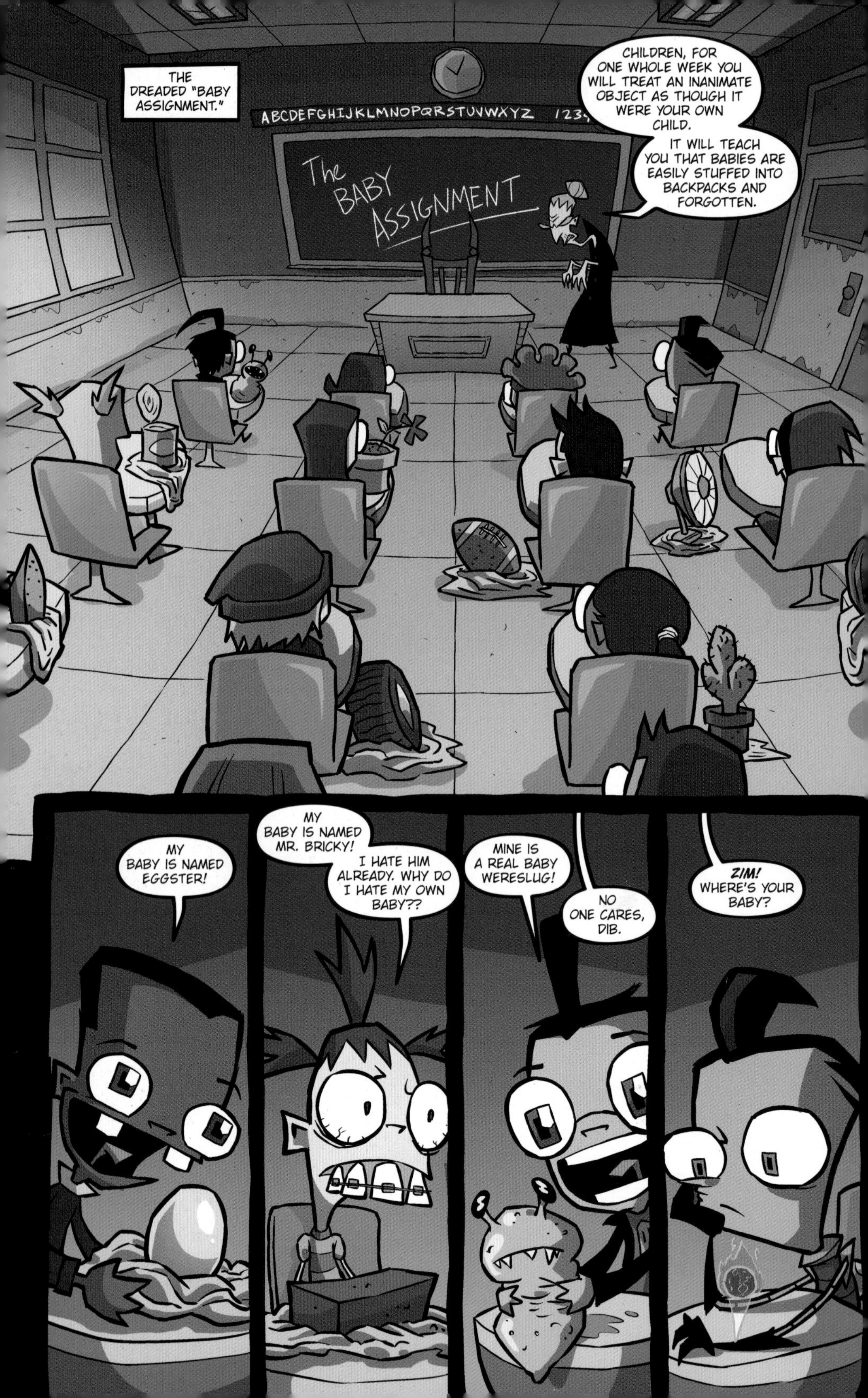
THE DREADED "BABY ASSIGNMENT."
CHILDREN, FOR ONE WHOLE WEEK YOU WILL TREAT AN INANIMATE OBJECT AS THOUGH IT WERE YOUR OWN CHILD.
IT WILL TEACH YOU THAT BABIES ARE EASILY STUFFED INTO BACKPACKS AND FORGOTTEN.
ABCDEFGHIJKLMNOPQRSTUVWXYZ 1234
The BABY ASSIGNMENT
MY BABY IS NAMED EGGSTER!
MY BABY IS NAMED MR. BRICKY!
I HATE HIM ALREADY. WHY DO I HATE MY OWN BABY??
MINE IS A REAL BABY WERESLUG!
NO ONE CARES, DIB.
ZIM! WHERE'S YOUR BABY?

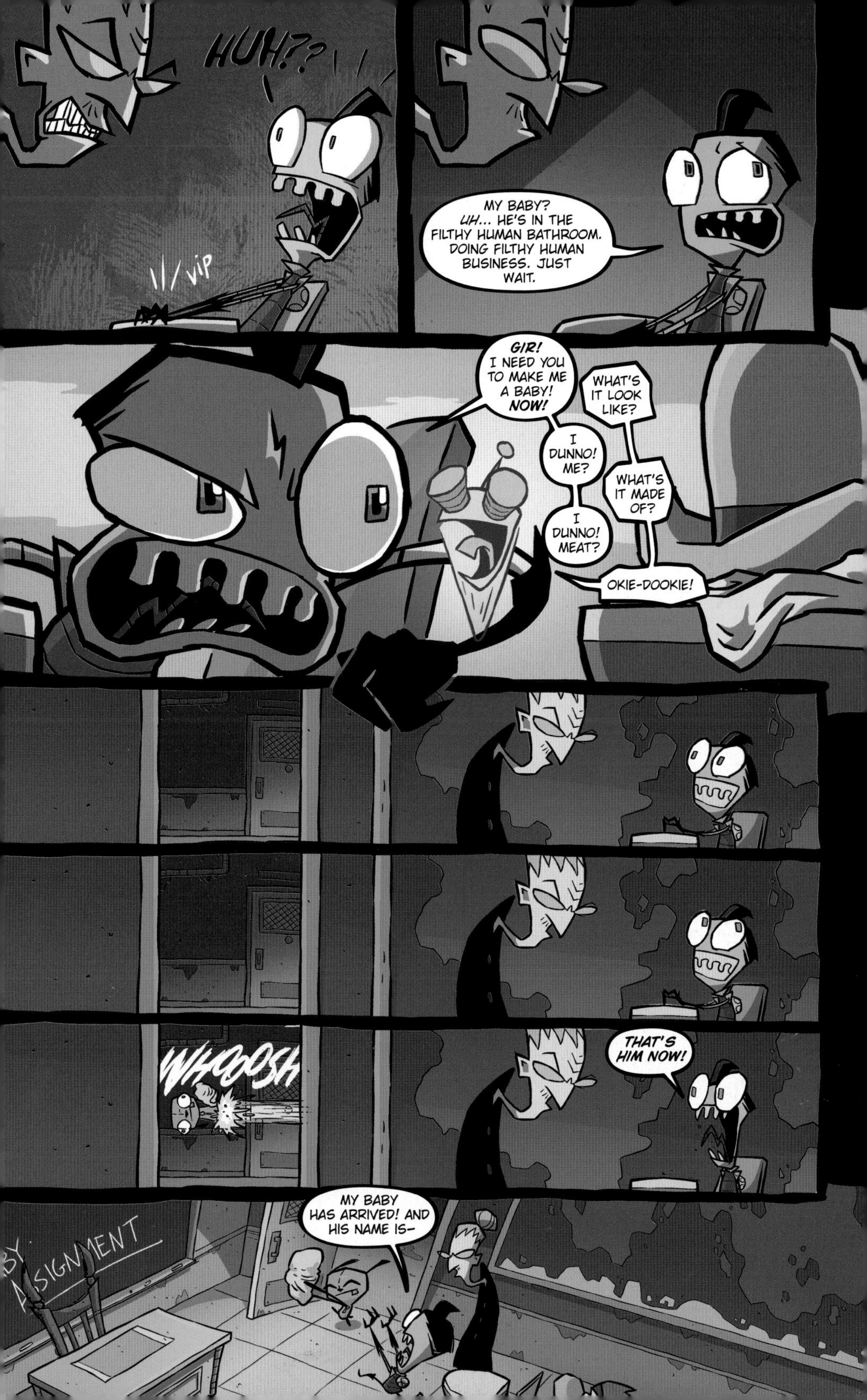
HUH??
VVVip
MY BABY? UH... HE'S IN THE FILTHY HUMAN BATHROOM. DOING FILTHY HUMAN BUSINESS. JUST WAIT.
GIR! I NEED YOU TO MAKE ME A BABY! NOW!
WHAT'S IT LOOK LIKE?
I DUNNO! ME?
WHAT'S IT MADE OF?
I DUNNO! MEAT?
OKIE-DOOKIE!
WHOOOSH
THAT'S HIM NOW!
MY BABY HAS ARRIVED! AND HIS NAME IS–
ASIGNMENT

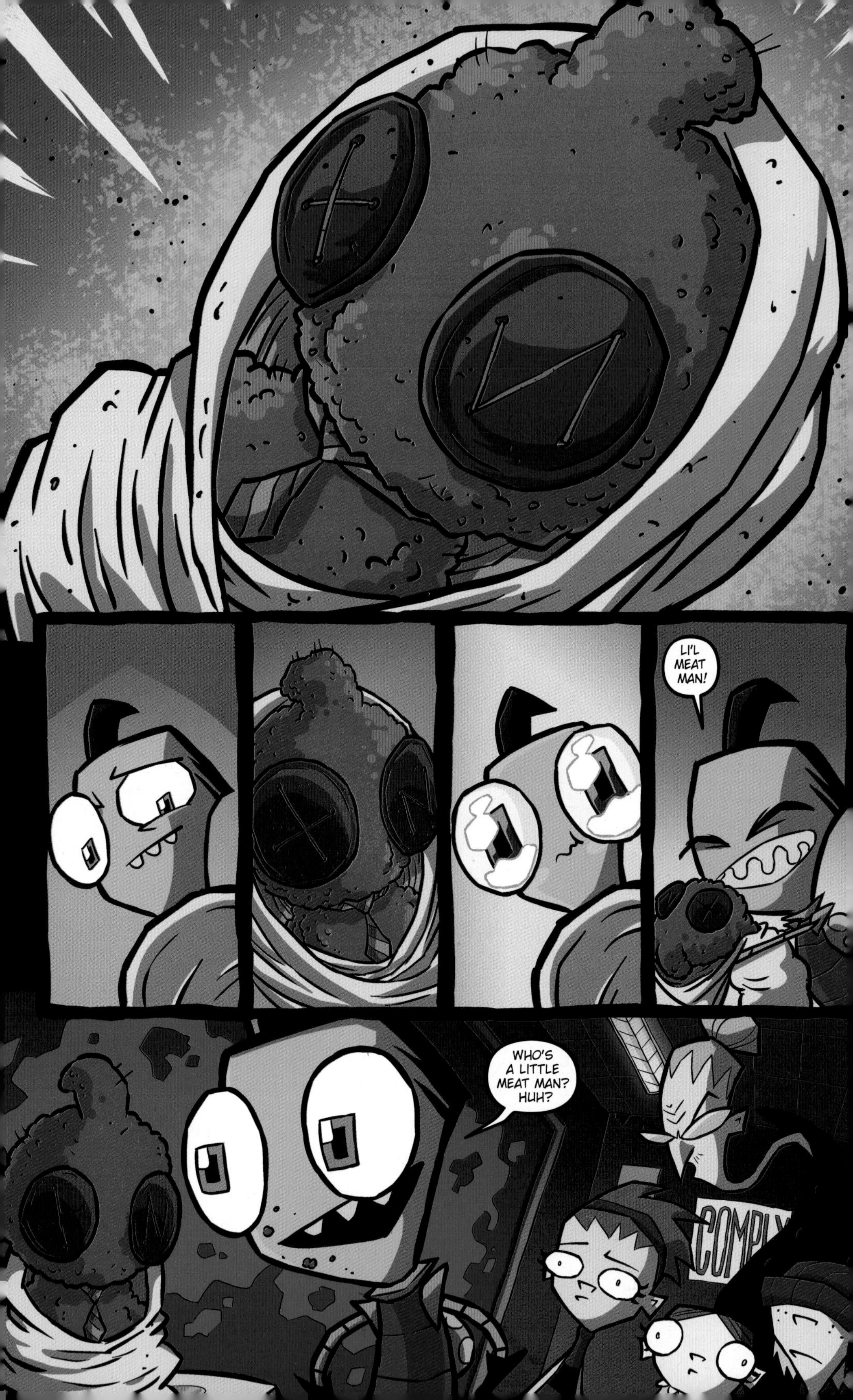
LI'L MEAT MAN!
WHO'S A LITTLE MEAT MAN? HUH?
COMPLY

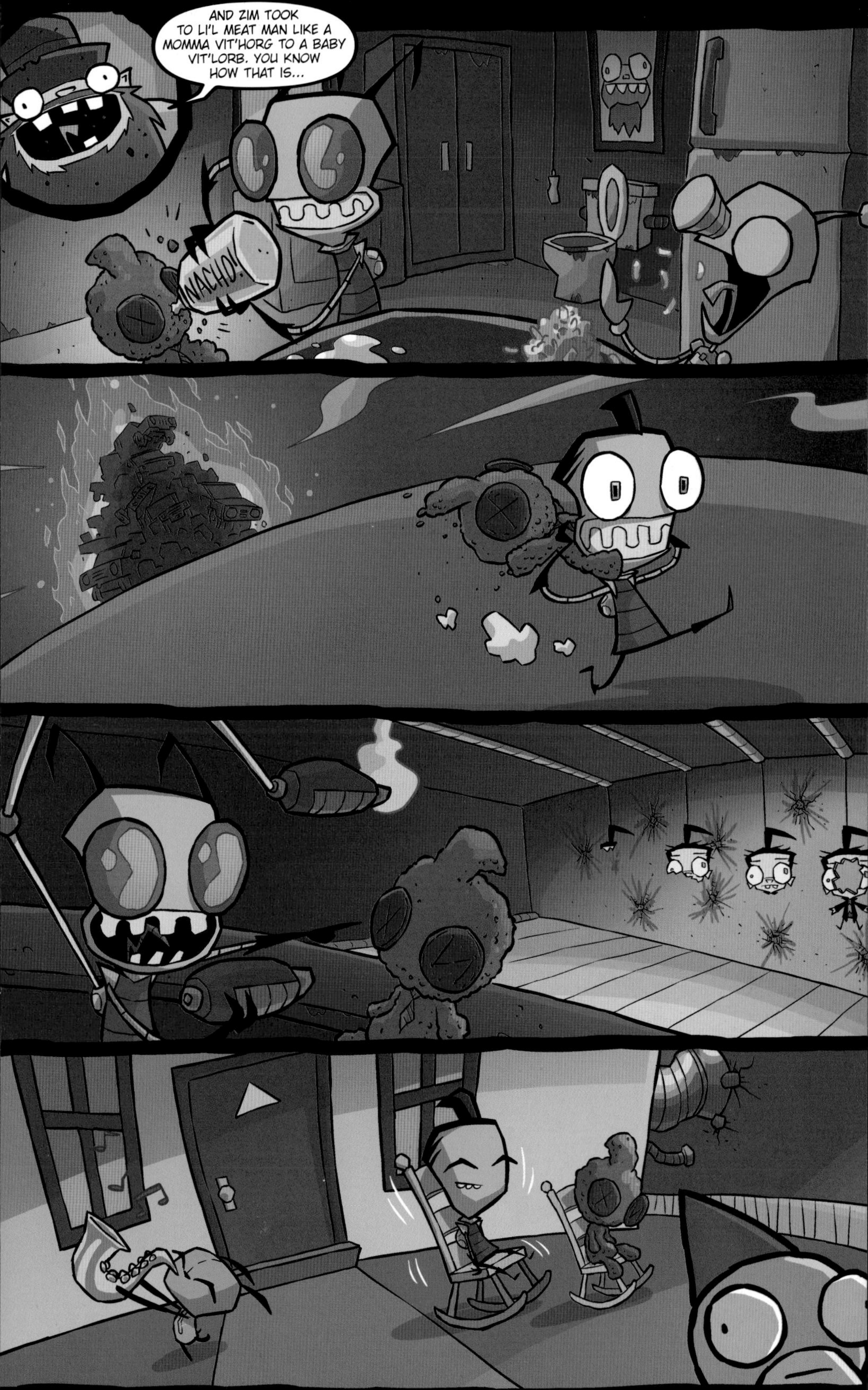
AND ZIM TOOK TO LI'L MEAT MAN LIKE A MOMMA VIT'HORG TO A BABY VIT'LORB. YOU KNOW HOW THAT IS...
NACHO!

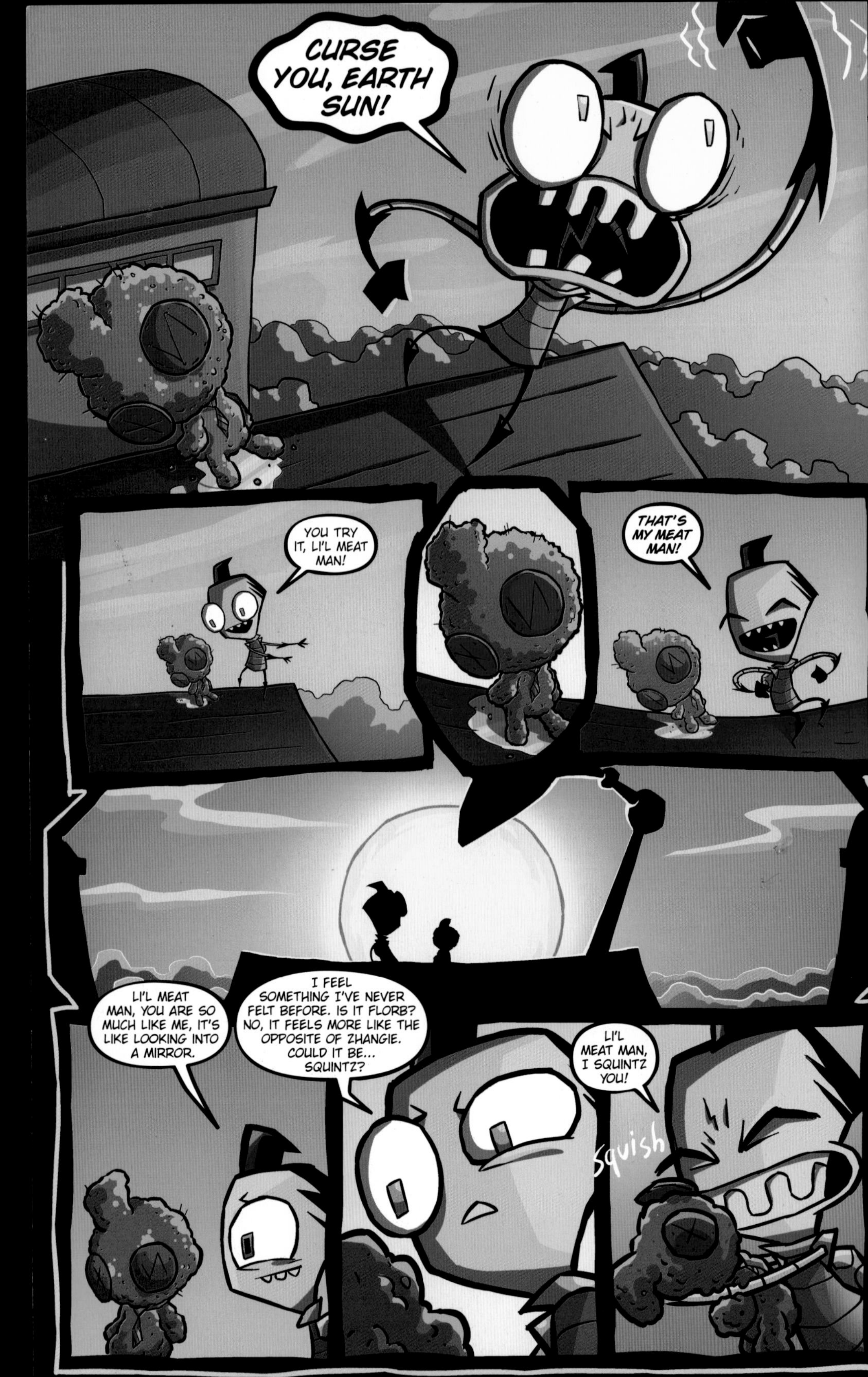
CURSE YOU, EARTH SUN!
YOU TRY IT, LI'L MEAT MAN!
THAT'S MY MEAT MAN!
LI'L MEAT MAN, YOU ARE SO MUCH LIKE ME, IT'S LIKE LOOKING INTO A MIRROR.
I FEEL SOMETHING I'VE NEVER FELT BEFORE. IS IT FLORB? NO, IT FEELS MORE LIKE THE OPPOSITE OF ZHANGIE. COULD IT BE... SQUINTZ?
LI'L MEAT MAN, I SQUINTZ YOU!
squish

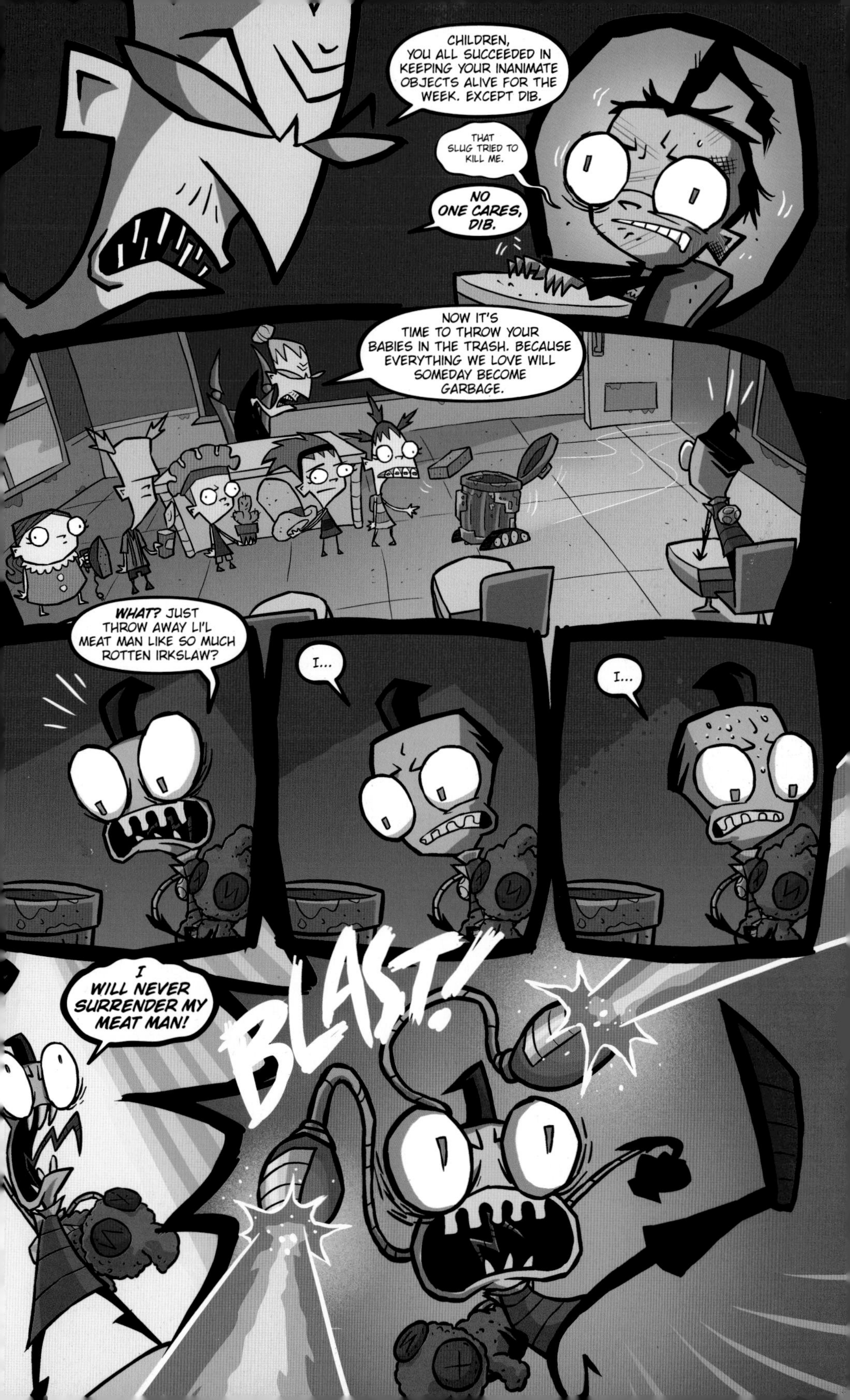
CHILDREN, YOU ALL SUCCEEDED IN KEEPING YOUR INANIMATE OBJECTS ALIVE FOR THE WEEK. EXCEPT DIB.
THAT SLUG TRIED TO KILL ME.
NO ONE CARES, DIB.
NOW IT'S TIME TO THROW YOUR BABIES IN THE TRASH. BECAUSE EVERYTHING WE LOVE WILL SOMEDAY BECOME GARBAGE.
WHAT? JUST THROW AWAY LI'L MEAT MAN LIKE SO MUCH ROTTEN IRKSLAW?
I...
I...
I WILL NEVER SURRENDER MY MEAT MAN!
BLAST!

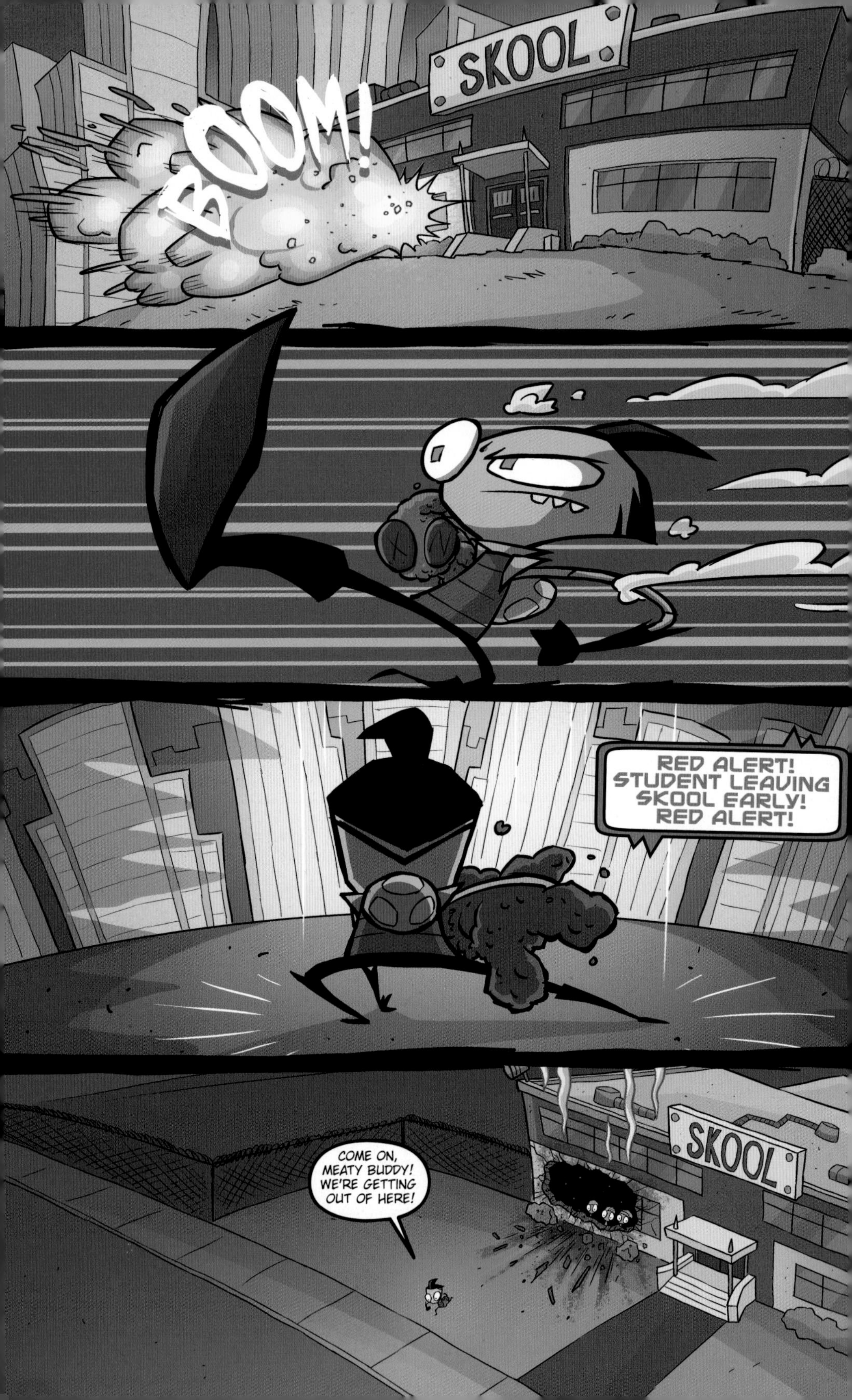
SKOOL
BOOM!
RED ALERT! STUDENT LEAVING SKOOL EARLY! RED ALERT!
SKOOL
COME ON, MEATY BUDDY! WE'RE GETTING OUT OF HERE!

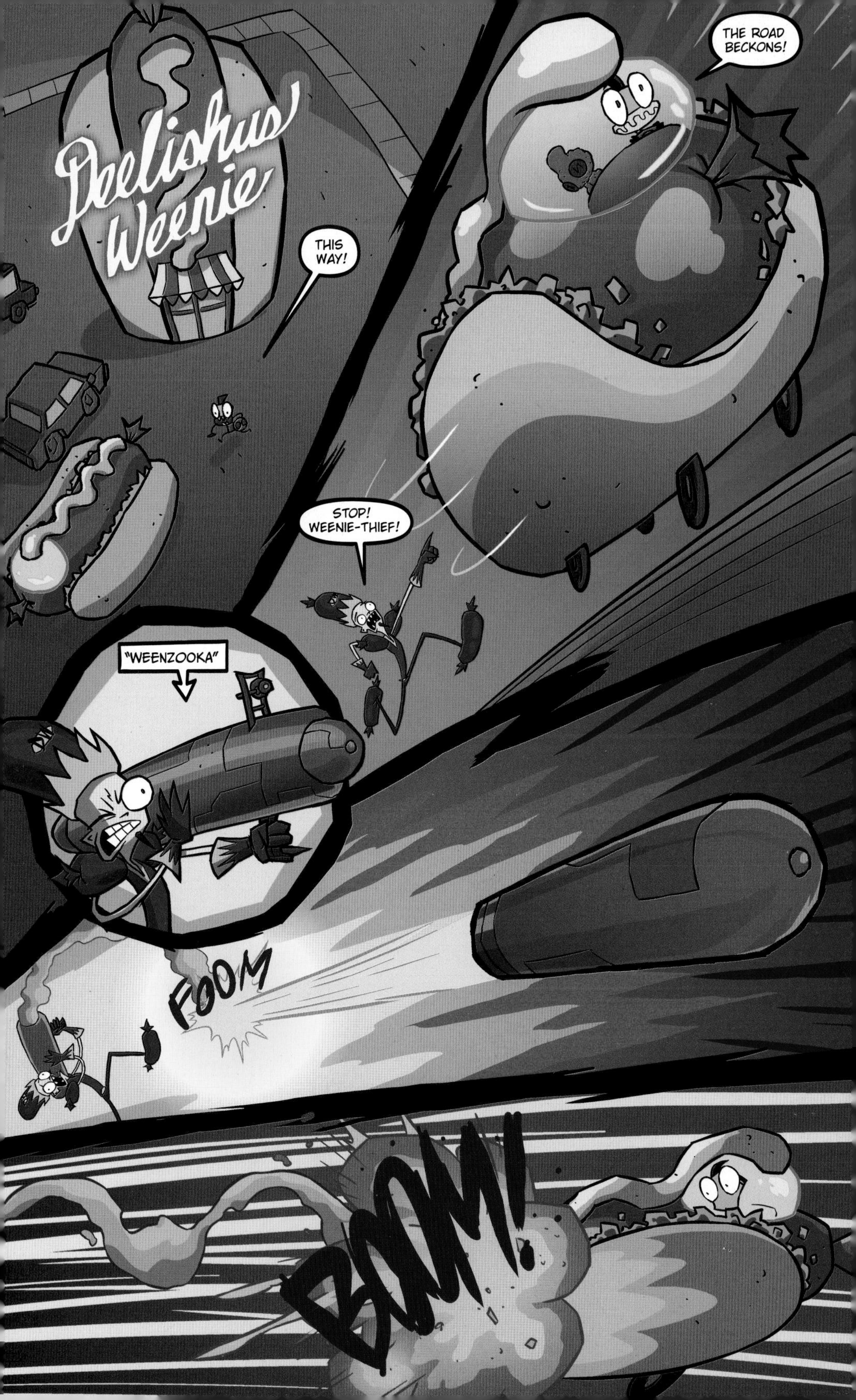
Deelishus Weenie
THIS WAY!
THE ROAD BECKONS!
STOP! WEENIE-THIEF!
"WEENZOOKA"
FOOM
BOOM!

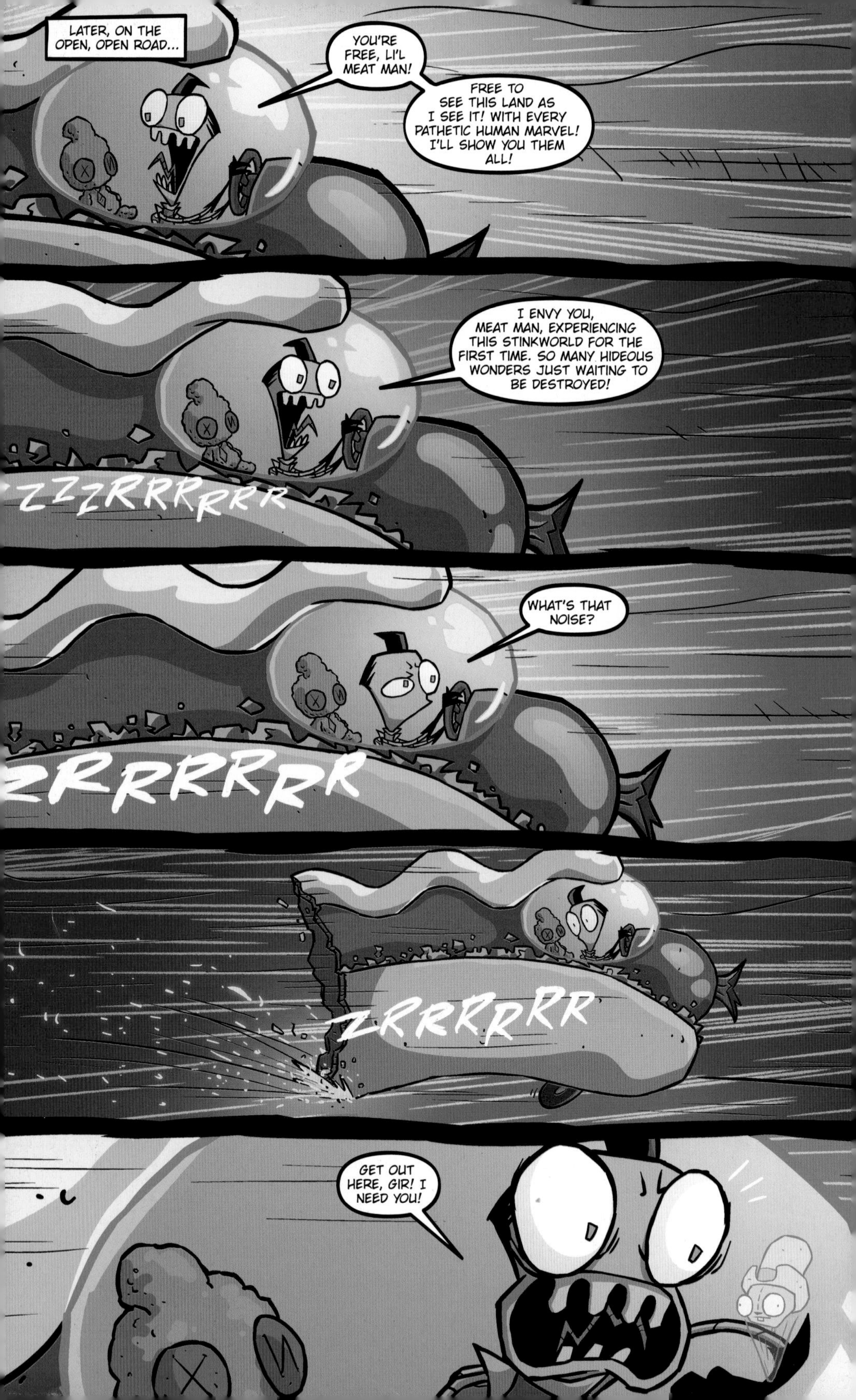
LATER, ON THE OPEN, OPEN ROAD...
YOU'RE FREE, LI'L MEAT MAN!
FREE TO SEE THIS LAND AS I SEE IT! WITH EVERY PATHETIC HUMAN MARVEL! I'LL SHOW YOU THEM ALL!
I ENVY YOU, MEAT MAN, EXPERIENCING THIS STINKWORLD FOR THE FIRST TIME. SO MANY HIDEOUS WONDERS JUST WAITING TO BE DESTROYED!
ZZZRRRRRR
WHAT'S THAT NOISE?
ZRRRRRR
ZRRRRRR
GET OUT HERE, GIR! I NEED YOU!

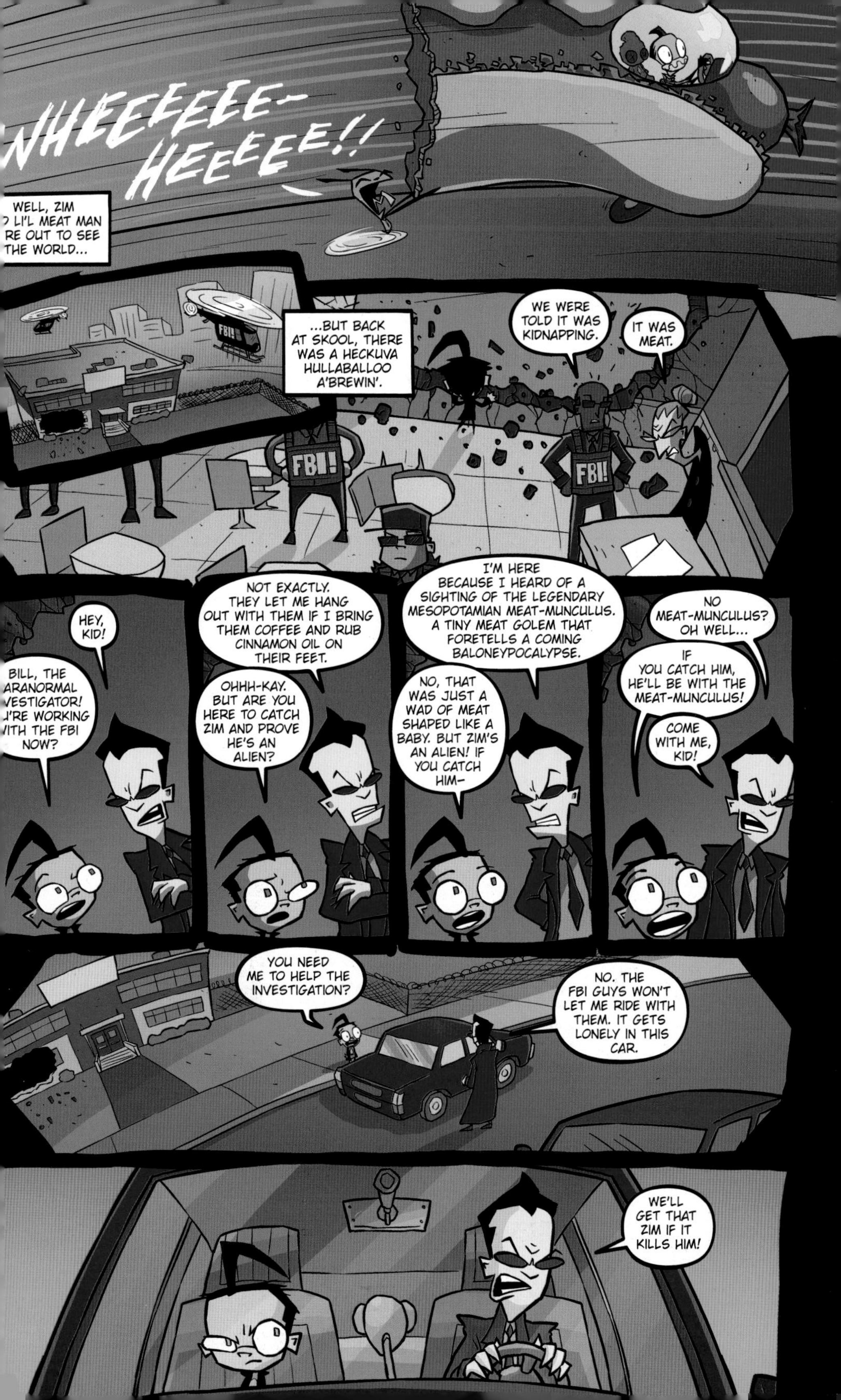
NHEEEEEEE-HEEEEEE!!
WELL, ZIM D LI'L MEAT MAN RE OUT TO SEE THE WORLD...
...BUT BACK AT SKOOL, THERE WAS A HECKUVA HULLABALLOO A'BREWIN'.
FBI!
WE WERE TOLD IT WAS KIDNAPPING.
IT WAS MEAT.
FBI!
FBI!
HEY, KID!
BILL, THE ARANORMAL VESTIGATOR! U'RE WORKING ITH THE FBI NOW?
NOT EXACTLY. THEY LET ME HANG OUT WITH THEM IF I BRING THEM COFFEE AND RUB CINNAMON OIL ON THEIR FEET.
OHHH-KAY. BUT ARE YOU HERE TO CATCH ZIM AND PROVE HE'S AN ALIEN?
I'M HERE BECAUSE I HEARD OF A SIGHTING OF THE LEGENDARY MESOPOTAMIAN MEAT-MUNCULUS. A TINY MEAT GOLEM THAT FORETELLS A COMING BALONEYPOCALYPSE.
NO, THAT WAS JUST A WAD OF MEAT SHAPED LIKE A BABY. BUT ZIM'S AN ALIEN! IF YOU CATCH HIM-
NO MEAT-MUNCULUS? OH WELL...
IF YOU CATCH HIM, HE'LL BE WITH THE MEAT-MUNCULUS!
COME WITH ME, KID!
YOU NEED ME TO HELP THE INVESTIGATION?
NO. THE FBI GUYS WON'T LET ME RIDE WITH THEM. IT GETS LONELY IN THIS CAR.
WE'LL GET THAT ZIM IF IT KILLS HIM!

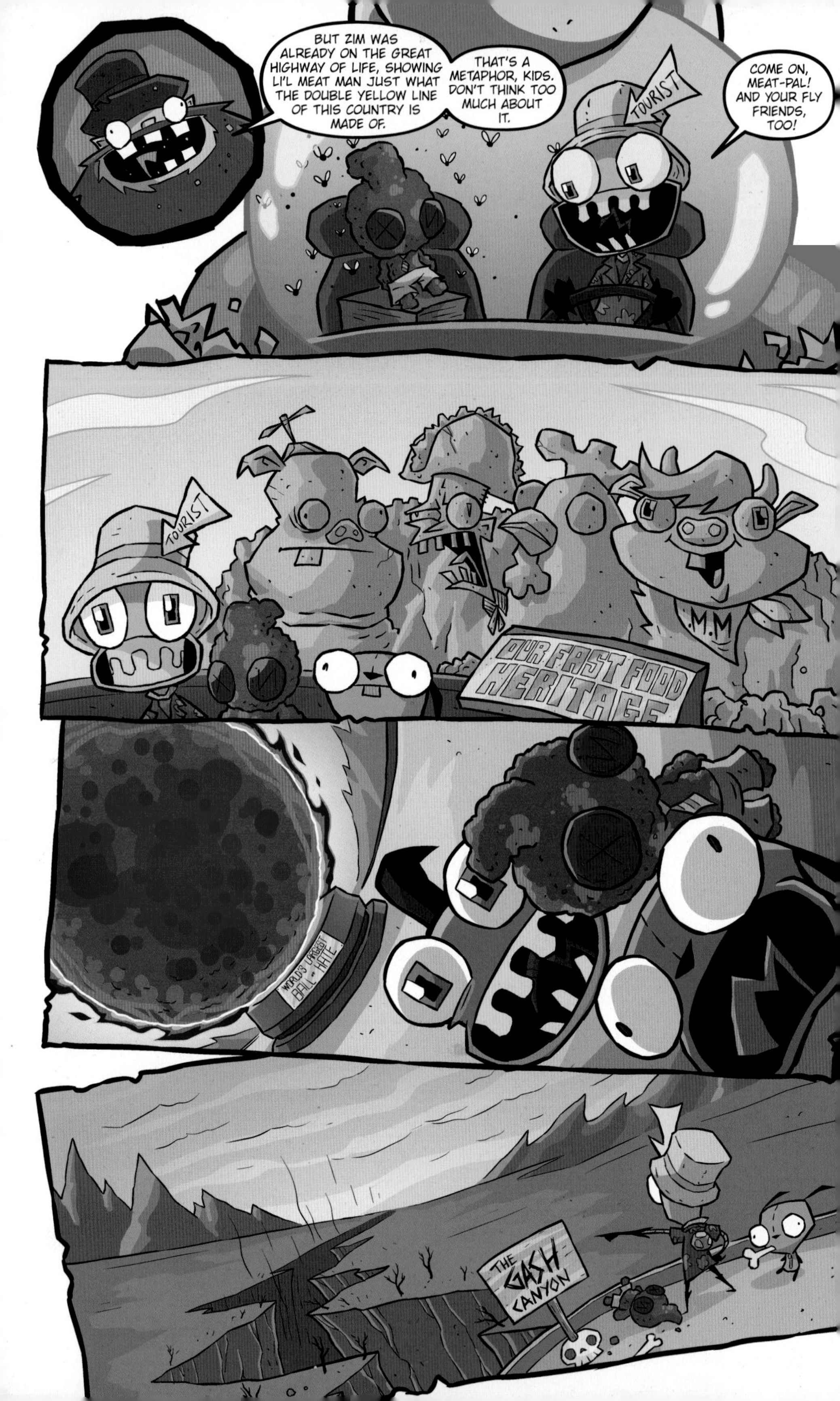

BUT ZIM WAS ALREADY ON THE GREAT HIGHWAY OF LIFE, SHOWING LI'L MEAT MAN JUST WHAT THE DOUBLE YELLOW LINE OF THIS COUNTRY IS MADE OF.
THAT'S A METAPHOR, KIDS. DON'T THINK TOO MUCH ABOUT IT.
COME ON, MEAT-PAL! AND YOUR FLY FRIENDS, TOO!
TOURIST
TOURIST
M.M
OUR FAST FOOD HERITAGE
WORLD'S LARGEST BALL O' HATE
THE GASH CANYON

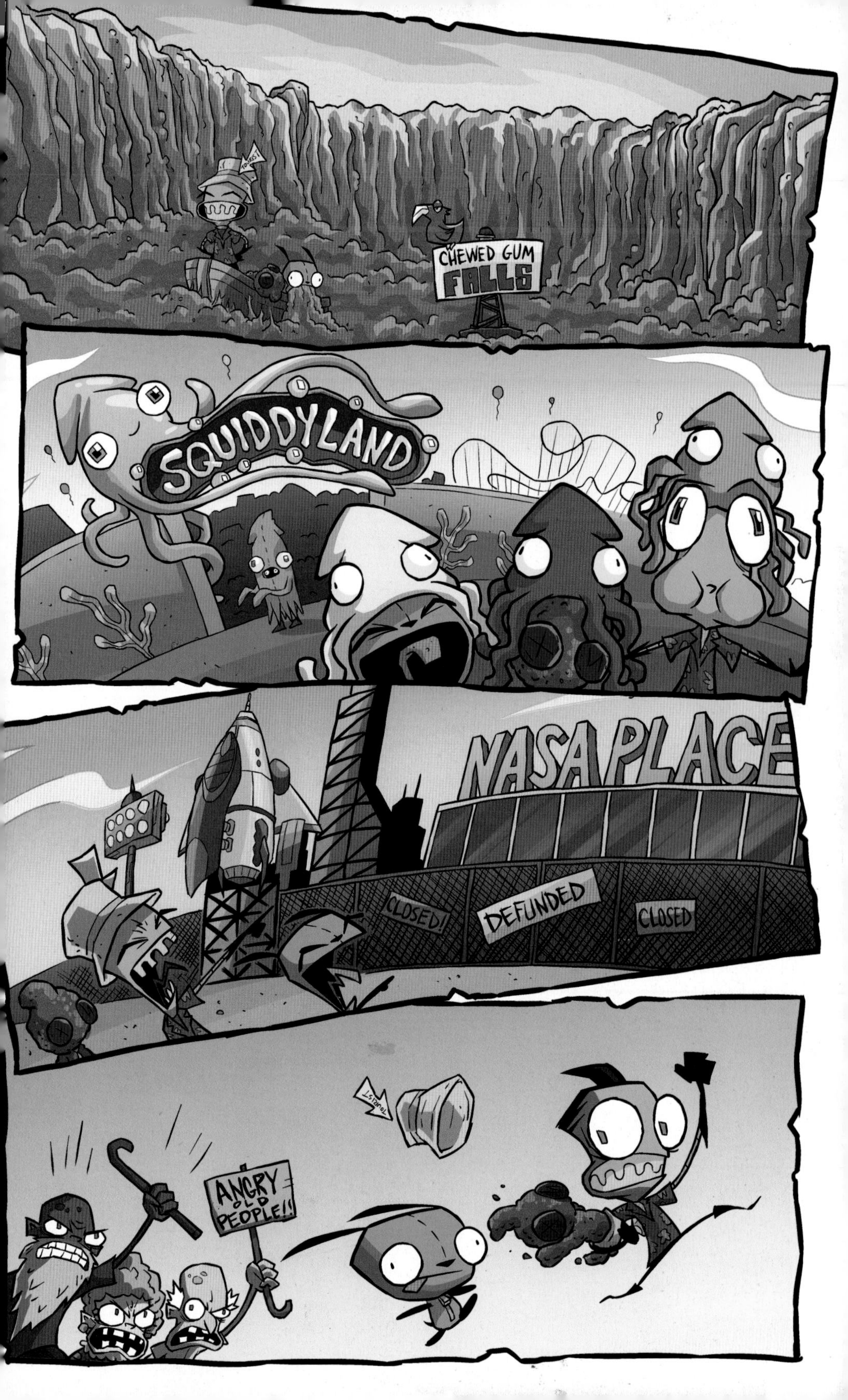
CHEWED GUM
FALLS
SQUIDDYLAND
NASA PLACE
CLOSED!
DEFUNDED
CLOSED
ANGRY OLD PEOPLE!!

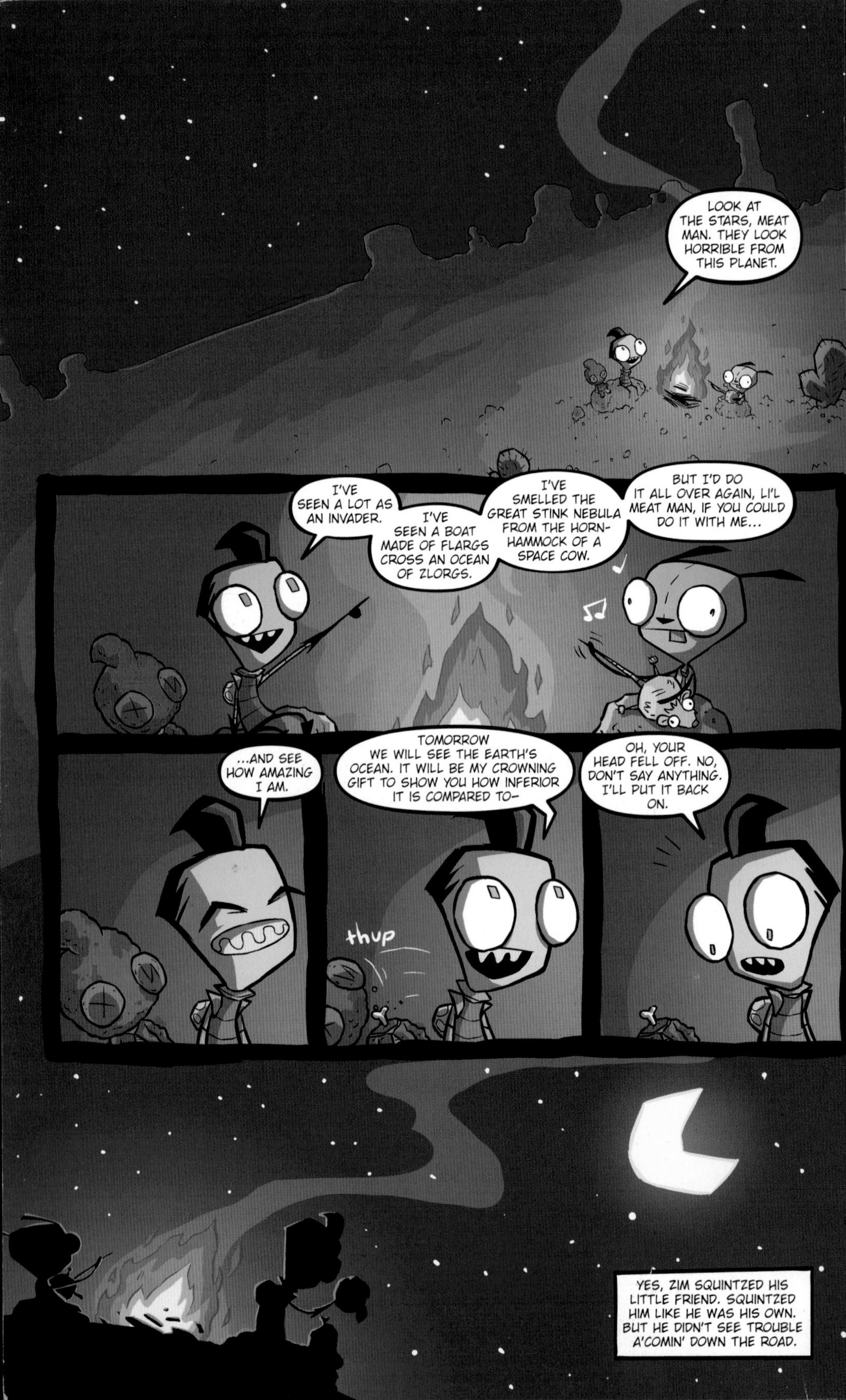
LOOK AT THE STARS, MEAT MAN. THEY LOOK HORRIBLE FROM THIS PLANET.
I'VE SEEN A LOT AS AN INVADER.
I'VE SEEN A BOAT MADE OF FLARGS CROSS AN OCEAN OF ZLORGS.
I'VE SMELLED THE GREAT STINK NEBULA FROM THE HORN-HAMMOCK OF A SPACE COW.
BUT I'D DO IT ALL OVER AGAIN, LI'L MEAT MAN, IF YOU COULD DO IT WITH ME...
...AND SEE HOW AMAZING I AM.
TOMORROW WE WILL SEE THE EARTH'S OCEAN. IT WILL BE MY CROWNING GIFT TO SHOW YOU HOW INFERIOR IT IS COMPARED TO—
thup
OH, YOUR HEAD FELL OFF. NO, DON'T SAY ANYTHING. I'LL PUT IT BACK ON.
YES, ZIM SQUINTZED HIS LITTLE FRIEND. SQUINTZED HIM LIKE HE WAS HIS OWN. BUT HE DIDN'T SEE TROUBLE A'COMIN' DOWN THE ROAD.

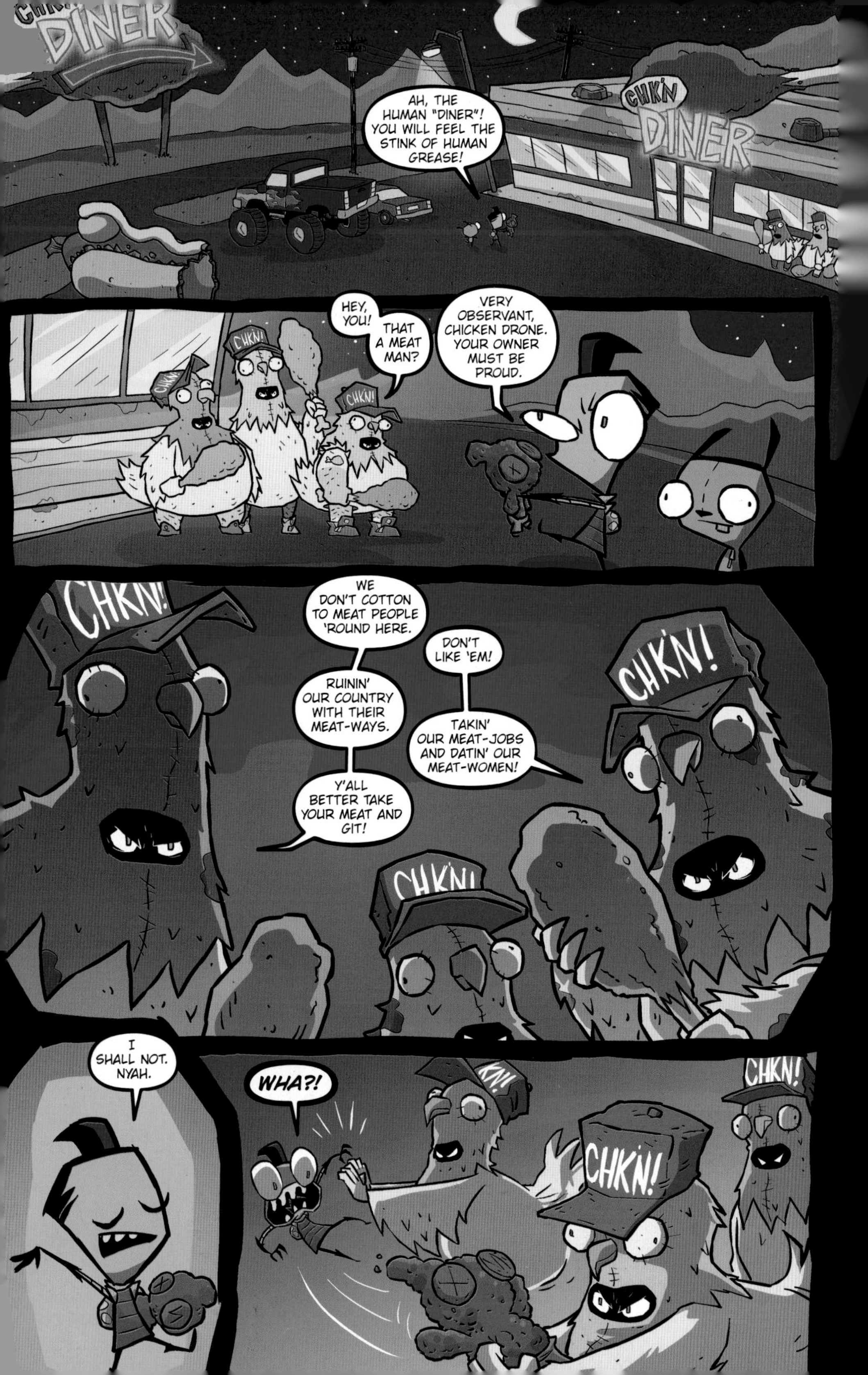

DINER
AH, THE HUMAN "DINER"! YOU WILL FEEL THE STINK OF HUMAN GREASE!
CHK'N DINER
HEY, YOU!
THAT A MEAT MAN?
VERY OBSERVANT, CHICKEN DRONE. YOUR OWNER MUST BE PROUD.
WE DON'T COTTON TO MEAT PEOPLE 'ROUND HERE.
RUININ' OUR COUNTRY WITH THEIR MEAT-WAYS.
DON'T LIKE 'EM!
TAKIN' OUR MEAT-JOBS AND DATIN' OUR MEAT-WOMEN!
Y'ALL BETTER TAKE YOUR MEAT AND GIT!
I SHALL NOT. NYAH.
WHA?!

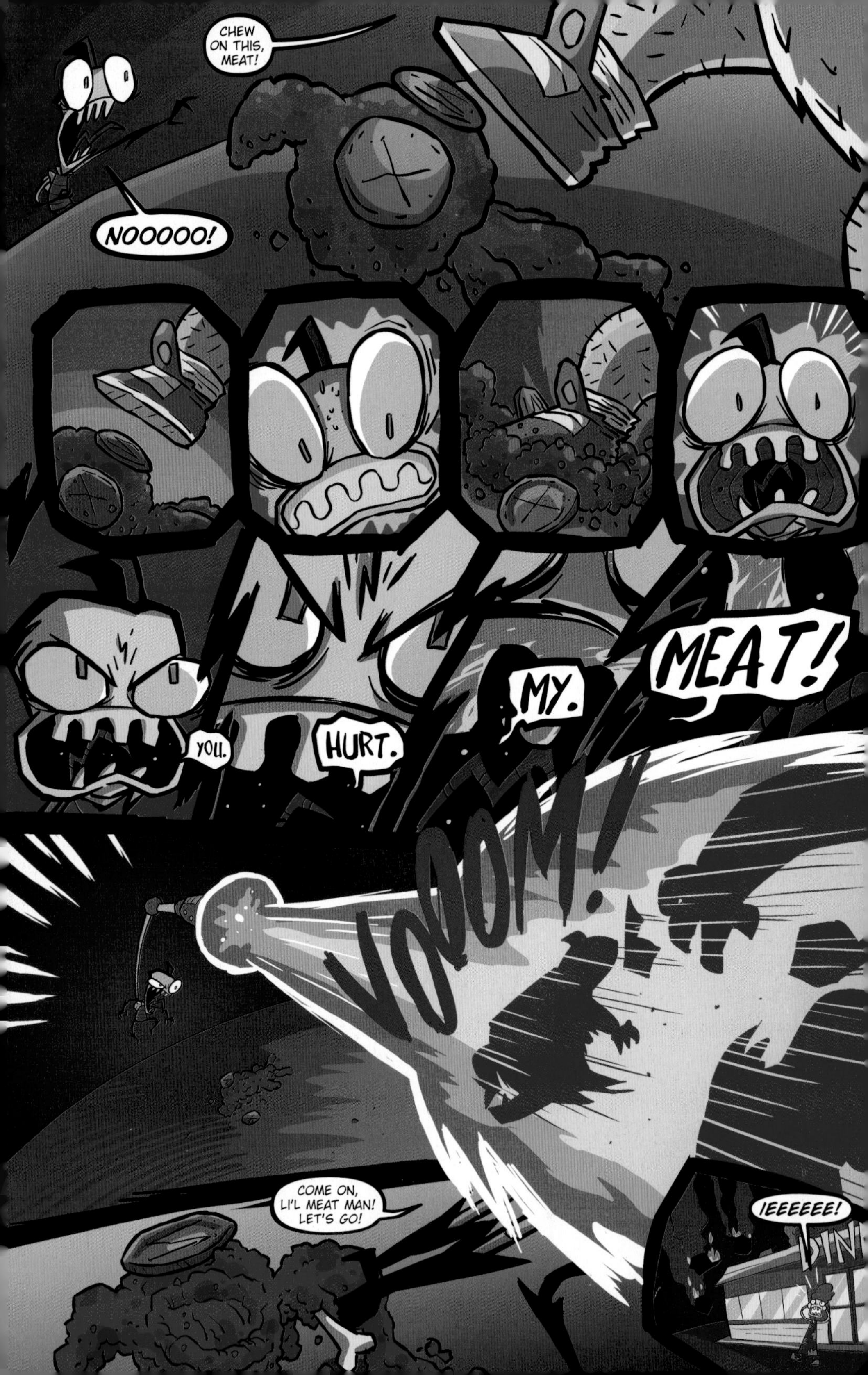
CHEW ON THIS, MEAT!
NOOOOO!
YOU.
HURT.
MY.
MEAT!
VOOOOM!
COME ON, LI'L MEAT MAN! LET'S GO!
IEEEEEE!

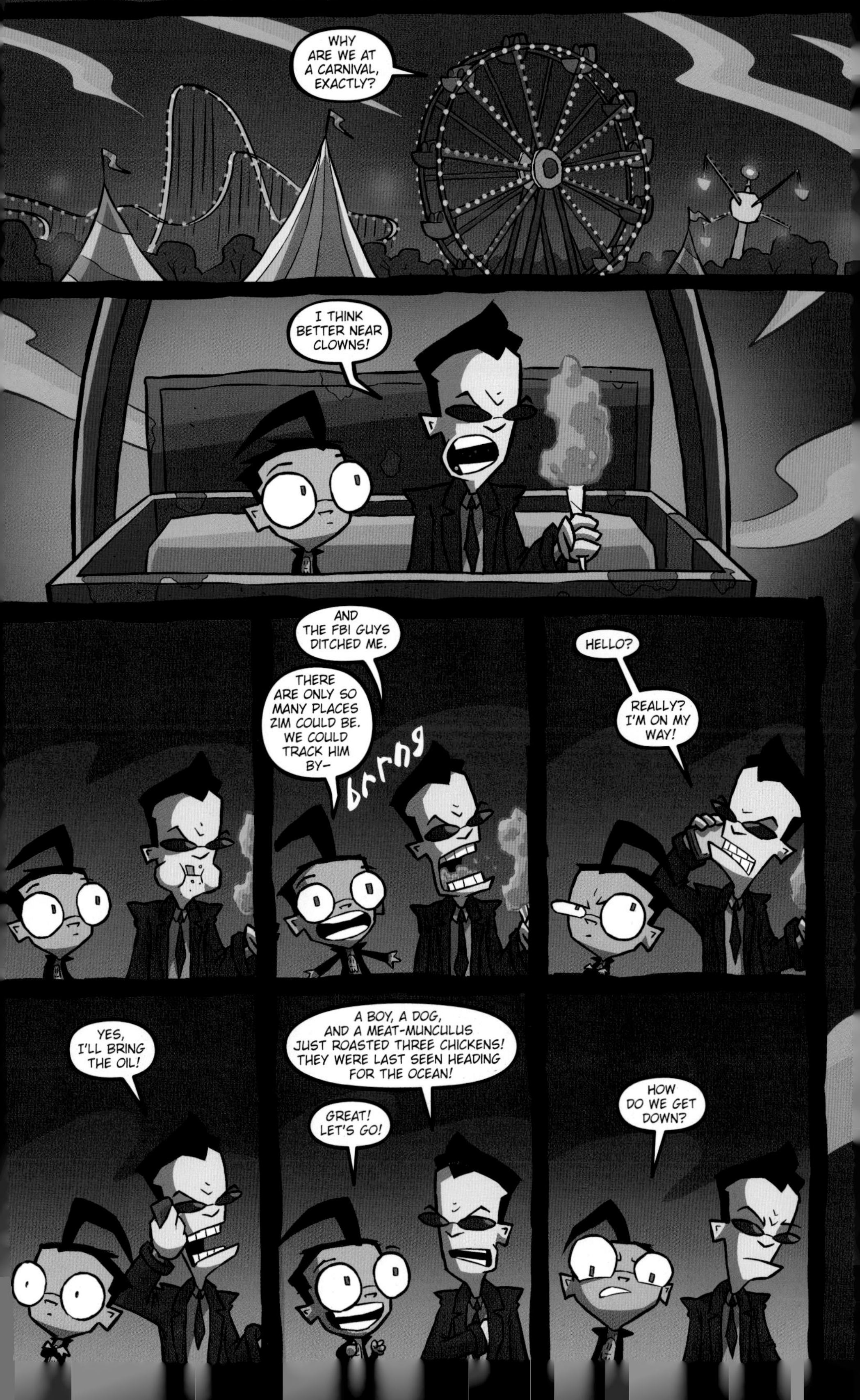
WHY ARE WE AT A CARNIVAL, EXACTLY?
I THINK BETTER NEAR CLOWNS!
AND THE FBI GUYS DITCHED ME.
THERE ARE ONLY SO MANY PLACES ZIM COULD BE. WE COULD TRACK HIM BY–
brrng
HELLO?
REALLY? I'M ON MY WAY!
YES, I'LL BRING THE OIL!
A BOY, A DOG, AND A MEAT-MUNCULUS JUST ROASTED THREE CHICKENS! THEY WERE LAST SEEN HEADING FOR THE OCEAN!
GREAT! LET'S GO!
HOW DO WE GET DOWN?

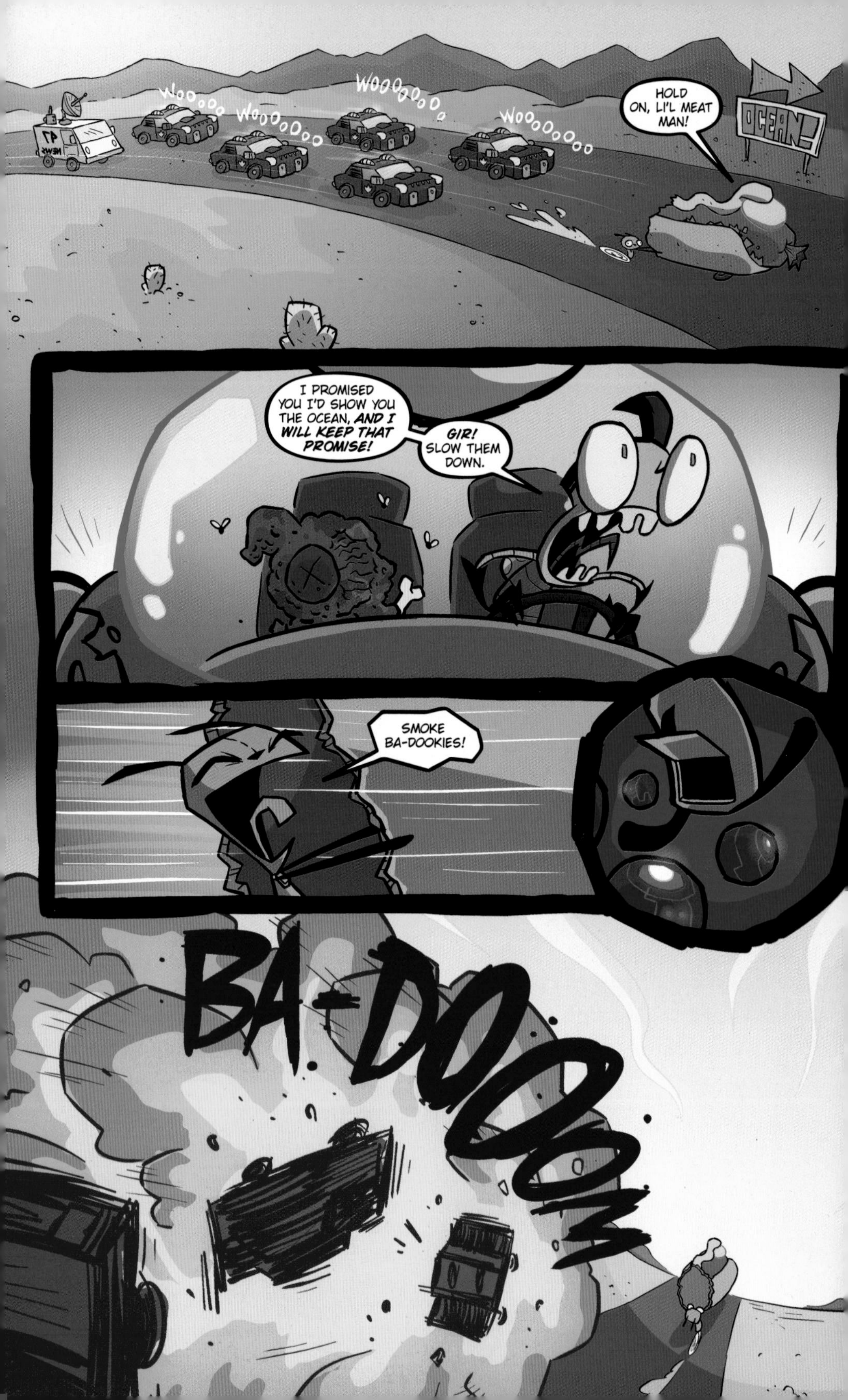
WOOOOOO
WOOOOOOOO
WOOOOOOOOO
WOOOOOOOO
HOLD ON, LI'L MEAT MAN!
OCEAN!
47 NEWS
I PROMISED YOU I'D SHOW YOU THE OCEAN, AND I WILL KEEP THAT PROMISE!
GIR! SLOW THEM DOWN.
SMOKE BA-DOOKIES!
BA-DOOOOM

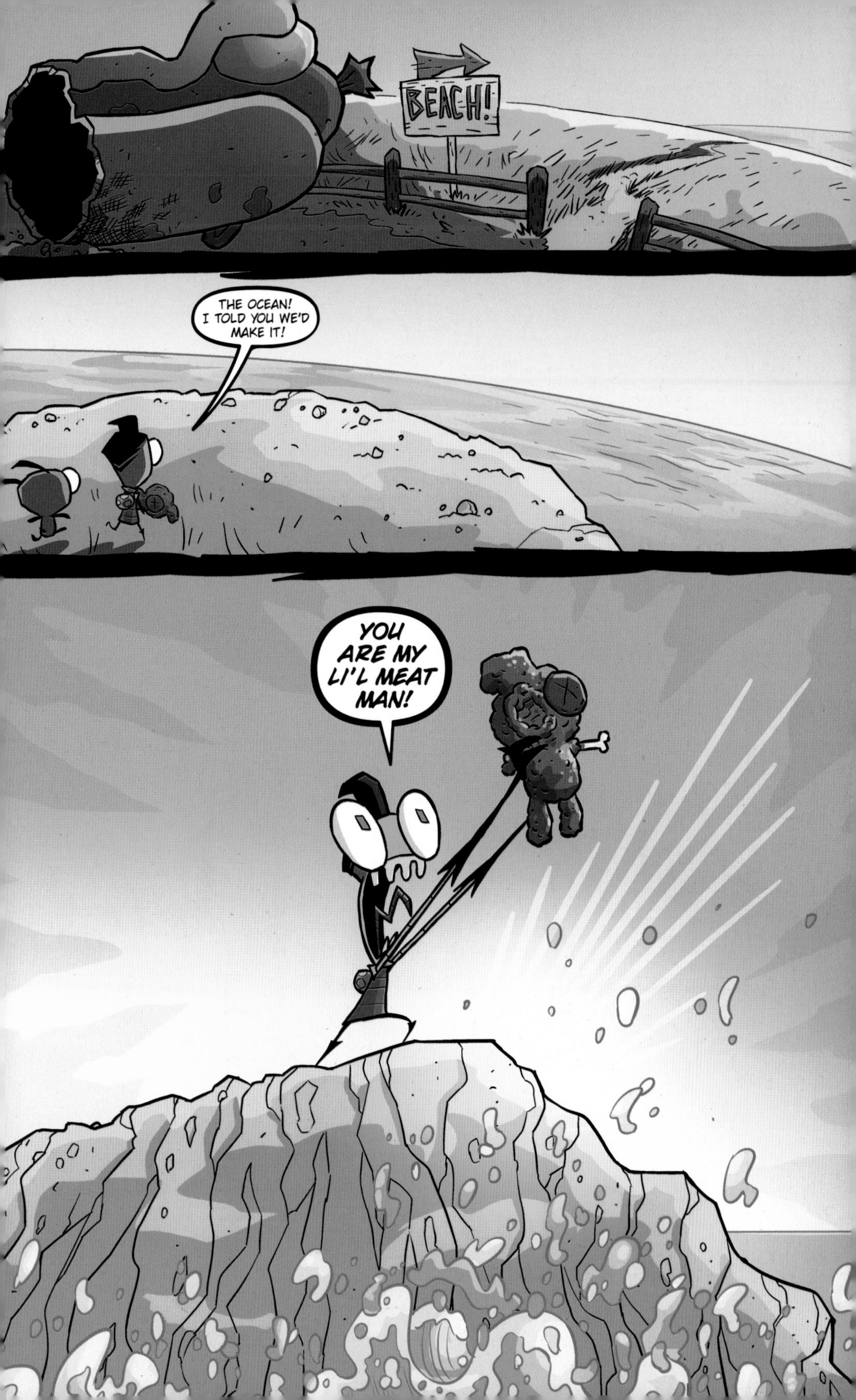
BEACH!
THE OCEAN! I TOLD YOU WE'D MAKE IT!
YOU ARE MY LI'L MEAT MAN!

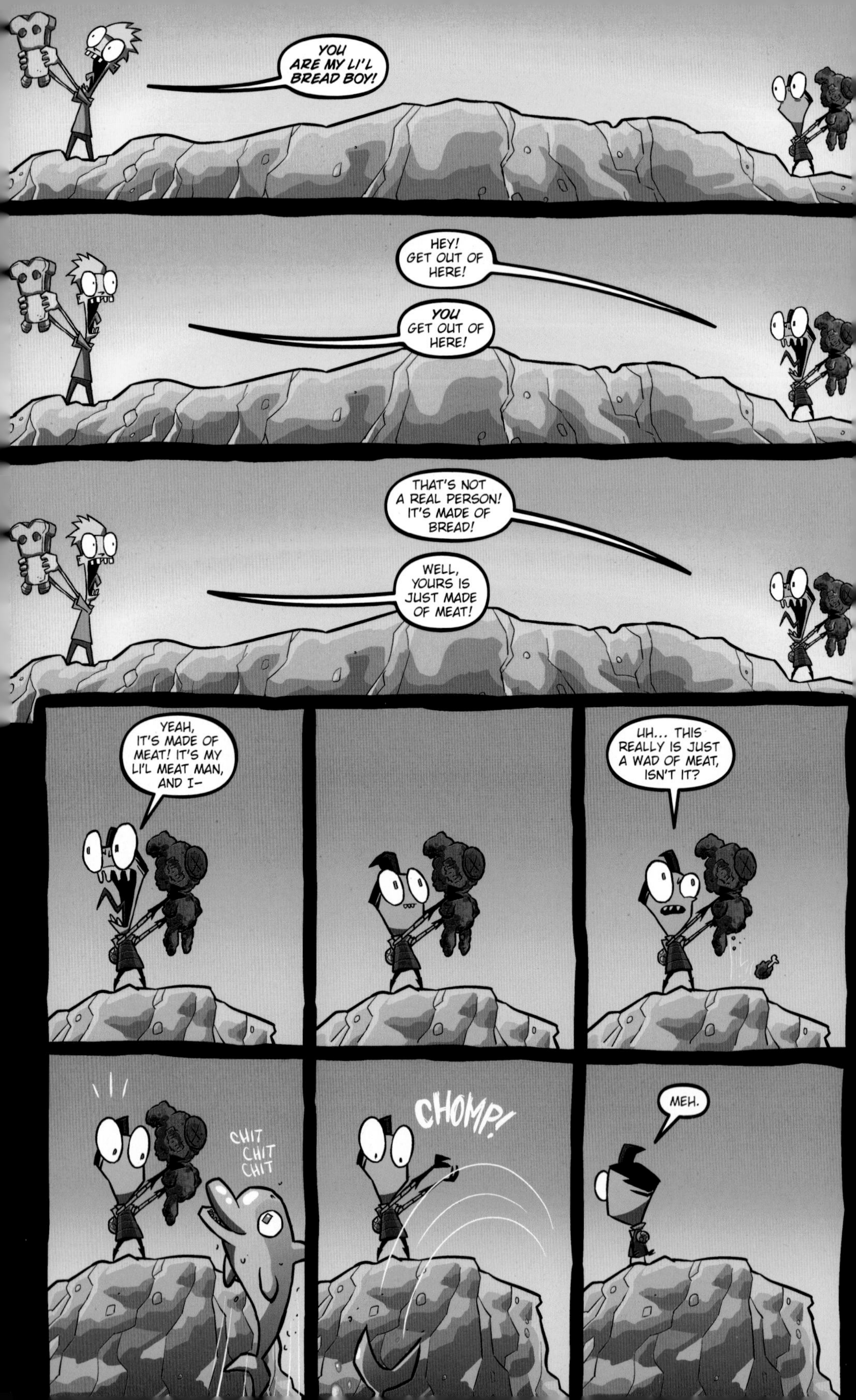
YOU ARE MY LI'L BREAD BOY!
HEY! GET OUT OF HERE!
YOU GET OUT OF HERE!
THAT'S NOT A REAL PERSON! IT'S MADE OF BREAD!
WELL, YOURS IS JUST MADE OF MEAT!
YEAH, IT'S MADE OF MEAT! IT'S MY LI'L MEAT MAN, AND I–
UH... THIS REALLY IS JUST A WAD OF MEAT, ISN'T IT?
CHIT CHIT CHIT
CHOMP!
MEH.

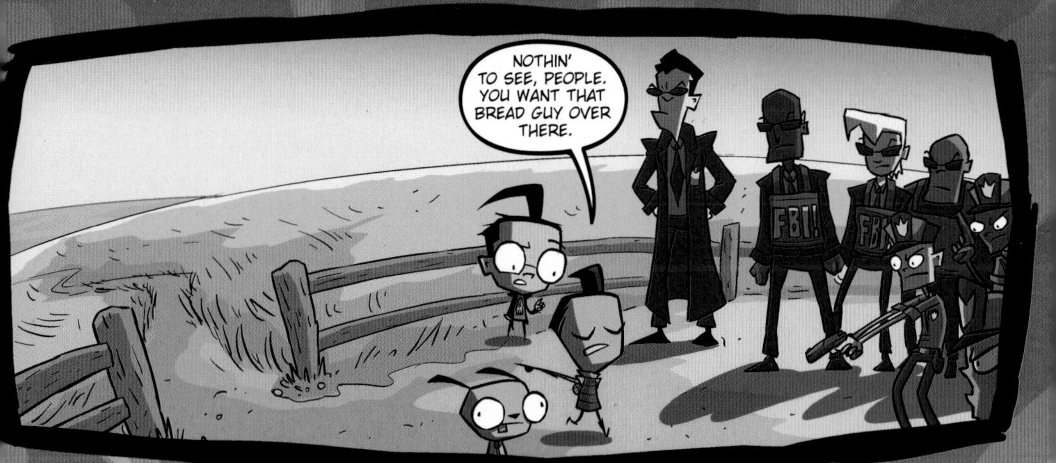
NOTHIN' TO SEE, PEOPLE. YOU WANT THAT BREAD GUY OVER THERE.
FBI
FBI

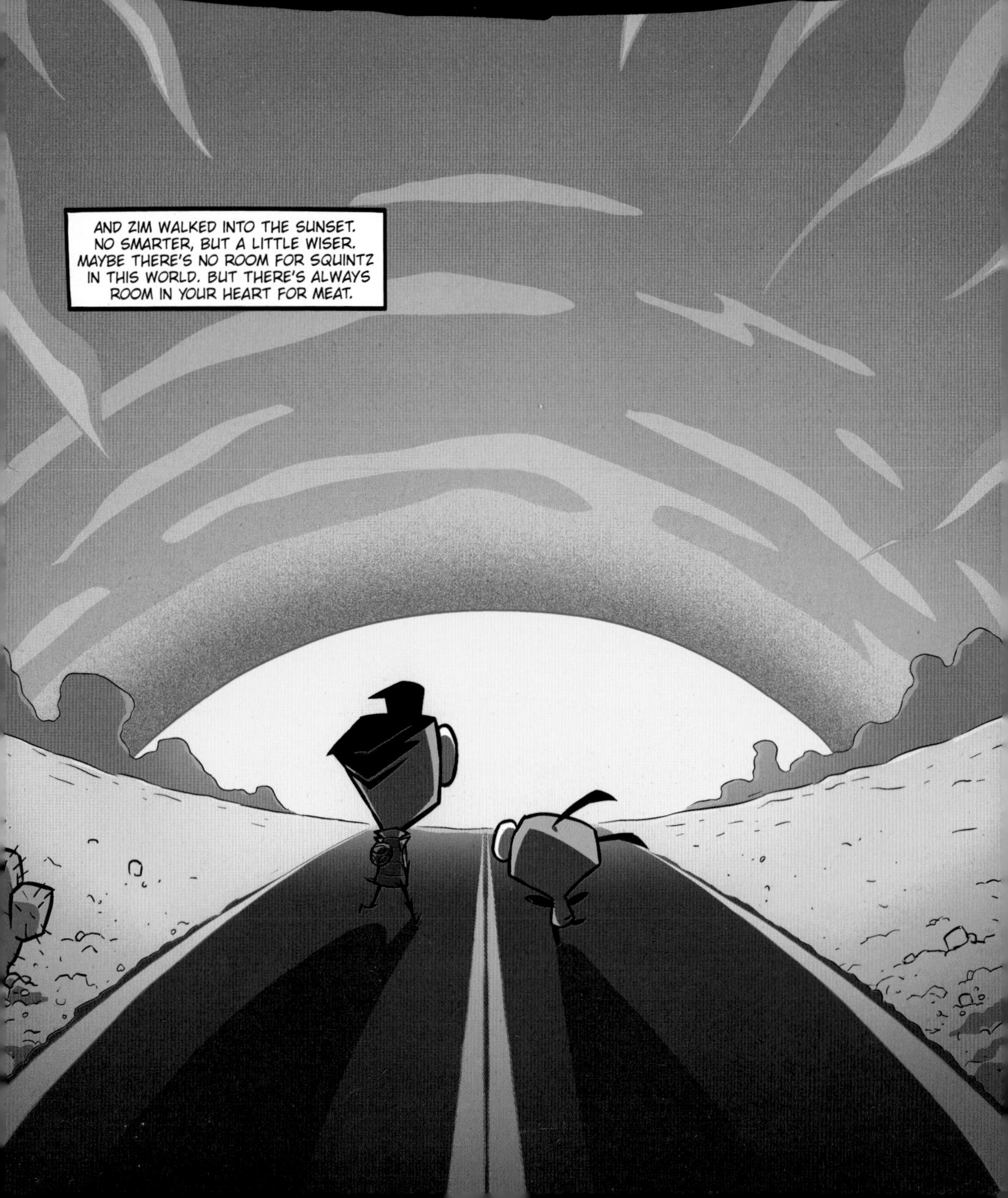
AND ZIM WALKED INTO THE SUNSET. NO SMARTER, BUT A LITTLE WISER. MAYBE THERE'S NO ROOM FOR SQUINTZ IN THIS WORLD. BUT THERE'S ALWAYS ROOM IN YOUR HEART FOR MEAT.

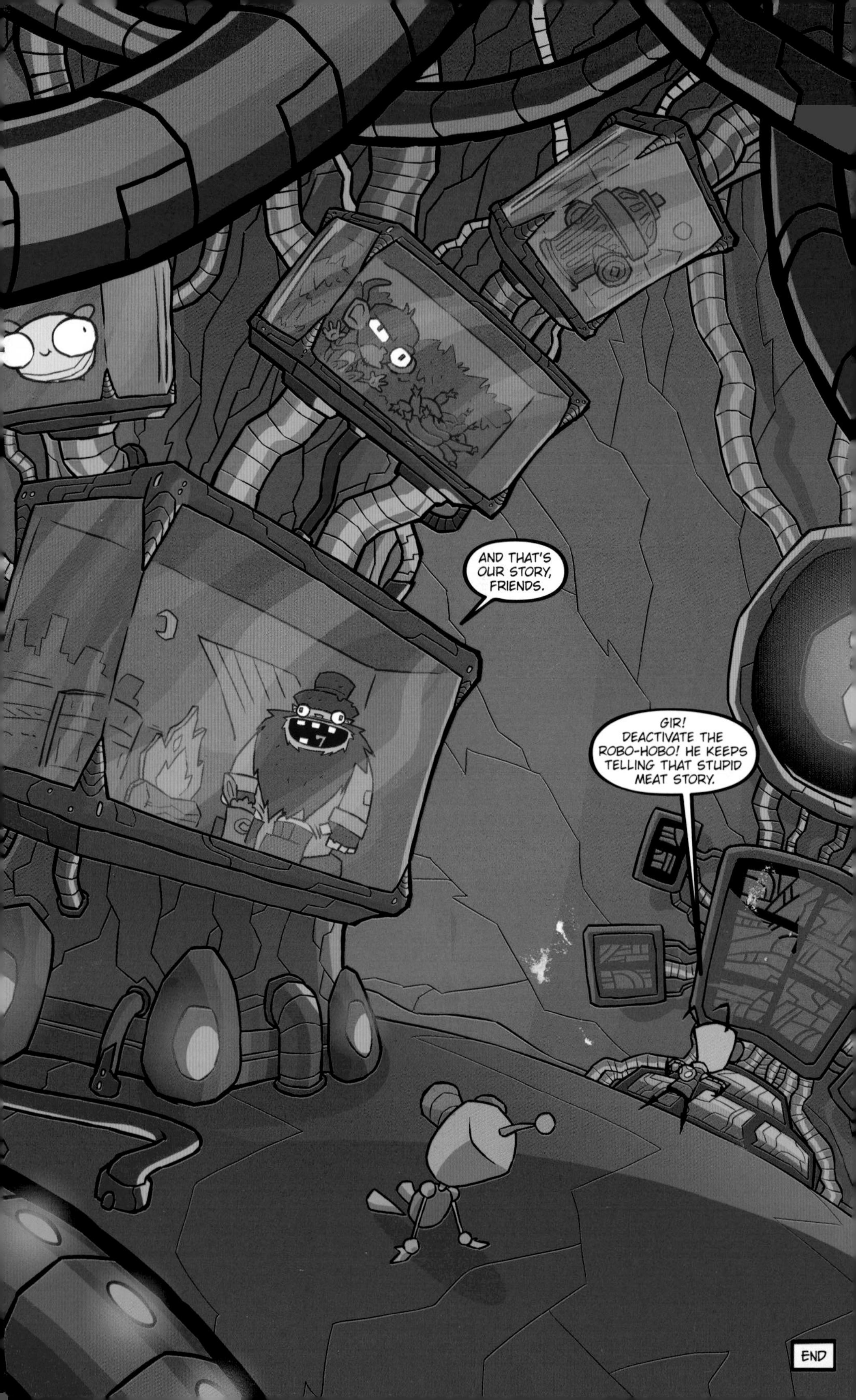
AND THAT'S OUR STORY, FRIENDS.
GIR! DEACTIVATE THE ROBO-HOBO! HE KEEPS TELLING THAT STUPID MEAT STORY.
END

CREATORS

JHONEN VASQUEZ

is a writer and artist who walks in many worlds, not unlike Blade, only without having to drink blood-serum to survive the curse that is also his greatest power (still talking about Blade here). He's worked in comics and animation and is the creator of *Invader ZIM*, a fact that haunts him to this day.

ERIC TRUEHEART

was one of the original writers on the *Invader ZIM* television series back when there was a thing called "television." Since then, he's made a living writing moderately-inappropriate things for people who make entertainment for children, including Dreamworks Animation, Cartoon Network, Disney TV, PBS, Hasbro and others. Upon reading this list, he now thinks he maybe should have become a dentist, and he hates teeth.

WARREN WUCINICH

is an illustrator, colorist and part-time carny currently living in Durham, NC. When not making comics he can usually be found watching old *Twilight Zone* episodes and eating large amounts of pie.

KATE SHERRON

is an artist, designer, and comic book writer whose comics credits include *The Amazing World of Gumball, Adventure Time, Rugrats, Labyrinth: A Discovery Adventure*, and, of course, *Invader ZIM*. Kate also wrangles hellbeasts in an amateur capacity and lives in St. Louis, MO.

FRED C. STRESING

is a colorist, artist, writer, and letterer for a variety of comics. You may recognize his work from *Invader ZIM*, the comic you are holding. He has been making comics his whole life, from the age of six. He has gotten much better since then. He currently resides in Savannah, Georgia with his wife and two cats. He doesn't know how the cats got there, they are not his.

KC GREEN

writes and draws comics for a long time, then a longer time happens where he is playing video games or watching the same five YouTube ASMR videos. The day starts again in much the same path, but instead maybe it's Wednesday and not Tuesday.

THE INVASION IS HERE!

INVADER ZIM

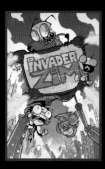

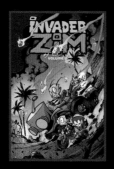

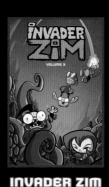

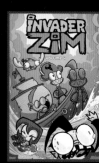

INVADER ZIM VOL. 1

Collects issues 1-5!

INVADER ZIM

INVADER ZIM VOL. 2

Collects issues 6-10!

INVADER ZIM
VOLUME 3

INVADER ZIM VOL. 3

Collects issues 11-15!

INVADER ZIM
VOLUME 4

INVADER ZIM VOL. 4

Collects issues 16-20

INVADER ZIM

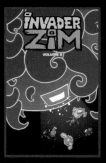

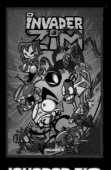

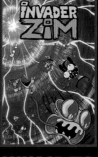

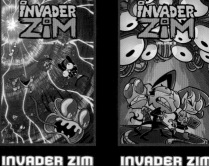

INVADER ZIM VOL. 5

Collects issues 21-25!

INVADER ZIM

INVADER ZIM VOL. 6

Collects issues 26-30!

INVADER ZIM

INVADER ZIM VOL. 7

Collects issues 31-35!

INVADER ZIM
VOLUME 8

INVADER ZIM VOL. 8

Collects issues 36-40

INVADER ZIM
VOLUME 9

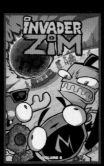

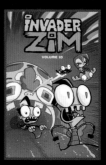

INVADER ZIM VOL. 9

Collects issues 41-45!

INVADER ZIM
VOLUME 10

INVADER ZIM VOL. 10

Collects issues 46-50!

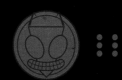